TO GLORIA

THE IMAGINED SLUM
Newspaper representation in three cities, 1870-1914

ALAN MAYNE

Leicester University Press
Leicester, London and New York

Distributed exclusively in the USA and Canada by St. Martin's Press

Leicester University Press
(a division of Pinter Publishers)
25 Floral Street, Covent Garden, London, WC2E 9DS, United Kingdom

Editorial offices
Fielding Johnson Building, University of Leicester
Leicester, LE1 7RH

Trade and other enquiries
25 Floral Street, London, WC2E 9DS *and*
St. Martin's Press, Inc., Room 400, 175 Fifth Avenue, New York, NY 10010, USA

British Library Cataloguing in Publication Data

A CIP catalogue record for this book is available from the British Library

ISBN 0 7185 1389 4

Library of Congress Cataloguing-in-Publication Data

A CIP catalog record for this title is available from the Library of Congress

Typeset by Saxon Graphics Ltd, Derby
Printed and bound in Great Britain by Biddles Ltd of Guildford and King's Lynn

Contents

List of plates

List of maps

Acknowledgements

I have many debts.

I am a beneficiary of contingent circumstance. Richard Rodger noticed an obscure conference abstract and invited me to write a paper for the *Urban History Yearbook*. Alec McAulay liked the paper, and had confidence that someone who distrusted facsimile machines could none the less write a book which would usefully expand upon it.

Tristan and Justin forgave me the missed opportunities for kite-flying in the updraughts around the Washington Monument. Gloria shared her lover with a Macintosh, drew my attention to James Cuming Walters in Birmingham, and helped me in the Library of Congress.

Other friends sustained me: Tom O'Neill in Melbourne, Michael Wreszin in New York, and Frances Gouda and Gary Price in Washington, DC.

Professional debts are legion. I never met H.J. Dyos, but his two-volume *The Victorian City* and his paper on London's slums in *Victorian Studies* started me thinking. So, too, did the ascerbic F.B. Smith, who challenged me to probe the Birmingham improvement scheme. Sam Bass Warner, Jr. provided the germ of an idea in his chapter in *The Pursuit of Urban History*, although when I met him he had already lost confidence in the approach that I was beginning to develop. Gunther Barth assisted me with his scholarship and gentle kindness. Asa Briggs encouraged me to pursue ideas in fields which were new to me, and his opinion was underlined when I read Andrew Lees's *Cities Perceived*. Greg Dening introduced me to rigorous new forms of history-making. Three archaeologists — Tim Murray, Iain Stewart, and Henry Miller — showed me the superficiality of reading texts as unproblematic reflections of material conditions in the past.

Four colleagues — Rhys Isaac, Ken Lockridge, Graeme Davison, and Anthony Wohl — were especially helpful in sharing ideas and provoking me to lift my game.

Anthony Wohl's colleagues helped me to pull the project's key themes together when I gave a paper at Vassar. Terry McDonald and David Scobey powerfully assisted that process when I spoke at Ann Arbor. Mike Lacey consolidated this learning process when he chaired a colloquium in Washington, DC.

The book could not have been completed without generous institutional support. The New South Wales Premier's Department awarded me a social history writing project grant, which enabled me to complete research work in Sydney. The Australian Research Council awarded two grants to facilitate research in Britain. The Australian–American Educational Foundation provided a Senior Fulbright Award to work at the University of California at Berkeley. The Woodrow Wilson International Center for Scholars, in the Smithsonian Institution, Washington DC, provided me with a fellowship, and it was there that much of this book was written. The maps were prepared by the Graphic Information Design Unit, in the Centre for the Study of Higher Education, at the University of Melbourne. The University of Melbourne awarded a publications grant to Leicester University Press.

The photographs of the Gullet, and the corner of Henn and Balloon Streets, are reproduced with the permission of Birmingham Library Services. All three are taken from a collection in the BCL entitled 'Photographs of buildings removed under the Birmingham Improvement Scheme of 1875'. The photographs of Queen's Place and Lynch's Court in Sydney are reproduced with the permission of the State Library of New South Wales, and are taken from the small picture file in the Mitchell Library.

Librarians and archivists guided me throughout the endeavour. I am particularly grateful to the staff of the Local Studies Department in the Birmingham Central Library, the British Public Record Office, the Cambridge University Library, and the University of Birmingham Archives; to their colleagues in the National Archives of the United States, the Library of Congress, and the Bancroft Library; and to the staff of the State and Mitchell Libraries in Sydney, the State Archives Office of New South Wales, and the archives of the Sydney City Council.

Antonia Balazs was a wonderful research assistant in Washington DC.

List of abbreviations

AONSW	Archives Office of New South Wales
BCC	Birmingham City Council
BCCHC	Birmingham City Council, minutes of the health committee, manuscript volumes in Local Studies Department, BCL
BCCIC	Birmingham City Council, minutes of the improvement committee, manuscript volumes in Local Studies Department, BCL
BCCP	Birmingham City Council, minutes of proceedings, manuscript volumes in Local Studies Department, BCL
BCL	Birmingham Central Library (Local Studies Department unless otherwise indicated)
BPD	*British Parliamentary Debates*
BPP	*British Parliamentary Papers*
BPRO	British Public Record Office
Bulletin	*San Francisco Bulletin*
Chronicle	*San Francisco Chronicle*
Daily Gazette	*Birmingham Daily Gazette*
Daily Mail	*Birmingham Daily Mail*
Daily Post	*Birmingham Daily Post*
Daily Telegraph	*Sydney Daily Telegraph*
Examiner	*San Francisco Examiner*
Herald	*Sydney Morning Herald*
LGB	Local Government Board
NA	National Archives of the United States
SCCA	Archives of the Council of the City of Sydney
SCC, LR	Letters received, in the archives of the Council of the City of Sydney
UBA	University of Birmingham Archives
V&P(NSW LA)	Votes and Proceedings of the New South Wales Legislative Assembly

Introduction

I

It is a hitherto unremarked oddity that so much attention was given in English-speaking societies during the last quarter of the nineteenth century, and the pre-war years of the twentieth century, to something which — in the senses commonly implied — never existed. I mean *the slum*. Charity workers, sanitarians, housing reformers, and urban planners all identified slums as spatial and social abominations. Their preoccupations focused upon the material conditions and social codes of inner-city living. They railed against slums as haunts of the criminal and dangerous classes, and as poverty traps whose entrenched inequalities questioned the real extent of social progress. These characterizations were further sensationalized and popularized by entertainers, who — in text, illustration, and guided tours — presented audiences with contrived spectacles of city low life which mocked the normal benchmarks of comfort and propriety in modern cities. The chief vehicle of slum sensationalism — the city press — asserted in 1901 that the slumland horrors of England's second-largest city, Birmingham, 'could scarcely be imagined'. So foreign did slums appear that conditions within them were such 'as few people imagine could be found out of heathendom'.[1]

Slums are myths. They are constructions of the imagination.[2] This is not to say, for example, that Chicago's turn-of-the-century poverty belt did not exist, or to downplay the shocking disequilibrium between it and Millionaire's Row. Nor is it to dispute the miserable living conditions that, by the late nineteenth century, had become the entrenched norm among the multi-storey tenements of Scottish cities. The deplorable life choices available to inner-city residents were real in material and absolute senses which do not extend to slums. I do not mean that slums were not real. They were, after all, a universal feature of big cities. Their reality, however, lay in the constructions of common-sense conviction, and in the certainties of public knowledge which common-sense understandings sustained, rather than in the material conditions of everyday living. To discuss slums is to deal with words, with discourse, with signs, and with the concepts they communicated, rather than with the social geography of inner cities. The term *slum*, encoded with the meanings of a dominant bourgeois culture, in fact obscured and distorted the varied spatial forms and social conditions to which it was applied. Universal in its application, it subsumed the innermost working-class districts of every city — notwithstanding their diversity of occupations, incomes, ethnic backgrounds, and household arrangements; and the variations in age, size, and labour and housing markets amongst cities — 'into one all-embracing concept of an outcast society'.[3]

Historians none the less insist that the essence of slums was their 'environmental reality'. Swayed by the dramatic and compelling qualities of surviving documentary evidence about slums, they have appropriated the word from the textual and graphic flotsam that was generated by discourse in the past. They have then sought to recast the term as a material reflection of the disequilibrium between wealth and poverty which undoubtedly characterized urban development under the stimuli of free-market capitalism. It has thereby become a commonplace that 'the slums helped to underpin Victorian prosperity'. To argue thus, however, that 'slums ... constitute a massive indictment of unregulated capitalism', is to apply an imaginative and value-laden construct as though it was a tangible and objective feature of all these cities.[4]

Historians, gullibly, have been allured by the disingenuous pledges given by bourgeois observers in the past, that their depictions were based upon strict empiricism. For example in Sydney, the oldest capital city of the Australian colonies, the *Daily Telegraph* introduced a sensational description of local slum conditions in 1884 with the disclaimer 'not [to] moralise on the subjects of progress and poverty or the filth in which the occupants ... live and die, it being our duty here to present the state of things as it presented itself before us.' Likewise when James Cuming Walters published his compelling series, *Scenes in Slum-Land*, in the *Birmingham Daily Gazette* during 1901, he emphasized that his articles 'deal only in facts', and the newspaper advertised the stories as 'pictures drawn from the life without exaggeration'. In the same year the American slumland publicist, Jacob A. Riis, whose *How the Other Half Lives* had startled New Yorkers during the early 1890s, wrote in his autobiographical *The Making of an American* that 'I am a reporter of facts'.[5]

Social historians have often, in self-serving assertion of methodological rigour, sought to distinguish between the supposedly reliable evidence of social surveys and reform discourse produced by the likes of Riis on the one hand, and the distortions attributed to slumland entertainers on the other. H.J. Dyos noted dismissively in 1967 that sensationalist writings about low life in Victorian London had turned 'the slums into a public spectacle, perhaps even a public entertainment'. Dyos detected an increasing divergence during the nineteenth century between the shallow sentimentality of slumland depictions in popular literature, which he ruled out of consideration in historical analysis, and the serious fact-finding and reform discourse about slums, which he drew to the attention of historians. This artificial distinction continues to skew analysis in the 1990s as historians distinguish between supposedly empirical observation and the stories by journalists and novelists which 'added sensationalism and a fictional gloss to this emerging factual basis'.[6]

The slums described by apparent fact-gatherers like Riis were not unproblematic reflections of social realities in the past. All slumland depictions were mediated by the cultural milieux within which they were framed, and upon which their creators depended for comprehension and credibility. The slum was employed by both reformers and entertainers as a potent trigger device which mobilized bourgeois interest because it dovetailed with basic axioms of prevailing common-sense opinion about the good and the bad in contemporary society. Consequently, as Graeme Davison has aptly noted,

The slum stereotype is the most serious stumbling block in the way of historians seeking to understand the life of ... [the] nineteenth-century underclass. It so pervades contemporary debate, influencing the selection of facts, the classification of statistical information and the construction of explanations, that it is difficult for historians to escape its influence. It portrayed lower-class life in essentially negative terms — *dis*ease, *dis*tress, *dis*order, *dis*affection — and always from a lofty middle-class point of view. It acted as a shutter closing the minds of contemporaries to the inner life and outlook of the poor.[7]

Historians nevertheless still cling to the term and to its presumed environmental essence. An obvious strategy which side-steps the stumbling-block noted by Davison is to extend Dyos' strategy of selectivity, and sift out from the slumland stereotypes the most obvious expressions of their creators' opinions. The intention thereby is to reconstruct the histories of inner-city working-class communities by reading against the grain of bourgeois slumland representations. The danger, however, is that by eliminating their original creators' judgements, historians are also obscuring the cultural milieux of the audiences for whom the depictions were intended, and the agendas which the stereotypes were intended to peddle. Moreover, not only are the moorings of slum representations to bourgeois opinion-making potentially obliterated, but the descriptive residue that remains is easily reworked into historically detached approximations of the inner-city working classes which reduce them to puppets who gesture at the tug of impersonal market-place structures. Their credibility as people has been dimmed, and with this an accurate sense of human agency and of social process.

In order to correct the shallowness of information thus culled from outside perspectives about the lives and outlooks of the city poor, historians have used slumland stereotypes as springboards for acts of their own imagination. By rephrasing imaginative licence as a scholarly method — empathy — they have sought to project themselves into the shoes of slum-dwellers through an innate capacity for fellow feeling. In so doing, they reify the phantoms of bourgeois imagination and further obscure the lives of the inner-city working classes. As Clifford Geertz notes, 'We cannot live other people's lives ... it is with expressions, representations, objectifications, discourses, performances ... that we traffic ... Whatever sense we have of how things stand with someone else's inner life, we gain it through their expressions, not through some magical intrusion into their consciousness.'[8]

This is a book about slums. However, it analyses them as products of discourse rather than perpetuating the illusion of their environmental reality. Instead of attempting to translate stereotypes about slums into anachronistic reflections of abstracted people from a remote past, it recognizes slums as constituting a genre of expression by real people who once lived in the present. The stereotypes have relevance in terms of those people's negotiations of public meaning, and the subsequently deleterious impact of public policy-making upon the material conditions of living in inner-city neighbourhoods. The imagined slum does therefore connect to spatial and social forms in so far as its stereotypes fed into schemes of slum clearance and 'city improvement', which in the nineteenth century began massively to intrude upon the actual conditions of working-class life in those inner-city communities to which the term *slum* was applied. The book is thus a rejoinder to historians who maintain that the post-structural 'linguistic left' has muddied historical analysis by introducing a spurious disconnection between language and culture on the one hand, and the material world and practical politics on the other.[9]

Slum stereotypes are not stumbling-blocks to analysis, but have historical value precisely on account of their distortions. Walters explained in the second series of his *Scenes in Slum-Land* that there 'would be small service or real benefit in drawing pictures of the vile dens allowed to exist in the poorer quarters of the city if we went no further and deduced no moral from the facts.'[10] Walters' moralistic musings tell us little about the conditions and rhythms of working-class life, but they tell us a lot about the hegemonic influence of bourgeois opinion. Because *slum* is so packed full with idiomatic meanings from the past, the term provides openings for historians to unravel the strands and festoons of past belief which made up evolving city culture, and which were translated into disruptive programmes of inner-city 'revitalization'.

II

A shared genre of slumland representation can be traced throughout the cities of the English-speaking world. Just as slums were conventionally represented as existing upon the margins of tolerable living conditions and acceptable behaviour, so too does this book go to the margins in order to explore the content and function of these common slumland depictions. This is evident in two immediate senses. First, the book focuses on provincial cities rather than, as is usual, upon the metropolitan cores. Second, in exploring the styles employed by the chroniclers and illustrators of city low life, it dwells upon the hack writers of the city press rather than upon the coterie of literary luminaries upon whom historical interest usually centres.

The book concentrates on three widely distant cities. The choices are, upon initial consideration, unlikely ones. In the United States, instead of concentrating upon New York's Empire City, the book looks across the continent to San Francisco. The city on the Golden Gate ranked ninth nationally in terms of size at the turn of the century. Proportionally, it had the highest ethnic-minority population of any large American city. San Francisco's immigrant 'slums' had for long been subjects of curiosity and concern. Chief among them was Chinatown, a label that was applied to the Chinese community centred around Broadway, and California, Kearny, and Stockton Streets. San Francisco city officials had announced in 1885 that

All great cities have their slums and localities where filth, disease, crime and misery abound; but in the very best aspect which 'Chinatown' can be made to present, it must stand apart, conspicuous and beyond them all in the extreme degree of all these horrible attributes, the rankest outgrowth of human degradation that can be found upon this continent.[11]

In Britain, rather than looking at imperial London, the book dwells upon the Midlands city of Birmingham. In 1895 a sanitary inspector for the Local Government Board said of working-class neighbourhoods he had just visited in the city that they constituted 'about the worst slum I have ever seen'. A local Liberal Party politician conceded in 1908 that it had often been said that 'Birmingham slums were the worst in England'. The slum stereotype was applied to neighbourhoods throughout the city, but by the 1860s the inner-city municipal ward of St Mary's, and especially the maze of streets to the south-east of Bull Street, were widely cited as constituting the centre of Birmingham's slumland. At the turn of the century, the adjoining parish of St Laurence, across Aston Road, was also being characterized as 'the very heart of the worst slum-region'.[12]

The third city selected for study is among the most unlikely choices of all. Sydney was the local hub of the settler society of New South Wales, on the periphery of the British empire. Yet Sydney was older and bigger than San Francisco. Its position as the largest city in the Australian colonies was eclipsed during the second half of the nineteenth century by booming Melbourne, capital of the adjoining colony of Victoria, but was regained early in the new century. Slumland pockets such as Durand's Alley and Queen's Place had since the 1850s been identified as existing behind the city's main business thoroughfares. During the last quarter of the nineteenth century the entire western portion of the city centre, running from George Street to Darling Harbour, became characterized as a sprawling slum region. Sydney, like San Francisco, contained a 'Little Canton' of Chinese immigrants which was conventionally cited as forming the lowest depths of slumland. However *slum* was applied more generally to include the inner-city's European poor as well: immigrant and native-born alike.[13]

I have chosen to concentrate upon these provincial cities in part because a key consequence of the nineteenth-century surge in urban development was that most city dwellers lived in constellations of urban places rather than in the handful of metropolitan centres with populations over a million inhabitants. These smaller urban places — on the frontiers of European settlement equally as much as in their economic cores — were networked components of an interactive urban world system. The exchanges amongst this hierarchy of towns and cities consisted not only of products and capital, or even of the movement of peoples. They also comprised the circulation of information and ideas. Slumland representation in provincial cities, echoing as it did reform discourse and modes of mass entertainment in London and New York, highlights the importance of cultural transmission in fashioning the horizons of city people in the past.

It is easy to note the derivative quality of provincial city culture. Commentators in San Francisco, whether lauding their city's achievements or bemoaning its shortcomings, expressed themselves by drawing comparisons with New York. It was natural that in Birmingham, too, local identity was fashioned through comparisons with the Great Wen. Slumland depiction was one amongst many strands in these comparisons. Walters wrote that 'Birmingham has ... slums worse than the East End of London.' In distant New South Wales slumland publicists expressed 'surprise ... to see places in so young a city as Sydney quite as bad, although not quite so numerous, as the very worst slums of London.'[14] Slumland representation in Sydney, Birmingham, and San Francisco was not, however, simply a reflection of metropolitan precedents. Local reformers and entertainers adapted the imported styles, and improvised as well. They were copied in turn in other cities. Provincial usage highlights the innovation and novelty that was generated by the flow of ideas between the cities of the urban network.

This diffusely innovative and mutually reinforcing process is especially evident in the daily press of these cities, which emerged during the last quarter of the nineteenth century as probably the most important arena of popular cultural production. An Italian who travelled through the Australian colonies during the early 1870s remarked upon 'the extraordinary number and circulation of newspapers' in the towns and cities he visited.[15] London alone boasted over one hundred suburban newspapers by 1880, and English provincial cities collectively sustained almost a hundred other daily newspapers. Fittingly, one of Manhattan's first skyscrapers was a news-paper office: the 1877 Tribune Building. During the 1880s Joseph Pulitzer's *New York World* consolidated journalism's emergence as a big business, combining sensationalism and editorial crusading. This new style of city journalism was not unique to the metropolis. Pulitzer's biggest rival, William Randolph Hearst had in fact matured his sensational press style in San Francisco during the 1880s and 1890s, in the struggle for circulation between his *Examiner* and the *San Francisco Chronicle*.

Representing big-city life was the biggest news story of the nineteenth century. Such journalism did not simply mirror cities. Press news — selective, judgemental, sensational — helped to create cities in popular imagination. Urban scale — the magnitude of population, the geographical dimensions of settlement, the pace of change — had left personal experience and personal knowledge insufficient as information sources about modern society. City journalism helped meet that need. Its audience was the primary labour force: male, skilled, regularly employed, and suburban. Newspaper influence upon public opinion was widely noted. Birmingham's flamboyant reform mayor during the mid-1870s, Joseph Chamberlain, privately spoke contemptuously of 'the fatal influence of so-called public opinion, i.e. the opinion of ill informed & commonplace people translated and transfigured by the unrivalled literary expression given to it by the writers in the London Press.' San Francisco's daily newspapers were frequently criticized as 'sensational sheets' which imitated the worst features of the New York press. The *San Francisco Examiner* responded to the jibe of 'yellow journalism' that was thrown at it by retorting that its press style was 'the kind of journalism that does things'.[16]

Slum sensationalism was an especially popular subject for the hard-hitting forays into public policy-making which newspapers such as Hearst's *Examiner* espoused. Such stories were an effective device for chasing newspaper sales: low-life revelations were a 'great coup' for newspaper editors over their competitors. Lurid tales of Chinatown violence, gambling, prostitution, and graft were the stock in trade of San Francisco journalism. The press in Melbourne and Sydney sustained a racy series of slumland exposés throughout the 1870s and 1880s. In Britain, slums became the subject of what Anthony Wohl calls 'a new type of popular reform journalism' during the 1880s, which was pioneered in London by George Sims and highlighted by William Stead's *Pall Mall Gazette*.[17]

Occasionally these journalists — provincial as well as metropolitan — achieved individual fame. Walters, for example, was a well-known figure in the British press. He was a leader writer and assistant editor for the *Birmingham Daily Gazette* when he wrote *Scenes in Slum-Land*. In 1906 he took charge of the *Manchester City News*, which he edited until his retirement in 1931. He was also prominent in literary circles. Most investigative journalists, unlike Walters, were anonymous figures whose stories have no claim to literary merit. Their reports, like those of the newspaper men in Sydney and San Francisco, are repetitious and open-ended. They are rushed instalments prepared for looming publishing deadlines, written with an eye to anticipating or building upon the copy of their competitors, filled with references to place marks and happenings that are obscure without local knowledge, often ponderous or awkward in style, and sometimes still containing the factual errors and grammatical slips of the first draft. What appear as flaws to our eyes are in fact the texts' essential moorings to the local contexts and concerns which animated them.

III

Newspaper discourse about slums highlights the dramatic essence of big cities. I use *drama* in two senses: first, to mean social drama — the multi-layered playing out in daily social life of ongoing mobilization and conflict;

second, to refer to the representations of the *modern city* in mass entertainment, which thereby sought to make cities comprehensible to their inhabitants. Social drama was an abiding feature of city living.[18] The scale, diversity, and novelty of city life, and the pace of urban change, made big cities contentious and perplexing places for their inhabitants. A multiplicity of social groups — some emergent, most of them marginal to power, a few enduring, others transitory in their influence, some formal in their organization, and many others based upon nothing more than the affinities of face-to-face encounters — constantly engaged themselves and one another in talk and action, setting forth agendas, begging audiences, demanding responses and resolutions of grievances and worries. Thus were determined and perpetually renewed the hierarchical structures of power, status, and significance in urban society. These ongoing negotiations and confrontations permeated everybody's daily lives and, still more so, public policy-making and administration. They were reflected in the prevailing discontinuities of city public opinion, the contingencies of decision-making, the indeterminacies of outcome.

Birmingham, Sydney, and San Francisco exemplify the indeterminacies of big cities. This book concentrates on each city during the unfolding of important inner-city redevelopment programmes up to the First World War: in Birmingham from 1875, in Sydney from 1879, and in San Francisco from 1900. Public policy-making in all three cities during these years took place amid crisis talk prompted by epidemic disease, and by environmental degradation that resulted from the inadequacies of housing supply and of provision for waste disposal. In all three cases, the search for palliatives led to important initiatives in slum eradication. Birmingham's City Improvement Scheme, which began in 1875 with plans to resume a large area of the central city, quickly became one of the best known examples of state-initiated urban renewal in the English-speaking world. The scheme's centrepiece — a grand new boulevard between New Street and the Aston Road — was proudly named Corporation Street in honour of the municipal achievement. Yet, as was pointed out by a critic of municipal policy in 1903, the 'original reason for making the street was that the line of houses through which it would pass was a slum.'[19] Sydney and San Francisco also experimented with 'improvement' programmes. Their initiatives have largely escaped the attention of historians. In Sydney, enactment in 1879 of the City of Sydney Improvement Act initiated a rolling series of municipal inspection tours throughout the remainder of the century to condemn insanitary inner-city houses. In San Francisco, the outbreak of bubonic plague in Chinatown during 1900 prompted a collaborative federal and municipal drive which continued into the 1930s to repair or tear down unhealthy buildings.

All three schemes unfolded amid controversy and indecision. The attitudes adopted by the city press highlight three extreme positions amid the diverse efforts to influence municipal policy-making. Sensational slumland stories appeared in the Sydney press throughout the 1880s. They had been written by journalists who accompanied the municipal officials on their tours to condemn insanitary housing. The stories applauded and sought to extend the principle of municipal slum clearance. Yet the applause was felt necessary in the first place because of the opposition to council policy that was being expressed by working-class tenants, by property owners, and by competing political and bureaucratic alignments.[20] Municipal policy-making in Birmingham was stingingly attacked by Walters' two series on *Scenes in Slum-Land* in the *Daily Gazette* during 1901. The first series consisted of 17 articles which appeared between March and early April. *Further Scenes in Slum-Land* was published as another 11 articles between April and May. They were consolidated and reprinted as two booklets later in the year. The stories attacked the City Council for failing to address the slum problem. Walters had 'for twelve months lived in various disguises in the worst of the slum dwellings.' His 'appalling revelations ... astounded the city. Official investigations were ordered, elections were fought on the problem, and at the request of the Bishop of Worcester a Sunday was devoted exclusively to sermons preached on Mr. Walters's articles.' *Scenes in Slum-Land* 'created [such] a violent public discussion' that Walters was sued for libel by the Medical Officer of Health and by the chairman of the City Health Committee, and the Health Committee was itself replaced by a new Housing Committee, made up of those who had championed Walters' allegations during the 1901 municipal elections.[21] Whereas slumland representations in the Sydney press generally endorsed the thrust of municipal slum-clearance policy, and the revelations publicized by the *Birmingham Daily Gazette* sought to discredit the City Council's anti-slum programme, the San Francisco press responded to slum clearance initiatives in Chinatown in another way altogether: with silence. Newspaper proprietors secretly agreed to ignore the municipal and federal programme in Chinatown lest publicity about plague harm the city's trade. They feared the commercial ill-effects of quarantine restrictions by other cities and foreign governments. Yet depictions of Chinatown vice continued to pepper the newspapers' pages.[22]

Notwithstanding the very different urban settings, and the varied political agendas which the journalists pursued, newspaper stories in the three cities drew upon a common style of slumland representation. They constitute one of the many strands of cultural performance which, by playing out and explicating the social dramas of urban life, sought to redress the indeterminacies of big-city living. Just as discontinuities of experience and belief, and contingencies of outcome, were part and parcel of city living, so, too, were the countervailing efforts to impose controls by 'cultural representations of fixed social reality'. Cultural performances, ranging through art, theatre, and both light and serious reading, functioned as 'a hall of ... magic mirrors in which social problems, issues, and crises ... are reflected as diverse images, transformed, [and] evaluated.' The entertainments 'probe a community's weaknesses, call its leaders to account, desacralize its most cherished values and beliefs, portray its characteristic conflicts and suggested remedies for them, and generally take stock of its current situation.' Because social dramas and the cultural performances which reflect upon them are embedded in power relationships, the meanings carried by representational conventions in the performances consolidate, perpetuate, and extend the belief systems of the dominant power groups.[23]

Characterizations of cities as *the modern city* — united in the bustling entrepreneurial energy of its people — were a central feature of such representation. Newspaper horror stories which cast slums as a universal antithesis of urban norms were a particularly potent vehicle for achieving this effect. There were, of course, many other representational themes and forms of performance. The widespread genre of late nineteenth-century utopian novels also 'provided mechanisms of ordering the confusing flux of social change and of charting its direction.' Popular theatre likewise thrived in cities whose size and diversity made their inhabitants strangers to each other, providing audiences with identifying markers for otherwise bewildering cityscapes. Yet, as William Taylor has written of cultural production in New York City during the nineteenth and early twentieth centuries, 'Most historians have assumed, mistakenly, that the public was sold entertainment that was sheer diversion and irrelevant to its needs, rather than being provided with cultural experiences that helped different groups within the population make sense of the new urban environment.'[24]

The daily press was ubiquitous to a degree which did not extend to the other media which addressed city themes. Moreover, perhaps only slum performances had sufficient spectacular attraction — what Dickens called an 'attraction of repulsion' — consistently to ram home a clear ideological message about consensus and continuity in the face of diversity and change. Slumland performances constructed an imagined schism between the good city and its antithesis in order to distil the essential core values of bourgeois common sense from the indeterminacies of opinion and choice in contemporary society. San Francisco's Chinatown was described characteristically in 1906 as 'the greatest pest hole of any modern city'. In the aftermath of that year's earthquake and fire which destroyed the district, it was recalled that Chinatown had 'appealed mightily to the imagination of melodramatists, authors of sensational tales, writers of specials for the Eastern press, and others who guide and stimulate the popular imagination.'[25]

The imaginary schism which entertainers and social reformers fashioned alike was achieved in part by following the convention of stereotyping that was common to all genres of city performance. Stereotypes are inherently bipolar and reductive, visualizing clear and absolute borders between normalcy and difference. They function thereby to externalize society's anxieties by projecting the sources of those anxieties on to villainous othersiders.[26] That these stereotypes of slumland schism could be sustained in popular imagination stemmed from their reflexive relationship to the accumulated local knowledge that was possessed by the individuals who interpreted them. The stereotypes' widespread attraction derived from the immediacy of their moral lessons to recurring themes in the daily dramas that were generated by the endlessly repeated conversations and confrontations of urban living.

Lights and shades in San Francisco (from Lloyd 1876)

The slum chroniclers' constant repetition of analogies drawn with borders and thresholds particularly appealed to, and built upon, individual experience. John Tagg wrote of slum representation in late nineteenth-century Leeds that 'What could not be known had to be imagined'. The most effective means of achieving this flight of the imagination from the known world to a contrived slumland netherworld was to echo the sense of crossing thresholds which punctuated everybody's personal lives. Arnold van Gennep argued that the 'life of an individual in any society is a series of passages from ... one defined position to another which is equally well defined.' The cross-over points for some of these acts of passage are marked by elaborate public ritual: for example, the ceremonies which accompany christenings, marriages, and funerals. Other thresholds are embedded in the daily routines of private life: crossing between home and street, and between kitchen and bedroom, are equally potent signifiers of changes in setting and appropriate behaviour. An extensive shared glossary of slumland signifiers was similarly employed by city journalists to signal a switch away from normal rules of credibility and, with this, from familiar to foreign environments.[27]

The conditions represented to newspaper readers as existing beyond the slum's threshold are none the less too surreal to become fully manifest. The slum is thus a glimpsed-at place. It is a liminal setting, a topsy-turvy land. It is a passing vision of how things might be without appropriate rules. Juxtaposed images of slumland and modern city, presented within frameworks which imitate the immediacy of personal experience, thereby sought to chart a wide consensus by visualizing key traits of bourgeois city culture in the hues of sound individual common sense. Representations of slums were moments in defining the parameters of legitimate social behaviour, and thereby endorsing the power structures in modern urban society.[28]

This book is divided into two parts. Part 1 is introduced by 'The modern city'. It reviews the representational conventions which depicted big cities as expressing modernity and progress. It also introduces the linked concept of *city improvement*, which was widely publicized as reflecting and extending the civilizing influence of modern market-place cities. Chapters 3 to 5 extend this theme, the first by studying plague eradication in San Francisco, the second by tracing the Birmingham Improvement Scheme, and the third by examining the evolution of slum-clearance practices by the Sydney City Council. The three chapters have another purpose. Presented in turn around the organizing themes of *drama, indeterminacy*, and *contingency*, they attempt to encompass the social and cultural milieux of city people which slumland representation addressed.

Part 2 is made up of four chapters and a brief epilogue. 'Showcase' summarizes slumland usage by reformers and entertainers. 'Threshold' examines the common representational forms which the city press employed in order to visualize and imaginatively cross the slum's borders. 'Slumland' pursues this theme as it probes the means by which the stories sustained the illusion of slum discovery, and illustrates the common-sense judgements which were embedded in them about the best direction of urban change. 'Faces of degeneration' studies the human types who are represented as personifying the slum, and unravels the tricks of narrative which served to vindicate bourgeois judgements about the lifestyles appropriate to modern city living. 'The just war' sketches the representations of slum abolitionists as Christian soldiers embroiled in crusades against infidels.

Notes

1 Walters, 1901a, p. 11; 1901b, p. 7.
2 See Ward, 1976, pp. 323–36. See also Mayne, 1990, pp. 66–84; 1991a.
3 Davis, G., Beyond the Georgian façade: the Avon Street district of Bath, in Gaskell, 1990, p. 144.
4 Gaskell, in ibid., p. 1. Dyos, 1967, p. 27. Englander, 1983, xi.
5 *Daily Telegraph*, 29 April 1884, p. 5, The rookeries on the rocks. Walters, 1901b, p. 24. *Birmingham Daily Gazette*, leader, 6 March 1901, p. 4. Lane, 1974, p. 154.
6 Dyos, 1967, pp. 22–4. Green, D.R., Parton, A.G., Slums and slum life in Victorian England: London and Birmingham at mid-century, in Gaskell, 1990, p. 17.
7 Davison, G., Introduction, in Davison, Dunstan, McConville,1985, p. 3.
8 Geertz, C., Making experiences, authoring selves, in Turner, Bruner, 1986, p. 373.
9 Watts, S., 1992, p. A40.
10 Walters, 1901b, p. 12.
11 San Francisco Board of Supervisors, 1885, p. 5. See map 1.
12 Report to the Local Government Board by Henry D. Crozier, 9 March 1895, in MH 12, No. 13371 (BPRO). *Birmingham Daily Post*, 14 October 1908, p. 11, Birmingham municipal elections. Walters, 1901b, p. 14. See map 2.
13 See map 3.
14 Walters, 1901a, p. 4. *Evening News*, 7 June 1886, p. 8, Under the Improvement Act.
15 Giovanni Balangero, quoted in Mayne, 1991b, p. 65.
16 Joseph Chamberlain to John Morley, 7 December 1875, in Joseph Chamberlain Correspondence, JC5/7, UBA. *Chronicle*, 23 May 1900, p. 6, Newspapers and the bubonic board. *Examiner*, 14 January 1902, p. 3, Yellow journalism blocks corrupt police job. See Barth, 1980, chapter 3.
17 William Stead, quoted in Wohl, 1977, p. 211; ibid., p. 205.
18 I borrow the term *social drama* from anthropologist Victor Turner. See Turner, 1982; 1985; Turner, Bruner, 1986.
19 The Reverend T.J. Bass to the Local Government Board, 18 April 1903, in HLG 1, box 146, folder 856.7041.04 (BPRO). See map 2.
20 See chapter 5.
21 *Manchester City News*, Mr. J. Cuming Walters: a journalist's long and varied career, no date (1931), and *Birmingham Daily Gazette*, 18 July 1933, Champion of slum dwellers, both in the Local Studies Department, Birmingham Central Reference Library. See chapter 4.
22 See chapter 3.
23 Moore, S.F., Epilogue: uncertainties in situations, indeterminacies in culture, in Moore, Myerhoff, 1975, p. 221. Turner, 1982, pp. 11, 13, 104–5. Bruner, E.M., Experience and its expressions, in Turner and Bruner, 1986, p. 19.
24 Kasson, 1976, p. 190. Snyder, 1989, p. 110. Taylor, W.R., The launching of a commercial culture: New York City, 1860–1930, in Mollenkopf, 1988, p. 108.
25 Dickens is quoted in Wohl, 1991, p. 89. Tyler, 1906, p. 308. Genthe, Irwin, 1909, p. 44. See chapter 6.
26 See Gilman, 1985.
27 Tagg, J., God's sanitary law: slum clearance and photography in late nineteenth-century Leeds, in Tagg, 1988, p. 131. van Gennep, 1960, pp. 2–3. See chapter 7.
28 See chapters 8 and 9.

Part 1

Cities

2

The modern city

I

When Max Weber visited the United States in 1904, he characterized its cities as 'a metaphor for capitalist modernity'. The equation between cities and modern times — used both in approbation and condemnation of urban change — had a long and wide currency amongst English-speaking peoples. The explosive growth of urban places during the nineteenth century had absorbed the attention of contemporaries since early in the century. They attempted to describe and thereby fathom their cities, 'groping for metaphors and frames of reference' that were sufficient for the task.[1] British cities were collectively described in 1881 as the 'epitome of modern times' and 'the indices of our advance'. In 1886 one observer, swayed by Birmingham's extravagant improvement scheme, commended the Midlands capital as 'the most fully developed example of the English city of the future'. The 'marvellous growth' of colonial capitals in the antipodes was upheld in 1891 as the 'most striking feature of Australian progress'. In the opinion of American social reform leader, Josiah Strong, the 'modern city is at the same time the most characteristic product and the best exponent of modern civilization.'[2]

The *modern city* is an abstraction. The phrase is linked only tenuously to the jarringly diverse spatial and social outcomes of urban development which it supposedly represented. Indeed, it was only as an abstraction that *the city* existed at all as a universal form. As a reference point in popular culture, however, it carried enormous power. When the British journalist William Stead visited the American Midwest during the early 1890s, he found that the new-style city press provided 'the cosmopolitan hetero-geneous mass of the residents of Chicago [with] a sense of the unity of their city'.[3] The modern city, as it was fashioned during the nineteenth century by bourgeois discourse throughout the cities of the urban network, emerged as a masterful uniting symbol of capitalist progress.

City chroniclers on both sides of the Atlantic were mesmerized by the magnitude of metropolitan forms. It had still been possible at the start of the nineteenth century to walk the length or breadth of London, although the city already contained a million inhabitants. By 1910 Londoners numbered well over seven million. The city's unparalleled mass led Charles Masterman to depict it as 'a mammoth of gigantic and unknown possibility'. New York was transformed during the same period of time from a town of 60,000 inhabitants to a metropolis of almost five million people. In 1906 Maxim Gorki likened New York's skyline to 'a vast jaw, with uneven black teeth. It breathes clouds of black smoke into the sky and puffs like a glutton suffering from his obesity ... Entering the city is like getting into a stomach of stone and iron, a stomach that has swallowed several million people and is grinding and digesting them.' These big cities bespoke raw power: dominance over their inhabitants, over hinterlands, adjoining regions, and, perceptibly, over the globe. The rapidity of population growth within such urban juggernauts overawed observers. Chicago's population mushroomed from 30,000 people at the middle of the nineteenth century to over two million by 1910. Snowballing populations imparted a sense of dynamism, of perpetual motion, of unrelenting pace. New York's elevated railroad — perpetually 'tearing along' — seemed to an Australian visitor during the 1880s to be symptomatic of the city's mood.[4]

Metropolitan vigour was conventionally equated with these cities' rampant commercialism. In 1889 one writer, striving to describe the essence of modern Glasgow, remarked upon the city's 'tenacious grip of business, its amazing power of adjusting itself to new conditions of commerce, its invaluable gift of finding compensation in some new industry when an old staple trade fails.' New York was characterized as the 'capitalistic center' of the nation: the 'magnificent embodiment of [the] titanic energy and force' of free market capitalism.[5] The boundless entrepreneurial energy of the age seemed to be encapsulated by Manhattan's skyline, which was increasingly given over to multi-storey towers during the 1870s and 1880s, and in the 1890s by a new generation of steel-frame giants. Henry James called them 'extravagant pins in a cushion already overplanted'. These new skyscrapers seemed 'alive with the instinct of competition, and strain each other to overtop its neighbours.' The tower blocks of corporate America, 'shooting upward to the fifteenth and twentieth stories', struck observers as giving 'architectural expression to the growth in wealth now going on, as perfectly as the castles and cathedrals of the middle ages expressed the power of the church and the baron.' They made manifest the representations of modern cities as 'the cutting edge of civilization and progress'.[6]

Although the chroniclers of city life focused their attention upon the metropolitan cores, the demographic and economic transformation of provincial cities was collectively even more remarkable a feature of the age (see Table 2.1). This is most clearly evident in the precocious growth of 'instant cities' in the regions of most recent European settlement. Sydney grew from some 54,000 people in 1850 to 482,000 inhabitants by the turn of the century, and to 630,000 by 1911. San Francisco's population expanded in the same period from 35,000 to 417,000 people. It is evident, also, in the accelerating growth of long-established towns in the British provinces, which rapidly became big cities under the stimuli of commerce and manufacturing. Birmingham was already a city of 73,000 people at the beginning of the nineteenth century. By mid-century its population had increased to almost a quarter of a million people, and by the turn of the twentieth century to over half a million inhabitants. Some 840,000 people lived within Greater Birmingham in 1910–11. Joseph Chamberlain crowed in 1884 that the pace of growth had made modern Birmingham 'really a new town; the increase of the population has been something very remarkable, almost equivalent to that of an American city.'[7]

2.1 Population increase in Birmingham, San Francisco, and Sydney, 1850–1920

Year	Birmingham	San Francisco	Sydney
1850	233,000	35,000	54,000
1860	296,000	57,000	94,000
1870	344,000	141,000	135,000
1880	437,000	234,000	221,000
1890	478,000	299,000	383,000
1900	523,000	343,000	482,000
1910	840,000	417,000	630,000
1920	922,000	507,000	900,000

Sources: Mitchell, 1981, p.86. Mitchell, 1983, pp.99, 103. Mayne, 1982, p.227. Vamplew, 1987, p.41.

These provincial cities were quick to claim metropolitan status of their own as regional market-place powerhouses. In thus appropriating from the representations of capitalist modernity which had been applied to metropolitan centres, the local boosters of other cities consolidated both the widespread currency and the universalizing features of modern city stereotypes. Liverpool, Manchester, and Birmingham were already by the early 1870s being described as 'almost metropolitan in wealth and population'. Birmingham boosters styled their city 'the Midland metropolis'; it was, they pointed out, 'a great factory place' and 'one of the most wonderful workshops of the world'.[8] A world away, in the Australian colonies, Melbourne was styled 'the metropolis of the Southern Hemisphere'. In 1888 — the centennial of European settlement — Alexander Sutherland published a two-volume celebration of the city and colonial progress, which he entitled *Victoria and Its Metropolis*. To the north, residents of Sydney defiantly called their own city the true 'metropolis of Australia'. Timothy Coghlan, the colony's statistician, applauded the 'spectacle of magnificent cities growing with wonderful rapidity' when he wrote *The Wealth and Progress of New South Wales* in 1897.[9] On the far Pacific shore, San Francisco was characterized by its business leaders as 'the metropolis, and principal port of the Pacific Coast', equal in 'rank ... with our great sister city on the Atlantic side'. Throughout the state, Californians referred to it simply as 'the City'. San Francisco's new metropolitan status 'among the foremost commercial cities of America' was represented as capping 'this ... age of progress'. In its commercial advance, they said, the 'City is but an index to [that of] the State'.[10]

When San Francisco was destroyed by earthquake and fire in 1906, some interpreted the disaster as a 'necessary' form of rebirth as the city evolved from a primitive frontier town to a modern market-place metropolis.[11] It was pointed out that most of the destroyed buildings had been squat and wooden, whereas the 'giant' new sixteen-storey headquarters of the *Call* newspaper — the highest building on the Pacific coast — still 'stood proudly erect' amid the desolation. The 'modern skyscraper' thereafter symbolized the emerging 'Modern City of Steel on the Ruins of the City that Was'. The pulse of San Francisco's remorseless modernity was predictably said to be business. In rebuilding the Bay City, it was taken as axiomatic that 'San Francisco's commerce is its meat. To rehouse this commerce fitly, even lavishly, was a first practical consideration. Its priority was never questioned.' The new city's commercial backbone was, appropriately, called Market Street, which — as it was rebuilt with 'more and more skyscrapers' — was characterized as quickly becoming 'the most modern street in the world'.[12]

San Francisco's reconstruction underlined another common feature of the boosters' modern-city imagery: its organic quality. A prideful sense of common citizenship was claimed to transcend the competitive individuality of market-place cities. The new modern forms of San Francisco were thus a 'product of the City's Collective Energy', and were grounded in the preparedness of its 'citizens to work in common for common ends'. The city's renewal was 'expressive of a civic spirit — a faith which the people have in their beloved city'. The Scottish city-planning pioneer, Patrick Geddes, likewise acknowledged and sought to consolidate this 'civic consciousness', and the 'common weal' which it sustained. Modern cities thus connoted far more than technological innovation and capitalist growth: 'Cities are not merely marts of commerce; they stand for civility; they are civilization itself.'[13]

The capitalist vigour and collective energy of modern cities was widely said to have energized the intellectual and artistic life of modern nation states. The American progressive, Frederic C. Howe, asserted in 1905 that the 'city has given the world culture, enlightenment, and education along with industry and commercial opportunity.' Free municipal libraries and art galleries in Manchester and Birmingham were claimed to epitomize the civility of these cities and in Birmingham were proudly called the city's 'brightest spot for many an artisan'. In the United States the landscape architect, Frederick Law Olmsted, contended that a 'city takes the rank ... of a metropolis' when it transcended narrow commercialism to foster 'other than purely money-making occupations'. By his definition, metropolitan status required the cultivation not only of 'ordinary commerce ... but [of] humanity, religion, art, science and scholarship'.[14]

The modern times which cities were thus represented as expressing were encapsulated by the phrase *city improvement*. The term referred to the headlong embrace of the new. It meant, in part, the application of new technologies, expressed, for example, in the electric glitter of night-time Broadway, in elaborate systems for water supply and waste removal, and in transport systems such as Melbourne's cable tram network, the world's largest. City improvement also meant the remodelling and renewal of inherited city forms, and the obliteration of the old and obsolete. The application of what, in New York, the novelist William Dean Howells in 1870 called the 'forces of demolition and construction'[15] was especially commended when it entailed the replacement of supposed slums with new places of business. This imperative was keenly felt, also, in the newer cities of the urban frontier. Businessmen in Sydney tapped community anxieties about epidemic disease during the mid-1870s as they unveiled plans to obliterate inner-city slums by railway extensions and wharfage improvement. Likewise in San Francisco, commercial rebuilding in the aftermath of 1906 was hailed as providing a unique opportunity for removing the city's slums.

Business interest in city improvement was matched by a groundswell of middle-class environmentalism which sought to remould the spatial forms and moral nature of modern cities. These goals crystallized in the urban planning movement, which began to take on organizational form late in the nineteenth century. City improvement was sustained, also, by governments. State sponsorship sometimes took the form of legislation in aid of private-enterprise construction work. These projects frequently went hand in hand with the destruction of working-class communities. The Manhattan approach works to the Brooklyn Bridge, for example, cleared a swath through the city's Fourth Ward, which the bridge's designer, John A. Roebling, predicted would 'greatly beautify and improve this part of the city which appears to need it more than any other'. The bridge's opening in 1883 was attended by the President, the State Governor, and the Mayors of New York City and Brooklyn. The celebration honoured not only the technological achievements but also the civilization of modern cities. As one shopfront display announced on opening day, just as 'Babylon had her hanging garden, Egypt her pyramid, Athens her Acropolis, Rome her Athenaeum; so Brooklyn has her Bridge.' In Roebling's opinion, the bridge was an emblem of New York's 'mission' in 'the great flow of civilization'.[16]

City governments sometimes participated directly in schemes of urban improvement. Municipal corporations in English cities had been active since the 1830s with public works to improve the health and comfort of their inhabitants. In Glasgow, local government intervention since mid-century to municipalize city services, to initiate urban renewal, to build parks, museums, an art gallery and imposing municipal centre, was attributed in 1914 with having entrenched a 'civic spirit' amongst its inhabitants, who were justifiably 'proud of the greatness of their city'.[17] Such initiatives were valued in part for their aesthetic value. During the rebuilding of San Francisco, for example, it was remarked enviously that the 'cities of Australia ... are laid out along liberal lines, with broad streets, parks, public squares, and beautiful modern buildings.' Municipal action was seen as having an egalitarian function as well. A Liberal Party spokesperson in Birmingham claimed during 1878 'that the work of the modern Town Council ... was [thus] an attempt to distribute amongst the great mass of our poorer citizens, advantages and benefits and blessings which would otherwise be the exclusive privilege of a few.' The defeat in 1894 of New York City's corrupt Tammany machine by a reform coalition pledged to wide-ranging city improvement prompted Jacob Riis to celebrate that 'Decency ... moved into the City Hall, where shameless indifference ruled before.' In 1905 Frederic Howe pointed to the enlarging scope of municipal interventions and argued that the 'humanizing forces of today are almost all proceeding from the city. They are creating a new moral sense, a new conception of the obligations of political life, obligations which, in earlier conditions of society, did not and could not exist.'[18]

The sense of municipal public service which supposedly thus under-pinned city civility was commonly said to have achieved its fullest expression in Birmingham's 'municipal gospel', which was implemented during the reform administration of Joseph Chamberlain in the 1870s. Chamberlain contended that his improvement programme had 'created a new sense of the responsibility of citizenship, and has given fresh incentive to public spirit and private munificence.' His allies asserted that municipal reformers thereafter looked to Birmingham in the same way 'as the eyes of the faithful are turned to Mecca'.[19]

Notwithstanding the Birmingham City Council's public ownership of water and gas, its building of parks, baths, and cultural facilities, attention most commonly centred upon a much more traditional aspect of municipal improvement strategies: the widening and extension of streets. The 'great "improvement scheme"' to build Corporation Street was cited 'as one of the most stupendous, courageous, and wise acts ever performed by a munici-pality'. Local improvement acts in Birmingham and other British cities since the 1850s and 1860s had sought to apply street-making schemes as devices for achieving inner-city renewal. However, the 1875 Cross Act upon which Birmingham's improvement scheme was predicated was intended to break through the impediments to these earlier street improvements, in order to embark upon larger-scale projects of urban revitalization. Birmingham's improvement scheme was credited with having 'bought up a great tract of slums and narrow passages in the heart of the city, and [with having] there laid out that now beautiful avenue called Corporation Street, which is one of the handsomest streets to be seen in any city in any part of the globe.'[20]

II

What do we recognize now from the discourse on big cities and their improvement? Historians have long tapped from it. In so doing, culled images of modern cities — Manchester, London, Pittsburgh, New York — have become convenient shorthands with which we seek to typify the uneven social outcomes of urban change under capitalism. These market-place cities, literally, were prisoners of progress. All were sustained by a 'floating market of unskilled labour'. And, axiomatically, in all of them can be seen the deleterious side-effects — poverty, inadequate housing, and community ill health — that flowed from this penny-pinching process. As the *Sydney Morning Herald* conceded ruefully in 1876, the 'handsome stores and warehouses that front our streets are but screens in many instances to human rookeries and rabbit warrens, where squalor reigns supreme, in the midst of an atmosphere of stinks.'[21]

We recognize, too, that city improvement, notwithstanding the rhetoric of city civility and public service, was as much a market-driven concept as the urban forms to which it was applied were market-place products. Sydney's Mayor and Health Officer voiced a widely current opinion among municipal officials when they commented in 1876 that all the 'courts and lanes ... off [the] main streets should, in our opinion, be cleared of these wretched tenements ... and the ground devoted to its legitimate use, the erection of substantial stores and warehouses.' It was, after all, a commonplace that good government meant business government. It followed, as a local Birmingham politician pointed out during 1878, that if city government was to function effectively, 'it was of the utmost necessity that men who understood business should be sent there.'[22] City reform strategies therefore required that business leaders intervene to wrest government from the hands of corrupt self-servers, and from the timid horizons and mean preoccupations of small business representatives. San Francisco's Democratic Mayor in 1900, James Duval Phelan, had in 1894 been instrumental in founding the city's Merchants' Association, and with its backing had led a group of businessmen-reformers who swept into office pledging to provide strong 'business government'. In Birmingham the civic gospel supplanted the older municipal screed of the economists, small-scale businessmen who had dominated local politics since early 1850s. They were pushed aside during the late 1860s and early 1870s as the city's business élite — nonconformists who had initially mobilized over the issue of state education — entered local politics. A network of related families — the Kenricks, Martineaus, Nettlefolds, and Chamberlains — dominated business and formed 'the aristocracy and plutocracy of Birmingham. They stand far above the town society in social position, wealth and culture; and yet they spend their lives, as great citizens, taking an active and leading part in the municipal, political and educational life of their town.' Birmingham under Chamberlain and his political successors was 'above all else ... a business city, run by business men on business principles.'[23]

We also easily recognize a third feature of market-driven urban change: the linkages between cities. Urbanization was remarkable not only for the raw scale of individual big cities, but for the proliferation of big cities within an interacting global network of urban places that were linked together by interlocking railway systems, shipping networks, and telegraph lines. Sydney, notwithstanding its geographical isolation, boasted an imposing central post office which was decorated with allegorical representations of the four quarters of the globe to which the city was linked by regular lines of communication. San Franciscans likewise felt confident of their harbour's place upon 'the World's Great Highway'.[24]

These networked cities functioned as the handmaidens of capitalist accumulation. They were economic hubs and communications nodes for their surrounding regions. Birmingham was described in 1908 as 'pre-eminently the market place of the Midlands. Not only does it produce an enormous volume of manufactures itself, but the major portion of the produce of the Midlands passes through the hands of its merchants.' The growth of Birmingham to become the second largest city in England was grounded in the expansion of coal-mining and iron-working in the Black Country region of South Staffordshire during the eighteenth century. Massive nineteenth-century growth in iron production until the 1860s enabled Birmingham entrepreneurs to consolidate the city's position as the region's commercial, distribution, and banking centre. It also became a finishing point for local products. The city thus emerged as a centre for the manufacture of jewellery, guns, brass products, buttons, and toys. Birmingham's ability to dominate new enterprises was facilitated by an extensive canal network, already completed by 1800, and was augmented by extensive railway construction during the first half of the century. As the iron industry declined during the second half of the century, and the Black Country switched to the manufacture of steel, Birmingham added engineering and metal-refining to its industrial staples. Entrepreneurs flocked to exploit the city's highly skilled and concentrated labour force.[25]

Whereas Birmingham's nineteenth-century development took place as the hub of an established region, urban development in the New World performed a gateway role, paving the way for the large-scale settlement and economic development of new regions. San Francisco, for example, had by 1900 — boosted by the Spanish–American War — become 'the chief port of entry and export' between the United States, China, Japan, and the Pacific. Its businessmen boasted that 'As New York is the gateway on the Atlantic side, so San Francisco is the gateway on the Pacific side, and the greater portion of the vast commerce of the Pacific is destined to pass through the Golden Gate.'[26] It had boomed during the second half of the nineteenth century as a handling centre for rural exports, thereby facilitating the establishment of Californian agriculture in 1860s and 1870s. The city consolidated its gateway role during 1880s by processing locally produced rural goods. Slaughtering and meat-packing, sugar-refining, milling, and the manufacture of boots and shoes became important city industries. San Francisco was among the top ten manufacturing centres in the nation by 1900.

The gateway function performed by market-place cities in the New World is highlighted by the rise of the colonial Australian port cities. Adelaide, hub of the South Australian wheat belt, was described in the early 1870s as 'a great entrepôt and market for grains and timber'. To dock in Melbourne or Sydney was to be enveloped in a 'forest of ships' masts ... on all sides'. Marine technological innovation, the opening of the Suez Canal, and reducing transport costs, had by the early 1870s firmly integrated the Australian run among the world's major shipping networks. The Australian port cities thereafter absorbed their hinterlands into the British trading system by developing them as new commodity markets. Sydney, for example, was a conduit to new lands for European settlement: the immigration intake from Britain to New South Wales boomed during the 1880s. It was a funnel for British investment capital, which during the 1870s and 1880s poured into infant colonial enterprises and government infrastructure developments such as railway construction. It was a service centre which underpinned local rural development by accumulating industries specializing in ship repair and construction, vehicle manufacture, the production of simple agricultural implements, and boot and shoe manufacture. It handled the growing volume of imported manufactured products which was consumed by the city's expanding hinterland. Simultaneously, it channelled the accumulating rural products of that hinterland to world markets. Harbourside rail yards handled 'an enormous and constantly increasing traffic' in agricultural produce, minerals, timber, and wool. A broker noted in 1890 that during each wool season drays 'almost monopolise the streets of the city' as wool was shuttled between the railways, the merchants' stores, and the wharves.[27]

In proportion to Sydney's successful accumulation of commercial functions as a gateway city for new regions, the evolving city became itself a mass new market to be tapped by capitalist entrepreneurs. It formed a dependable and multi-layered market for wage labour. Moreover, mass city living generated large new potential markets for accommodation, for food and drink, for amusements and novelties, for personal services, for city news and information. It encouraged the flow of private investment capital into increasingly speculative markets for urban land and building construction in the 1870s and 1880s, which in addition to sustaining a mania for suburban living resulted in a redevelopment and commercial building boom which remodelled the central city as a specialized business district. Mass city living, like the rural industries which the gateway city sustained, generated a multiplicity of commodities to be marketed for private profit.

To argue that cities collectively are market-place creations is unexceptionable. The determining influence of market cycles upon city economies, the sway of businessmen within city municipal halls, and the intrusive effects of entrepreneurial agendas upon the inner-city neighbourhoods, are immediately evident in the following three chapters on municipal improvement strategies in San Francisco, Birmingham, and Sydney. There is none the less a danger lest we appropriate too readily from past characterizations of modern cities as we strive to encapsulate the nature and consequences of market-driven urban change. The risk in so doing is that we unintentionally perpetuate an abstraction — the modern city — rather than unravelling as fully as we might the fractured and patchworked urban forms to which this concept was applied. The modern city — proud and optimistic in its celebration of modernity and community — was in fact a necessarily countervailing influence to the confusion and dismay with which city-dwellers often reacted to the discontinuous and kaleidoscopic qualities of urban society, and to the unpredictable and uneven outcomes of rapid change. The diversity and formlessness of urban mass led some inhabitants to characterize their cities a 'labyrinth of human ways'. One Birmingham resident shook his head in 1907 that 'there is no plan, system or organisation. Everything is chaotic and go as you please.' The 'clashing contradictions' of these market-place cities were highlighted by the grandiose improvement schemes which sought to modernize city centres by sweeping away their unsightly and unproductive slums.[28]

Notes

[1] Weber is quoted by Katznelson, I., Reflections on space and the city, in Mollenkopf, 1988, p. 285. Wohl, 1991, p. 80.

[2] Coleman, 1973, pp. 166–7. Macdonald, 1886, p. 234. *Daily Telegraph*, 2 May 1891, p. 4, Australian cities. Strong, 1907, p. 16.

[3] Stead, 1964, p. 335.

[4] Masterman's *From the abyss* is quoted in Wohl, 1991, p. 79. Gorki's *The city of the yellow devil* is quoted in Marqusee, 1988, p. 10. Adams, W. E., *Our American cousins*, is quoted in Still, 1956, pp. 206–7.

[5] Lees, 1985, p. 200. *The Public*, 13 January 1900, quoted in White, 1989, p. 37. Still, 1956, p. 228.

[6] Henry James, *The American scene*, quoted in Still, 1956, p. 257; George W Steevens (1896) is quoted in ibid., p. 206. *The Social Economist*, December 1893, is quoted in White, 1989, p. 152. Buder, 1990, p. 68.

[7] Chamberlain, J., in *BPP*, 1884–5, question 12,358, p. 443.

[8] *BPP*, 1871, p. 177. Ralph, 1890, p. 99.

[9] Twopeny, 1883, p. 2. *Daily Telegraph*, 28 November 1895, p. 2, Municipal elections. Coghlan, 1897, p. 600.

[10] Chamber of Commerce of San Francisco, 1902, p. 30. Merchants Exchange, 1907, p. 9. Glennan to Wyman, letter, 30 November 1902, in Marine Hospital Service, Box 551, NA. Board of Trade of San Francisco, 1893, pp. 9–10. Chamber of Commerce of San Francisco, 1875, p. 5.

[11] Park, 1906, n.p.

[12] Searlight, 1906, p. 20. Tyler, 1906, pp. 303–4. Linthicum, 1906, pp. 48, 255. Steele, 1909, pp. 47, 79. See also Anon, n.d. (1908).

[13] San Francisco Board of Supervisors, 1908–9, n.p. Merchants Exchange, 1909, p. 11. Geddes is quoted in Lees, 1985, pp. 238–9. Bancroft, 1907, p. 4.

[14] Ayles, W.A., in minutes of evidence, *BPP*, 1909, p. 431. Howe is quoted in Lees, 1985, p. 202. Olmsted is quoted in Scobey, 1989, p. 238.

[15] Howells is quoted in ibid., p. 2.

[16] Shapiro, 1983, p. 72. Klein and Kantor, 1976, p. 154. Scobey, 1989, p. 231.

[17] Lees, 1985, p. 237. See Fraser, 1976, pp. 154–75.

[18] Bancroft, 1907, p. 17. *Birmingham Daily Post*, 28 October 1878, p.5, The municipal elections. Riis, 1904, p. 132. Lees, 1985, p. 250.

[19] Chamberlain, 1894, p. 652. Dolman, 1985, p. 1.

[20] Chamberlain, 1894, p. 652. Dolman, 1985, pp. 1–2, 10. Ralph, 1890, p. 107.

[21] Klein and Kantor, 1976, title page. Menton, H.J., in *BPP*, 1909, p. 342. *Sydney Morning Herald*, 19 August 1876, p. 4, editorial; and see Fitzgerald, 1987.

[22] *Votes and Proceedings of the New South Wales Legislative Assembly*, 1875–6, question 272, p. 625. *Birmingham Daily Post*, 23 October 1878, p. 7, The municipal elections.

[23] Anon, n.d. (1902), p. 40. Webb, 1938, p. 150. Ralph, 1890, p. 99. See Briggs, 1952; Hennock, 1956; Fraser, 1976, chapter 4.

[24] San Francisco Chamber of Commerce, 1893, p. 3.

[25] *BPP*, 1908, p. 81. See British Association for the Advancement of Science, 1950; A history of Warwickshire, in Pugh, 1964.

[26] Board of Trade of San Francisco, 1899, p. 18. ibid., 1901, p. 20.

[27] Giovanni Balangero, quoted in Mayne, 1991b, p. 67. *V&P(NSW LA)*, 1888–9, pp. 599–602. John Henry Geddes, minutes of evidence, question 789, in *V & P (NSW LA)*, 1890.

[28] Walker, 1962, p. 97. Ayles, W.H., in *BPP*, 1909, p. 431. Pike, 1981, p. 26.

3

Drama: eradicating plague from San Francisco, 1900–1909

'Disaster and ... horror'[1]

Dramatic events convulsed San Francisco during the first decade of the twentieth century. The spectacular climax was an earthquake and fire which destroyed most of the city in April 1906. Telegraph news splashed the story in headlines across the world. Three days after the event, the *Sun* newspaper published a nostalgic pean to 'The City That Was: A Requiem of Old San Francisco'. The lament was coupled with predictions of rebirth. San Francisco would 'rise ... out of the ashes ... a modern city'.[2] The events of 1906, retold with an eye to the likelihood of their repetition, have obscured other early twentieth-century city dramas. This chapter addresses three of these: the bubonic plague epidemic of 1900–05, the sensational exposés of San Francisco's oriental slumland which accompanied the epidemic, and the reappearance of plague in 1907–9.

Some 110 people died from bubonic plague in San Francisco between 1900 and 1904.[3] Health officials believed that many more deaths were concealed. Almost all the epidemic's victims were Chinese, and they had all lived in or near the city's Chinatown. Dramatic news of the first-ever appearance of the Black Death in mainland United States broke in March 1900. A global pandemic had spread from China since the mid-1890s. Plague caused 180,000 deaths in Canton during 1894. Millions died in India. The San Francisco Board of Health rushed to avert another catastrophe. Urged along by federal medical officials of the Marine Hospital Service (renamed the Public Health and Marine Hospital Service in 1902) who were stationed in the city, the Board cordoned off the whole of Chinatown and — as it had done during Chinatown's smallpox epidemic in 1876 — rushed volunteers to spray disinfectant, scour the sewers, and begin house-to-house inspections of the district.

In Washington, DC, the Supervising Surgeon General[4] of the Public Health and Marine Hospital Service, Dr Walter Wyman, immediately sent a plague expert — Dr Arthur H. Glennan, his bureau chief in New Orleans — to check the reports. Anticipating the worst, Wyman telegraphed advice to

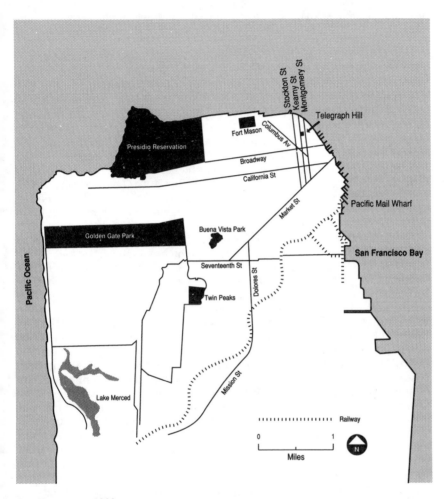

San Francisco, 1900

the city authorities, and kept a close watch on events through Dr Joseph J. Kinyoun, the Service officer in charge of the Angel Island federal quarantine station in San Francisco Bay. Late in 1900, Wyman sent Dr Joseph H. White, the officer commanding the entire Division of Domestic Quarantine, to take charge of federal operations. Acting on White's advice, Wyman appointed a federal Plague Commission to assess the unfolding emergency.

Prodded into action by the Commission's report, which was released in March 1901, the State Board of Health joined city authorities and the Marine Hospital Service in a renewed blitz of medical inspections and disinfecting work throughout Chinatown, which began in April 'under the advice and direction' of Dr White.[5] In addition the city Board of Supervisors, prompted by White, ordered that insanitary buildings in Chinatown be declared public nuisances and destroyed. Cleansing operations were wound down in June, after almost 1,200 houses had been disinfected. For the next year it seemed that an epidemic had been averted.

That hope was dashed by a surge of new cases during the second half of 1902. Glennan, now chief quarantine officer in Cuba, was again sent to assess the situation. In December, with plague deaths climbing towards 100, the Surgeon General personally visited San Francisco. A new plan was worked out in February 1903 between Wyman, the Mayor, and the state Governor to throw even more resources into the plague prevention measures in Chinatown, under the formal direction of the Public Health and Marine Hospital Service. Dr Rupert Blue, who had been attached to the federal plague-prevention squad in San Francisco since 1901, was placed in charge. By the end of March, the whole of Chinatown had been inspected, and hundreds of premises sprayed and limed. Every week thereafter, hundreds more houses were reinspected and disinfected, as were dwellings in the adjoining 'Japanese territory' and the 'latin quarter slums'.[6]

The city authorities simultaneously 'commenced ... a vigorous assault' to tear down 'the old wooden rookeries' which had been tacked on to buildings in Chinatown, choking the rear alleys and courts.[7] Insanitary buildings were simultaneously condemned as unfit for human habitation, and closing orders were issued until they were adequately repaired. The clause against buildings unfit for human habitation had been enacted in 1876, during the smallpox emergency in Chinatown. It was used by the City Board of Health in 1880 in an attempt to condemn the whole of Chinatown as a nuisance, but the experiment was stymied by legal impediments. The Board tried again to issue closing orders between 1888 and 1890, and each year secured the repair or demolition of a scattering of old and insanitary buildings in Chinatown. City officials sought to employ the clause on a more extensive scale in Chinatown during 1896, and as a consequence 'numerous premises ... were torn down to the ground'.[8] However, this initiative was stopped late in the year when Chinatown property owners obtained a court injunction to restrain the Board. Fear of plague in 1903 muted the earlier opposition. By mid-October, 160 buildings had been torn down and another 70 houses closed. In February 1904, when representatives of the city's commercial associations, the Public Health and Marine Hospital Service, the Board of Supervisors, and the city and state Boards of Health met to formalize terms for extending their collaborative programme for another year, it was resolved that all underground dwellings in Chinatown should be condemned as unfit for human habitation and destroyed.

The plague eradication programme in Chinatown was not wound down until the first quarter of 1905, a year after the last known cases of plague. Blue was applauded on all sides for successfully preserving 'San Francisco's high sanitary state and commercial prosperity'. Wyman trumpeted that plague had been beaten by the 'united and harmonious efforts' of federal, state, and city authorities.[9]

Adding to the drama of Black Death in San Francisco were sensational depictions of the city's Chinese 'netherworld'. Chinatown was held accountable for introducing and sustaining such an alien pestilence. Plague dramatically underlined the district's reputation as a fetid slum. Vivid newspaper photographs of condemned buildings, whitewashing teams, and burning garbage, all accompanied by lurid commentaries, affirmed long-held popular beliefs that Chinatown was indeed a 'Hotbed For All Sorts Of Disease'.[10]

San Francisco's Chinatown was the largest Chinese settlement outside China. Its core spread over 12 city blocks, and a significant Chinese presence extended across 20 blocks. Chinatown's population in 1900 fluctuated between 12,000 during the summer and 15,000 during the winter, when labourers returned from the Alaskan salmon canneries, and from fruit picking and ranching in the Californian hinterland. San Francisco's Chinese population had halved since 1890, the result of restrictive federal legislation, and continued to decline until the 1920s. The Chinese Exclusion Act of 1880, which was periodically extended until 1945, suspended the immigration of Chinese labourers. In 1887 the Scott Act prohibited the return of Chinese once they had left the United States, and in 1892 the Geary Act required all Chinese residents in the United States to obtain a certificate of eligibility in order to remain in the country.

The City Board of Health declared sensationally that the sanitary inspections prompted by plague had resulted in them 'discovering' in Chinatown 'the most degraded, filthy, immoral and unsanitary location within the boundaries of the United States of America'. The board warned that this 'wretched' district, 'honeycombed' by underground passages in which the sick were secreted to evade the health inspectors, represented 'a constant menace to the health of the community'.[11]

Federal medical experts concurred. Kinyoun characterized Chinatown as a place 'of filth and refuse', inhabited by 'the lowest cooly [sic] class ... [who] live under the worst hygienic conditions imaginable.' In 1901 the federal Plague Commission, guided by city police detectives, confirmed that the poorer inhabitants of Chinatown were living in 'shockingly unsanitary' conditions, and drew attention to opium addiction and prostitution. White, who directed the three-tier cleansing programme in Chinatown which was set up after the Commission's report, was so disgusted by the amount of filth which the disinfecting teams uncovered that he called 'the thorough cleansing of Chinatown ... almost a physical impossibility'. He predicted that 'almost every block in Chinatown I frankly believe will have to be gutted.' His successor, Blue, labelled the buildings in Chinatown 'excrescences', and characterized the entire district as filthy, overcrowded, and 'a hotbed for all manner of infections'.[12]

The State Board of Health, which toured Chinatown in April 1903, also expressed shock at 'its extremely bad sanitary condition'. In the following month the State Board urged the total destruction of Chinatown, citing 'the presence in the heart of the great city of a large alien and unassimilable population ... [as] a constant and serious menace to the health, commerce and industries, not only to the city itself but also of the State and even the Nation at large.' The State Board, federal officials, and the city's commercial associations all applauded the city for its demolition work in Chinatown. The daily press, too, rejoiced that 'many old rookeries are being torn down', and applauded the new 'era of improvement in Chinatown' that had been prompted by the disease scare.[13]

The appearance of plague prompted a spate of proposals by improvement clubs, commercial associations, and the daily press between 1900 and 1904 for the wholesale demolition of Chinatown. Some favoured a municipal street improvement scheme to run 'a great thoroughfare' through the district. Others suggested a bond issue to raise enough capital 'to condemn and purchase the entire district, clear off the buildings, rectify the grades, widen the streets, close the blind alleys, repave and resewer the district and sell off the lots for building purposes.' Business leaders suggested spending up to $10 million to replace Chinatown with a park. Responding to these suggestions, the City Board of Health recommended that 'Chinatown ... cannot be rendered sanitary except by total obliteration. It should be depopulated, its buildings levelled by fire and its tunnels and cellars laid bare; its occupants should be colonized on some distant portion of the peninsula.' Plans were prepared late in 1902 by the Board of Supervisors 'for cutting two avenues on an extensive scale' through Chinatown, but the scheme was set aside because of the heavy cost.[14]

Fresh dramas — earthquake, fire, and renewed pestilence — piled upon the earlier dramas of Black Death and slumland discovery. On the morning of 18 April 1906 a massive earthquake rocked San Francisco, and with the water mains destroyed, fires raged uncontrolled. Four days later, when the fires went out, 520 city blocks were blackened and 25,000 buildings lay in ruins. At least 460 people were dead, and 300,000 more were left homeless. Chinatown had been destroyed. The city's commercial centre was gutted.[15]

A year later, in May 1907, plague reappeared in the devastated city. The likelihood of epidemic disease again dramatically underlined the 'deplorable condition' of sanitation in the city. Health officials acknowledged that 'vast accumulations' of filth had been allowed to accumulate, and conceded 'the disgustingly unsanitary condition' of many of the city's remaining buildings.[16] San Francisco's commercial associations, anticipating the likely quarantine of the port and anxious to avoid another body blow to the city's economy, urged intervention by the Public Health and Marine Hospital Service, under the direction of the tried-and-trusted Rupert Blue.

Plague in 1907 had initially appeared about the wharves and on the site of Chinatown, but subsequently spread throughout the city. With Chinatown being compulsorily rebuilt with rat-proof buildings, very few Chinese died as the disease spread. In neighbouring Oakland, by contrast, a city of 225,000 people across the bay, the large Chinatown remained 'very insanitary' and was targeted by the cleansing teams. In San Francisco, 25 blocks in the heart of the unburnt city, containing the Japanese and Italian quarters, were earmarked because of their alleged overcrowding and filth. However, health officials conceded that infected rats infested all San Francisco's timber dwellings, planked yards, basements, and garbage bins. The city's nine miles of wooden docks were especially 'rat-riddled', as were the sprawling wholesale fruit and vegetable section behind the water front, and the bayshore area of old wooden slaughterhouses known as Butchertown.[17]

Rats also swarmed in the burnt-out districts, amid the rubble which still littered streets and vacant allotments, inside damaged and destroyed sewers, and among the many temporary stables. Thousands of refugees lived in temporary shacks made from scraps of sheet iron and timber, many of them located in congested and insanitary camps. By the time the epidemic subsided early in 1908, 159 plague cases had been reported, resulting in 78 deaths. Another seven deaths were reported in Oakland. Plague remained endemic among rats in the bay area, and spread to squirrels. A handful of new human cases were uncovered in Oakland and surrounding counties during 1911, and in 1925 another outbreak occurred in Oakland and in Los Angeles.

When plague had reappeared in San Francisco in 1907, the Public Health and Marine Hospital Service immediately began to inspect and fumigate shipping, and again offered assistance to the City Board of Health. However, the city government, already reeling from the disasters of 1906, had insufficient funds to sustain an effective plague eradication programme, and telegraphed President Theodore Roosevelt in September to ask the federal health officers to take charge. In July 1908 the Mayor telegraphed Roosevelt that the magnitude of plague prevention and eradication measures was beyond the city and state, and asked the Public Health and Marine Hospital Service to take over full control and bear the cost.[18]

Rupert Blue was again sent to San Francisco and assumed control of a force of almost 750 doctors, inspectors, and labourers. Plague cases were sent to an isolation camp, their houses fumigated, and their contents disinfected or burned. Gangs of labourers placed rat traps, laid poison, and set about rat-proofing buildings by concreting basements, floors, yards, passageways, and sidewalks. House-to-house and garbage-can inspections were instituted. Rat-infested buildings were ordered destroyed, as also were large numbers of insanitary refugee shacks and stables. By the end of 1909 over 730 houses had been torn down.[19]

In January 1908 the Mayor appointed a Citizens' Health Committee to help Blue by mobilizing the community against the 'impending pestilence'. At year's end, Wyman reported confidently to Congress that Blue had received

the hearty support and cooperation of the ... governor of the State, the state board of health, the mayor of San Francisco, the board of supervisors of the city and county of San Francisco, the city board of health, the police department, the citizens' health committee, the state medical association, and committees from various improvement clubs, labor organizations, trades councils, mercantile bodies, and women's clubs.[20]

In March 1909 a banquet in Blue's honour was held in San Francisco to commemorate the eradication of bubonic plague. Ostentatiously staged in the middle of a city street, the banquet sought to ram home the message that San Francisco's streets were now 'clean enough to eat from'. Blue, his reputation cemented, went on to become Surgeon General of the renamed and expanded Public Health Service in 1912. In San Francisco, with returning confidence, the Chamber of Commerce asserted that 'To-day San Francisco can be pointed to as possibly the cleanest city in the civilized world.' The chamber characterized the reconstruction and improvement of the city as being 'undeniably one of the world's wonders'.[21]

Federal plague eradication measures in San Francisco continued after 1909 upon a smaller scale until the First World War. Federally employed labouring staff poisoned and trapped rats, rat-proofed buildings, pulled down shacks and stables, and removed garbage. City inspectors worked under federal direction, systematically reinspecting premises and enforcing new municipal sanitary ordinances. In 1916 federal operations in the city were transferred back to the municipal authorities, although the Public Health Service continued to maintain a squirrel-free zone around the bay cities until turning this task over to the State Board of Health in 1936. The Service still operated a plague laboratory in San Francisco and continued to supervise a scaled-down programme of rat-trapping and rat-proofing by the City Health Department. From the mid-1920s, the Public Health Service again provided staff to help the city sustain sanitary inspections and rat-trapping. This assistance was maintained throughout the 1930s. Every year during the 1920s, as a result of this collaborative work, between 100 and 200 buildings were referred to the Board of Health for condemnation as unfit for human habitation. Between 1920 and 1932, 1,400 buildings were torn down at the Board's orders.

'... the most complicated situation I have ever known'[22]

Telling the story of catastrophe and renewal in San Francisco involves three more dramas. The first is historiographical. Perplexingly, after the initial sensational press coverage in 1900 of plague in Chinatown, public discourse on the subject abruptly ceased. This occurred despite the massive gearing up of plague prevention and eradication measures. Just as surprisingly, most of this early press sensationalism, although hostile to Chinatown, sought to deny the existence of plague and to belittle the health officials who diagnosed it. The second drama partially explains the first. Reporting the news of plague and slum clearance stopped as the result of a cover-up, arranged at a secret meeting between the State Governor and representatives of the San Francisco press, and perpetuated in covert agreements made with the Marine Hospital Service.

The third drama is enmeshed in the first two. As such, it is fully comprehensible only if we wrench ourselves loose from our own expectations of dramatic significance in order to moor early twentieth-century newsmaking to the local horizons and particular preoccupations which animated it. In so doing, dramas of a different order become evident. The story of plague becomes a story of conflict. Social drama — the ongoing process of social conflict and conflict resolution — comprised the everyday essence of big-city social interaction and public policy-making: 'In San Francisco plague met politics ... There was open popular hostility to the work of the sanitarians, and war among the City, State, and Federal health authorities.'[23]

The twin plague emergencies unfolded amid controversy and apparent contradiction. Notwithstanding Wyman's public assertions of community mobilization in support of the eradication programmes, health officials privately fretted about community indifference to the plague danger. Kinyoun had announced with frustration in 1900 that these 'people seem to be perfectly indifferent whether or not bubonic plague exists in San Francisco, so long as they can sell their products and make large percentages on their investments.'[24] The establishment of the Citizens' Health Committee in 1908, far from highlighting community support of Blue's programme, was in fact an emergency effort intended to overcome indifference and hostility.

The State Board of Health had reported in 1903 that 'Everything that sanitary science can suggest and money can do is being done to put Chinatown in a healthful condition.' This apparent confidence was skin-deep. The motives and competence of the health authorities were in fact widely derided during both plague outbreaks. The *Examiner* noted that 'One of the features of the situation is the readiness of laymen to put their opinions against those of the doctors in regard to the existence and symptoms of disease.'[25]

Ridicule of scientific medicine was expressed most vociferously by the city press. The City Board of Health had been 'ridiculed' by the press in 1876 when it announced that smallpox was epidemic in Chinatown. Now, in the early 1900s, journalists sneeringly dubbed the City Board of Health the 'bubonic Health Board', characterized its diagnosis of plague a 'fake' and 'swindle', and lampooned its eradication measures as a 'farce'.[26] The *Chronicle* characterized the link which the Public Health and Marine Hospital Service drew between infected rats and plague as 'humbug', and continued to deny throughout the second outbreak of plague at the end of the decade that the illness was 'genuine plague'. Despite the discovery of the plague bacillus in 1894, the newspaper scoffed that 'this whole germ theory is yet in its infancy' and reiterated earlier allegations that the laboratory diagnoses in 1900 were the fumbled results of 'scientific busybodies'. Defying the Public Health and Marine Hospital Service's definitive pronouncements of a flea–rat connection in the spread of plague, the *Chronicle* continued to call the rat theory of plague transmission a 'farce', and the anti-plague programme thus a waste of time and money. Blue worried that 'a good many ignorant persons have accepted these derogatory statements as truths and have used them against our work.'[27]

Notwithstanding the general rush in 1900 to condemn Chinatown on account of the stories of filth and overcrowding which accompanied the cleansing operations, the *Examiner* was almost alone in conceding the presence of plague in the city, and in supporting eradication measures which extended beyond Chinatown. The City Board of Health complained that it had become the subject of an 'editorial fusillade' of 'virulent press criticism', which had influenced 'the opinion of a large percentage of the public into one of pronounced and aggressive enmity toward the Board'. Even at the end of the first joint plague eradication programme by federal, city, and state health authorities in June 1901, the City Board commented that the attitude of the press remained so 'extremely unsatisfactory' that the people of San Francisco continued to 'delude themselves' about the threat of plague.[28] Although a special conference of the states, meeting in

Washington, DC in February 1903 to discuss the plague emergency in San Francisco, pressured the city and state authorities to acknowledge the presence of plague in California and to instigate decisive eradication measures under the direction of the public health service, the *Chronicle* still vehemently denied the truth of the epidemic.

During the second epidemic of 1907–9, the City Board of Health reported that the press in general remained 'openly antagonistic' to the health authorities, and the State Board of Health likewise railed against 'malicious' newspaper commentaries which 'persisted in either denying the existence of the disease, or minimizing the danger.' The State Board fumed that 'the result was entire apathy on the part of the public, and the danger grew.'[29]

The conflicts generated by competition between medical and lay common sense were intensified by contending styles of journalism. Telling the city's morning news was dominated by the struggle for circulation between the *Chronicle* and the *Examiner.* The former was owned by Michael De Young, characterized by Blue as 'a strange, stubborn man [who] ... likes to be consulted about San Francisco affairs'.[30] The managing editor was John P. Young. The *Examiner,* teetering on the brink of bankruptcy when it was bought by mining millionaire George Hearst in the 1880s, was so quickly turned around by his son William Randolph Hearst that by the turn of the century it enjoyed the largest newspaper circulation in the state. Its sales were greater than those of the *Chronicle* and the *Call* combined. Hearst strove to make city affairs newsworthy. Typical of his style was the newspaper's sensational exposures during 1900 and 1901 of Chinatown gambling and police corruption, which prompted investigation by state legislature, humiliation for the millionaire Democrat reform Mayor, James Duval Phelan, and the discrediting of his police chief. John Young sneered that the *Examiner* 'was more intent on attracting attention to itself by doing things out of the usual than it was concerned about the formation or interpretation of public opinion.' Hearst's methods were disparaged by the *Chronicle* as 'yellow journalism', an epithet which the *Examiner* defiantly adopted as a shorthand term for its ongoing 'crusade for pure and effective city government'.[31]

A similar clash of newspaper styles was played out every evening, as the *Call* strove to protect its leading share of newspaper sales from the *Bulletin.* The latter, a staid paper until Fremont Older became managing editor in 1895, was rapidly revitalized. Chasing big circulation, the *Bulletin* adopted 'the methods of the most sensational evening papers of the Eastern metropolis'.[32] Fremont Older introduced big-type headlines, abundant illustrations, and launched flamboyant exposés of municipal protection rackets involving prostitution and gambling in Chinatown.

Journalistic rivalry was compounded by the newspapers' sharply divergent political affiliations. The *Chronicle* was conservative Republican in stance. The *Call,* moderate Republican in tone, was a mouthpiece for its owner, the businessman John D. Spreckels. Its editorial staff were labelled 'lackeys of the plutocracy' by Hearst.[33] The *Bulletin,* like the *Call* and the *Chronicle,* had long been Republican in sympathy, but after its sale to the businessman R.A. Crothers, Fremont Older switched its editorial policy to support Phelan's Democrat reforms.

Hearst's *Examiner* also leaned to the Democrats, and was consequently savaged by its Republican rivals as being 'the very backbone' of the City Board of Health when plague was first diagnosed in 1900. Yet by 1900 the *Examiner* was distancing itself from Phelan's pro-business administration as organized labour and capital lined up more and more against one another. By 1902 Hearst, who was running for Congress in New York in preparation for a drive at the Democratic nomination for President in 1904, was keen to demonstrate to the east that the Californian labour movement was solidly behind him. The *Examiner* therefore supported Mayor Eugene E. Schmitz's corrupt Union Labor Party administration which replaced Phelan, earning from the *Bulletin* the epithet 'the official organ of the grafting administration'. Schmitz repaid Hearst by travelling east in October 1902 to speak in his New York campaign.[34]

Bubonic plague highlighted other social dramas. Some, involving protests by property owners and the Chinese, were specific to the epidemic. Other conflicts represented longer-standing antagonisms, being played out upon a new stage. The forcible closure or demolition of insanitary property put city officials in conflict with property owners, whose objections were pressed within the Board of Supervisors and surfaced in the city press. These tensions were exacerbated by reformist proposals for comprehensive slum clearances. The suggestions prompted the Chinatown Property Owners' Association to ridicule as 'bosh' the widespread representations of Chinatown as being underpinned by a 'foul subterranean' network of tunnels and lairs.[35]

Chinese anger spilled out on to the streets. At the beginning of the epidemic in 1900, attempts to undertake a sanitary survey of Chinatown and to launch a mass innoculation programme stalled in the face of Chinese resistance. The sanitary inspectors found their entrance to houses barred. The innoculation campaign prompted demonstrations, stone-throwing, and proclamations by highbinder tongs (highly organized gangs) threatening any Chinese who co-operated. Medical staffs were mobbed and their fumigating apparatus destroyed.

The initial quarantine cordon around Chinatown and federal ban on the movement of uninnoculated Asians prompted Chinese and Japanese diplomatic protests, and late in May a federal court granted a Chinese injunction application against both restrictions. Federal courts in June threw out a second sanitary cordon around Chinatown, declared restrictions on interstate travel by Asians unconstitutional, and grilled Kinyoun for possible contempt of the first court order. The federally guided anti-plague programme in Chinatown during 1901 was initially delayed because of Chinese objections, and when it did begin White quickly concluded that the Chinese were systematically concealing plague cases and deaths from his staff. White protested that the Chinese Consul General in San Francisco was 'the ringleader' behind Chinese opposition.[36] Blue encountered equally determined Chinese resistance during the federal programme in Chinatown in 1903, and when demolition work began the wrecking crews had to be guarded by police.

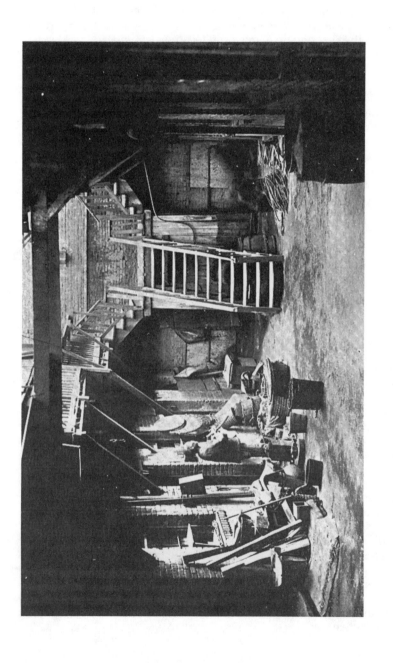

Court of Chinese rookery, Chinatown, San Francisco (from Rieder 1904)

General community responses to Chinese anger, however, were dismissive. The attitude of San Franciscans was well expressed by Mayor Phelan in 1900, when he swept aside Chinese complaints with the comment that they were 'fortunate, with the unclean habits of their coolies and their filthy hovels, to be permitted to remain within the corporate limits of any American city'.[37]

The State Board of Health reported fulsomely at the conclusion of the second plague epidemic that California 'owes a great deal to the steady co-operation and support of the United States Government in the eradication of this dangerous disease from the bay cities'.[38] Wyman, too, in his public statements repeatedly drew attention to the co-operation and harmony which he said had all along characterized relations between the federal, state, and city authorities during the plague emergencies. The reality had been very different. Relations between federal and state health officials were acrimonious until a new state administration was sworn in early in 1903. Although the two groups thereafter worked together closely, relations between federal officials and City Hall — which had hitherto been warm — became increasingly strained after Schmitz was elected Mayor late in 1901. Relations between city and state governments were uniformly bad until 1912, when a progressive reformer was elected Mayor with joint Republican and Democratic endorsement.

In 1900 the Republican Governor, Henry T. Gage, and his State Board of Health had vehemently denied the presence of plague. So great was the mutual suspicion between state and federal authorities in California that Gage hired a private detective agency to 'shadow' Marine Hospital Service officials. The latter relied on coded telegrams to communicate between San Francisco and Washington. The Marine Hospital Service blamed the State Board of Health for having 'led Governor Gage astray' by feeding him misleading medical advice. A majority on the State Board doubted the plague diagnosis, and cold-shouldered the doctors who had diagnosed it. Their hostility focused upon the State Bacteriologist, Dr H.A.L. Ryfkogel, who was driven from office. Their antagonism also extended to the City Bacteriologist, Dr W.H. Kellogg, and to Kinyoun, who had confirmed the two local bacteriologists' diagnoses. Kinyoun became the embattled target for 'vituperation and vials of wrath' from the Governor and his allies. Further 'hard feeling' was generated when Ryfkogel joined the Marine Hospital Service's San Francisco plague eradication team and in 1902 became acting City Bacteriologist.[39]

This friction encompassed far more than competing medical reputations. Federal officials concluded that the 'concealment' party was tied up with 'state pride'. Kinyoun noted that newspaper depictions of him as 'a scoundrel of the deepest dye' were grounded in the allegation that he 'was attempting, by circulating reports which were not true, to destroy the reputation of "the great State of California".' State sensitivities enmeshed with city parochialism. Wyman was attacked in the San Francisco press for having 'brazenly enroll[ed] himself among ... the official calumniators of San Francisco'. Newspaper vilification of the City Board of Health was likewise grounded in indignation that the Board was attempting 'to fasten upon San Francisco the stigma of being a bubonic plague infected city.'[40]

Local sensitivities were intimately bound up with the contentious subject of federal–state power-sharing. Federal health authorities had, during the last quarter of the nineteenth century, vigorously sought to build up a uniform national system of public health administration. Their object was contested by big city governments. It was further complicated by the constitution, which reserved to the states under their local police powers the responsibility 'to secure the comfort, happiness, and health of the people'.[41] The exclusive nature of these powers had, since early in the century, been gradually unravelled by the Supreme Court. At the turn of the century, however, federal statutory authority and the majority opinion of law-makers both in Congress and state legislatures still limited the jurisdiction of federal health officials to providing the states with advice and co-operation.

Federal quarantine legislation in 1890 had enabled the President to enforce regulations drawn up by the Marine Hospital Service to prevent the interstate spread of cholera, yellow fever, smallpox, and plague, wherever local administration was judged inadequate by the Surgeon General. The quarantine law of 1893 greatly expanded Marine Hospital Service oversight of state and local health jurisdictions, requiring the service to scrutinize state and local safeguards against infectious disease, and to enforce additional regulations if necessary. The caveat, however, was that federal intervention should take the form of co-operation and aid rather than outright direction. This 'spirit of cooperation and friendly assistance' was further codified by Congress in 1902, when it required the new Public Health and Marine Hospital Service to hold annual conferences with state health authorities.[42]

Wyman, ambitious to transform the Marine Hospital Service into an agency with overriding national health functions, therefore pressed for incremental federal legislation which expanded his Service's responsibilities in collaboration with local health authorities. He simultaneously scouted for local emergencies where Marine Hospital Service advice and financial assistance could be used to enhance the federal agency's reputation as senior party. Local authorities which spurned Wyman's proffered assistance could thereby be branded as pariahs for upsetting the Marine Hospital Service's loudly proclaimed commitment to harmony of action. Their bad example could be pointed to in order to press for greater federal powers in cases where local authorities refused to co-operate for the national good.

The strategy ultimately worked brilliantly in San Francisco. President Roosevelt pointed to the Public Health and Marine Hospital Service's containment of plague as proof of the need for a strong federal health service. In the aftermath of Blue's successful plague eradication programme, handsomely supported by federal funding, the state of California and the city of San Francisco both owed a debt of gratitude to the Public Health and Marine Hospital Service for protecting them from harsh and protracted quarantine restrictions by other states and foreign governments. Moreover, city and state had both learned from the experience that neither possessed the resources and expertise to prevent the importation of infectious disease. At a conference between state and federal health officials in 1903, the new secretary of the California State Board of Health sought to appease other state representatives who had accused California of having hampered White's and Glennan's plague eradication work by emphasizing that the Board was now 'working in perfect harmony and accord under the general direction of Doctor Blue, of the United States Public Health and Marine Hospital Service. There is no friction in any part of the machine.' At the end of the epidemic in 1909 the State Board pointed to the experience as affording 'a practical demonstration' of the need for the Public Health and Marine Hospital Service to become a national department of health.[43]

State policy had been altogether different in 1900. The Marine Hospital Service had then been watched jealously lest it seek to intrude upon Californian jurisdictions. The City and State Boards of Health had both been in conflict with the Marine Hospital Service over quarantine regulation ever since the building of a federal quarantine station at Angel Island had been approved in 1888. Health administration in San Francisco thus had already become a political arena for federal and state competition. These conflicts were exacerbated by plague. Gage, who stacked the State Board with members who ridiculed the plague diagnosis, was accused of having 'intruded politics into health matters'. At the Washington plague conference early in 1903, other state medical representatives scorned the credibility of California's sanitary authorities, saying that they were created as political 'tools'.[44]

Californians countered that outside critics were being deceived by 'A Worked-Up Plague Scare'. The rumours, they said, had been hatched by San Francisco's commercial rivals in Seattle and had been propagated by Wyman, whom John Young accused of having 'conceived the idea of creating a national health body, which was to have a place in the president's cabinet.' Young predicted that the effect of caving in to Wyman's meddlings would be 'to practically turn over the business of caring for the health of the state to the Marine Hospital Service.'[45] When the federal Plague Commission was appointed early in 1901 Gage attempted to stymie the investigation, and demanded that President William McKinley appoint a new commission made up equally of state representatives.

Wyman wielded power under the 1890 Quarantine Act to request the President to intervene where inaction of the sort that the Plague Commission was likely to reveal was endangering the national health. Knowing the danger but loath to capitulate to federal authority, Gage confidentially told White that he was prepared to accept a joint cleansing programme in Chinatown under White's direction, so long as the Commission's findings were kept confidential. When Wyman insisted that the Governor acknowledge the presence of plague, Gage gave ground and in late February formally requested Washington to take charge, pledging co-operation with the Marine Hospital Service. However, Gage simultaneously sent his own commission to the capital, which won from McKinley a pledge that state sovereignty would be respected, and that the Governor was not to be forced against his will to acknowledge the presence of plague. The state commission then hammered out an agreement with Wyman for Marine Hospital Service direction of joint plague-eradication works.

The joint programme launched in 1901 was a shambles from the start, despite Wyman's determined perpetuation of the myth of harmonious co-operation as the basis for legitimizing continuing federal engagement in Californian affairs. The chairman of Gage's commission to Washington, John Young, returned to San Francisco claiming that Wyman had admitted to the delegation that there was no serious disease menace. White, incensed, reported to Wyman that Young continued to write hostile editorials in the *Chronicle*, which by 'still harping on "No Plague"', would 'seriously handicap and possibly destroy my usefulness'.[46] Another attempt was made to discredit federal intervention late in 1902, in response to the sending of Glennan to California on a fact-finding mission about the spread of plague beyond San Francisco. Under a Page 1 banner headline, 'Plague Fake Is Exposed', the *Call* announced that Glennan had really been sent because of Wyman's doubts that plague existed at all, and that Glennan had concluded from his investigation that the supposed plague bacillus found in San Francisco was really only chicken cholera. Glennan indignantly retorted that the report was 'malicious and false in every particular'.[47]

The agreement over joint action collapsed in the middle of 1902. White was told bluntly by John Young that the programme 'should have stopped long ago', and 'that the Service continued its Plague investigations here without due warrant.' Couching the dismissal in terms of state rights, Gage announced that the 'State authorities are now, and always have been, abundantly able to look after the health conditions of the State without interference.' White angrily called this 'a direct insult', but federal oversight of plague eradication measures was legally dependent upon the continuing willingness of the state and local authorities to co-operate with the Marine Hospital Service. Gage's attitude therefore forced Wyman to wind down the federal programme in San Francisco to providing advice to the beleaguered City Board of Health. Even these small-scale operations were hampered by the state authorities, which for the remainder of 1902 persisted in denying the existence of plague and hence the need for any form of collaborative work with the Marine Hospital Service.[48]

Checked by state rights sentiment in California, Wyman turned to the new 1902 statutory requirement for his Service to confer regularly with state health authorities in order to try to win his arguments before a wider forum. The issues were canvassed at a conference of state boards of health in New Haven in October 1902, and as a result of resolutions passed there, and of subsequent requests by other states, a special plague conference was summoned by Wyman to meet in Washington in January 1903. Rumours circulated the country that Wyman had announced at New Haven that there had already been 2,000 plague deaths in San Francisco. The *Bulletin*'s Washington correspondent telegraphed that as a result of the conference other states were contemplating 'drastic measures' to quarantine the city, and to call upon the federal government 'to step in and take charge' unless the city and state authorities formally conceded the existence of plague and acted decisively to suppress it. The cable caused key city health officials, politicians, and businessmen to meet in emergency session to consider how to stave off federal intervention. The new Republican Governor elect, George C. Pardee, privately conceded the presence of plague to Public

Health and Marine Hospital Service officials and expressed his prepared-ness to co-operate. Gage himself, in a final message to the State Legislature on the eve of the Washington conference, presented a 'wordy denial' of plague but finally recommended that the city and state act to remove Chinatown.[49]

The conference was a triumph for Wyman, and a disaster for his Californian opponents. The *Chronicle* complained that the delegates had set out 'to make it appear that San Francisco is a plague infected city', and that as a result, 'the Eastern press has been filled with editorials and statements which convey the impression that the disease is raging in our midst and carrying off thousands of victims.'[50] The conference concluded that the existence of plague in San Francisco had been established beyond doubt, and authorized uniform quarantine restrictions on the city. Delegates demanded that decisive action be taken by the city and state authorities under the direction of the Public Health and Marine Hospital Service, and threatened to quarantine the whole of California if preventive measures were not quickly put in place. Wyman had needed unanimity, if his rhetorical commitment to harmonious consultation and collaboration was to have credibility. He got it. The Surgeon General wooed the delegates by emphasizing his determination 'always ... to recognize fully the authority of the State and not attempt to do anything to override it.' However, Wyman and his senior officers in San Francisco had already stretched that undertaking to the limit by intervening to prevent the Californian State Board of Health from attending the conference. Glennan privately told Pardee that 'the reprehensible conduct' of the Board had stripped them of any legitimacy. He engineered the new Governor's temporary appointment to the Board of a strong advocate of the Public Health and Marine Hospital Service, who was then ordered to attend the conference.[51]

Victorious on the conference floor, the Public Health and Marine Hospital Service still needed a formal invitation to take control in the west. Armed with the conference resolutions, Wyman stepped up the pressure on the city and the state to fall into line. On 2 February Glennan pushed through a resolution by the city's joint mercantile committee — representing the City and State Boards of Trade and peak San Francisco business organizations — acknowledging the presence of plague in Chinatown, and calling upon the Governor and Mayor to institute a plague-eradication programme 'under the supervision of the Public Health and Marine Hospital Service'. The resolution was rushed to Pardee and Schmitz on the same day and formally endorsed by both. Late in the month, with federal direction entrenched and Pardee undertaking to replace Gage's nominees on the State Board of Health, Glennan wrote gleefully to Wyman: 'All opposing interests have withdrawn and the contentions of the past few years are dissipated'.[52]

The combativeness evident in federal–state relations over public health administration in San Francisco also coloured dealings between city and state government, and the internal workings of city politics. When plague first appeared, the Mayor and his nominees on the City Board of Health were Democrat. Federal health officers found that the Republican Governor and the Democratic Mayor 'do not agree upon anything, and will never get together.' The City Board, moreover, was 'ready and willing and anxious to fight any effort of the State board to supersede them.' Denial of plague and belittling of the City Board by the Republican State board and its press allies were thus political acts. Sensational exposés of Chinatown filth and of bumbledom by 'Mayor Phelan's bubonic Health Board' were deliberately shaped so as to illustrate Republican assertions of the 'utter incompetence' of Democratic City Hall.[53]

Health administration was intimately tied to city politics. It was commonly alleged by the Republican press that Phelan's Board had, 'by creating a scare, [hoped to] force the Supervisors to be more generous with money.'[54] Sanitary administration in San Francisco had for decades been paralysed by inadequate funding. Even Phelan's Democratic reform regime, elected in 1896, had brought no relief. Swept into office with strong support from business, Phelan championed his backers' calls for economy in city administration. In 1900, with funds exhausted, the staff of the health department worked on without pay. Marine Hospital Service officers in San Francisco regularly noted that the City Board of Health lacked the funds and staff adequately to inspect and cleanse Chinatown.

When in 1900 the City Board announced the discovery of plague, Phelan's business allies worried about the implications for trade. The Board of Supervisors debated whether to ask the Mayor to sack his health board. Phelan, anxious to distance himself from a potential electoral liability, beat a tactical retreat. Kinyoun reported that Phelan was holding the Board back until after the November municipal elections so as not to invite criticism of his administration. Even after Phelan's re-election, Kinyoun complained that 'the peculiar conditions, largely political, ... seemed to deter the health authorities from doing anything toward the eradication of plague infection in San Francisco'.[55]

The volatility of San Franciscan electoral politics considerably complicated plague eradication measures in the city. Phelan's administration relied not only upon the support of business, but upon organized labour. San Francisco's labour movement was the strongest in the nation. It was composed largely of skilled workers who had been unionized during 1880s. In 1896 these craft unions established a Building Trades Council. The 1890s depression led also to the emergence of new unions among the city's less skilled work-force, which were represented after 1893 by the San Francisco Labour Council. A protracted teamsters' and waterfront strike late in 1901, led by the head of the new Teamsters' Union, Michael Casey, destroyed the Democrats' local power base. When the strike collapsed unionists deserted Phelan, accusing him of having used the police to protect strike breakers. Businessmen complained that Phelan had not been decisive enough. The *Examiner*, intent upon retaining labour support, switched from being an ally to a harsh critic of City Hall. In the November 1901 municipal elections Schmitz, president of the Musicians' Union and the United Labor Party candidate, was elected Mayor.

Schmitz had been picked for the office by renegade Republican district party boss, Abe Ruef, who had built up influence in the United Labor Party after failing to win control of the city's Republican Party machine in the 1901 primaries. Although Ruef controlled the Mayor, the United Labor Party was outnumbered by Democrats and Republicans on the Board of Supervisors. Even the Deputy Mayor was a Democrat. The United Labor Party was also despised by the Republican state authorities in Sacramento. Gage remarked dismissively of Schmitz's administration 'that he wanted nothing to do with that crowd in San Francisco'.[56] Moreover, the United Labor party was detested by the mainstream Republican press. Ruef and Schmitz therefore sought to reduce their political isolation by attacking Phelan's beleaguered Democrat nominees on the City Board of Health.

The Marine Hospital Service, dependent upon city support to sustain the work of plague eradication, noted with alarm that the new Mayor 'shows a distinct disposition to hinder the Plague work here.' He was, said White, 'prejudiced against the Board and the idea of Plague having ever been in San Francisco'. In March 1902 Schmitz abruptly sacked the Board's Democrat members and sought to replace them with his own nominees. The Mayor formally denied that plague had ever existed in San Francisco, and alleged that the Board's actions had brought disrepute upon the city. The tactic seemed to work. The Republican press, notwithstanding their disdain for Ruef's machine, disliked the Democrat Board even more, and splashed banner headlines celebrating the removal of the old 'bubonic board'. They were joined by the pro-Schmitz *Examiner*, which now accused the board of 'flagrant abuse of power'.[57]

Phelan's Board fought back with a court injunction restraining Schmitz, and legal proceedings begun by Ruef and Schmitz to remove them from office were blocked by the Republican state Attorney General. Matters were further complicated by bitter faction fighting within the United Labor Party during 1902, which resulted in Casey briefly seizing control of the party from Ruef. Casey, installed as president of the Board of Health, won appropriations from the anti-Schmitz majority in the Board of Supervisors to continue sanitary work in Chinatown in defiance of the Mayor throughout 1902. He was supported by boards of health in other states, which passed resolutions condemning Schmitz's meddling. Matters were still further complicated because the City Board deliberately ran down its anti-plague operations, anxious not to harm the chances of the Democratic candidate in the gubernatorial elections in November 1902.

Schmitz privately 'admitted' the existence of plague to Wyman when the Surgeon General visited San Francisco at the end of the year.[58] However, at the same time he instituted fresh court proceedings against the City Board, which were again rejected in May 1903. That setback was compensated for by Ruef's recapture of the United Labor Party organization. Casey retaliated by urging unionists to vote for the Democratic candidate in the 1903 mayoral elections. Ruef in turn whipped up the labour movement's anti-Chinese sentiment and, supported by Hearst's *Examiner*, Schmitz won with an increased majority.

In the election's aftermath, Blue predicted glumly that Schmitz would immediately move 'to oust' the Board of Health.[59] However, the Mayor still did not command the loyalty of the Board of Supervisors. The latter, in a slap in the face to Schmitz, voted additional funding to continue the work of the disinfecting staff and wrecking crew in Chinatown. In the new year Schmitz appointed new members to the Board of Health, denied the truth of the latest plague cases, and announced that he would stop the work of house inspection, disinfecting, rat-trapping, and wrecking. Blue interceded with the Mayor, and the State Board weighed in with a resolution expressing confidence in the Service and calling for work to continue. Democrat leaders in the Board of Supervisors undertook to vote additional funds. The Supervisors continued to vote funds until Blue was satisfied in February 1905 that the disinfecting and wrecking work was completed.

Faction fighting over plague funding was just one front in the many conflicts generated in city politics as Ruef's machine sought to maximize graft opportunities. Phelan and Democrat reformers organized to expose municipal corruption. Their object was championed by Fremont Older at the *Bulletin*. The newspaper had backed the Democrats in the 1903 city elections in order to save Phelan's reforms from a relapse into corrupt politics. Disappointed in that object, Fremont Older in 1904 launched a relentless press campaign to discredit the Union Labor Party administration. The *Bulletin* focused, as ever, upon Chinatown protection rackets involving gambling, opium, and prostitution.

By 1905 Californian Republican leaders, as well as the Democrats, were becoming alarmed by Ruef's rising power. Concerned that Ruef might capture the Republican nomination for Governor for Schmitz, they formed a Republican League which collaborated with the Democrats against Schmitz in the 1905 municipal elections. The Mayor appealed for labour solidarity. Strongly backed by the Building Trades Council, the Union Labor Party won a stunning victory, at last winning control of the Board of Supervisors. The sordid excesses in municipal corruption which this set in train paved the way for the most sensational confrontation of all in San Francisco public life. City Hall systematically extracted payoffs from brothel owners, gambling-hall and dance-house proprietors, restaurateurs, saloon keepers, and from the utility, telephone, city transit, and railroad corporations. Meanwhile Fremont Older, financed by Phelan and his friend Rudolph Spreckels, who ran San Francisco's Gas and Electric Company, set in train investigations that would bring the entire administration crashing down. President Roosevelt, concerned that the United Labor Party might enter national politics, provided federal agents to lead the investigation.

The San Francisco graft prosecution began in October 1906 amid considerable press sensationalism. In the new year, in return for grants of immunity, the entire Board of Supervisors confessed. Ruef himself confessed in May in return for a promise by the prosecution to request immunity. His testimony paved the way for Schmitz's trial in June. He was found guilty of extortion and sentenced to five years. The office of Mayor was declared vacant and the discredited Board of Supervisors were ordered to resign. Schmitz successfully appealed his conviction, but late in 1908 Ruef was put on trial, convicted and sentenced to 14 years. Schmitz was again prosecuted in 1912, but acquitted. Ruef was released in 1915.

'... the policy of hiding the truth'[60]

Initially it seems unlikely — given the divergent agendas that were being pursued by federal, state, and local authorities, the combative nature of city and state politics, and the rivalry between the daily newspapers — that any consensus could have been reached, still less sustained, among the contending parties to cover up news of plague in Chinatown. Here, surely, was a spectacle that the contending parties could manipulate in the telling in order to score points off their rivals. Chinatown, after all, served as the daily butt of lurid press sensationalism regardless of the the political affiliation of the newspapers. The *Chronicle*'s initial focus on Chinatown filth in 1900 to discredit Phelan was matched by the *Bulletin*'s focus from 1904 on Chinatown gambling and prostitution in order to discredit Schmitz. The *Examiner*, intent upon boosting its circulation and keen to discomfort its political adversaries, filled column after column with stories of slave girls in Chinatown brothels.

Perplexingly, news of plague in Chinatown, and of the massive works of slum improvement, appeared only in intermittent dribbles in the San Francisco press. Kinyoun was already complaining by telegram in 1900 that 'People here absolutely in dark as to correct situation, on account of local papers refusing publishing any matter pertaining to epidemic.' White privately advised Wyman in 1901, 'You can depend upon the Newspapers to lie about the matter and barring an epidemic, keep it quiet for another year.' The *Chronicle* conceded the substance of these criticisms even as it dismissed gossip about a cover-up. The press, it said, had simply 'refuse[d] to give currency to the cooked-up reports of the bubonic Health Board.' The same implicit acknowledgement was made by Schmitz when he sought to dismiss the City Board of Health in 1902. The Mayor, as he denounced the Board, simultaneously praised 'the united press of city' for having 'refrained from giving undeserved and undue publicity to your reports.'[61]

Widening press silence about plague was rooted in fear of the likely commercial harm to San Francisco if the presence of plague was acknowledged. The biggest fear was not plague at all, but quarantine. By refusing to make plague news, the press sought to counteract the statements coming from Kinyoun and the City Board of Health. Their reports, it was feared, had resulted in San Francisco being 'heralded the world over as an infected port', and invited disastrous quarantine restrictions upon the city's commerce. The federal quarantine officer, said the *Bulletin* bitterly, was 'busily engaged in hurting the business of the merchants, shippers, transportation companies and, indeed, all the people of San Francisco.'[62]

The newspaper managers' sentiments reflected concerns widely evident among Californian businessmen. The state Republican delegation which travelled east in 1900 to endorse McKinley's renomination took time to lobby the President to remove Kinyoun's quarantine safeguards on shipping at San Francisco. When cities in other states and in Canada threatened to impose restrictions against the city's commerce, special meetings of San Francisco's mercantile bodies were called to protest against such 'oppressive and unjust quarantine'. White reported to Wyman in 1902 that the continuing cover-up of plague news stemmed from 'the fear that if the existence of the disease should be recognized by the State, commerce would be most seriously hampered by the quarantine measures which would be imposed by other States, and even should other states not quarantine, it is believed that immigrants would hesitate to settle here, and that farm-products would be looked upon with injurious suspicion in eastern markets.' San Franciscans feared that any acknowledgement of plague would be used against them by Seattle and Vancouver, intent on wresting from San Francisco its position 'as the principal port of entry' on the west coast. The joint mercantile committee, established in 1903, was intended to counter the 'slander' emanating from the cities of Puget Sound and British Columbia, which were accused of seeking to profit commercially from any injury done to San Francisco.[63]

Denial of plague, abuse of Kinyoun and the City Board of Health, and the increasing reliance upon secrecy, were not simply *ad hoc* and unconnected responses by individual journalists to the harmful commercial implications of quarantine upon Californian business. They were the result of long-established networks of power-sharing and mutual reward between business, politicians, and the owners and managers of the city press. It dawned upon Kinyoun that an 'understanding ... seems to exist' between the *Call*, the *Chronicle*, the *Bulletin*, and the Chamber of Commerce, which was reflected in a 'premeditated' campaign both to cover up the incidence of plague and to secure his dismissal.[64]

Kinyoun concluded that this covert influence did not originate with the press or even local business associations. It came instead from the political bosses who controlled public affairs in the city and the state. Kinyoun condemned the efforts by 'the Governor and his sycophantic editorial and political business staff' to prevent publication of the federal plague commission findings. He was especially scornful of 'Governor Gage's organ "The Chronicle"'.[65] John Young chaired Gage's plague commission, and worked so deceitfully on his behalf that White refused to deal with him. Gage's deputation to Washington in 1901 included not only Young, but Fremont Older from the *Bulletin* and the *Examiner*'s business manager. Political cronyism was deeply entrenched in the San Francisco press and paid the newspaper proprietors useful pocket money. Fremont Older was matter of fact in acknowledging that Phelan had paid the *Bulletin* for its support. The Republican candidate for Mayor in 1901 sneered that the *Chronicle*'s owner, Michael De Young, was 'outraged' by lack of patronage positions offered him by the Republicans, and had complained that the Democrat Phelan had been more generous.[66]

Intimate as relations between pressmen and politicians were, however, the ultimate controlling influence over newsmaking in San Francisco was held by big business. The state's most powerful business empire was Southern Pacific Railways. The Southern Pacific line, completed in 1883, linked San Francisco with New Orleans via Los Angeles and Texas, and connected the city with Portland and Seattle in the north. The company belonged to the business portfolio of New York banker E.H. Harriman, who also controlled Union Pacific–Central Pacific's original 1869 transcontinental line between San Francisco and Chicago. The allied railroad companies used their near monopoly of transcontinental railways in California to dominate economic activity in the state. Southern Pacific controlled San Francisco's Pacific Mail and Occidental & Oriental steamship companies, and most of the waterfront in San Francisco and Oakland. The Harriman companies thus controlled trade between California, Asia, and Europe.

Their great American rival was another New York banker, J.P. Morgan, whose steamship line connected at Seattle with James J. Hill's allied Great Northern transcontinental line. The two conglomerates locked horns during 1901 in a stock-market struggle to win control of the Northern Pacific line to Portland. When neither side won, a compromise was worked out whereby the stock of all the western lines other than the independent Santa Fe line to Los Angeles was put into a joint holding company which was owned by the Morgan and Harriman groups. A federal anti-trust prosecution begun by Roosevelt in 1902 led in 1904 to a court order to dissolve this monopoly.

Kinyoun's troubles began when the federal quarantine officer's activities in San Francisco became an irritant to Southern Pacific's far-flung trading connections. He warned Wyman that Southern Pacific's 'predominating spirit of commercialism ... seems to be omnipresent and controls everything here.' It was, he said, 'an open secret that these railroad corporations control and influence the press in San Francisco.' Fremont Older conceded that the *Bulletin* had been on Southern Pacific's monthly payroll until it had abandoned the Republicans, and that the *Evening Post* was effectively owned by the railroad company.[67]

Southern Pacific also dominated city and state politics. Its political boss, William F. Herrin, maintained a network of political influence to which the party wire-pullers of both Democrat and Republican machines were beholden. Ruef wisely deferred to Herrin. Southern Pacific stood behind Schmitz's dismissal of the City Board of Health. The emergency municipal conference called in response to the *Bulletin*'s New Haven telegram was attended not only by Ruef and Fremont Older, but representatives of Southern Pacific, too. The State Governor was another satellite of Herrin. Southern Pacific had engineered Gage's election in order to maximize business opportunities for itself. White confidentially advised Wyman that Gage was 'acting under instructions from Southern Pacific'. Herrin was a member of Gage's state commission which travelled to Washington in 1901. The state medical representative appointed by Gage to work with Glennan in 1903 was the chief surgeon of Southern Pacific Railroad. His replacement, nominated by Pardee, was the current chief surgeon of Southern Pacific in San Francisco. Herrin had engineered Pardee's own nomination by the Republicans when it became clear that Gage could not supply enough patronage positions to secure renomination. Glennan warned Wyman that although 'I think Pardee ... means to do right as near as possible, ... [he] may be constrained a little by political exigencies.'[68]

It was this web of influence between big business and politics which generated the cover-up of plague news. Blue reported in 1901: 'I believe the Railroads and other monied interests of the whole State ... back ... [Gage] on account of his stand in the plague matter.' Hoping that Gage's departure would end the impasse between federal and state medical authorities, White sounded out Pardee and his Democrat rival in the lead up to the 1902 gubernatorial elections, but found that neither candidate 'would deem it politic to express the opinion that Plague existed here'.[69]

Neither was it politic for any local newspaper to break ranks. The City Board of Health had reported obliquely to Phelan in 1901 that as the result of 'powerful influences', in March newspaper coverage of plague and of anti-plague measures in Chinatown suddenly ceased. Kinyoun, in his coded telegrams and private dispatches to Washington, was more forthright. He reported to Wyman early in March that Herrin, together with the president of Pacific Mail and the managers of the *Chronicle* and the *Examiner*, were on their way to Sacramento by special train for a 'secret conference' with Gage. The result, he said subsequently, was an agreement that no newspaper would mention the results of the federal Plague Commission, and that a delegation be sent to Washington to intercede with McKinley to withdraw federal interference.[70] The secret mission of the state negotiating team which met Wyman in Washington to ratify the forms of federal–state collaboration had in fact been to destroy the very basis of such an agreement.

The situation was more complex than even Kinyoun realized. First, in spite of the apparent unanimity of opinion between businessmen, politicians and pressmen, the alliance was in fact characterized by internal tensions, and there existed considerable fluidity of opinion among business organizations concerning the most appropriate responses to plague. Second, in attempting to capitalize upon these uncertainties, the Marine Hospital Service itself resorted to secret understandings to hush up the eradication measures. In so doing, Wyman deceived and isolated Kinyoun, who was posted away from San Francisco at his own request in May 1901.

Although San Francisco's peak business associations had initially responded to news of plague with studied silence, they and their Southern Pacific colleagues — concerned that secrecy about plague was in fact hurting the city's commerce by breeding exaggerated rumours outside California — met in June 1900 to consider 'How can we convince our sister States and the entire Nation that there is no danger.' A spokesman for Southern Pacific warned that the impression was spreading throughout the nation 'that the black plague was rampant in San Francisco.'[71] The meeting pledged support for the City Board and Kinyoun. Led by the manager of Pacific Mail, who urged that decisive action was needed to stave off hostile quarantine measures by other states, participants began a subscription fund to assist the cleansing programme in Chinatown, and a standing committee was appointed to mobilize business support. Business leaders followed up this initiative by calling on press proprietors to fall into line.

Behind the façade of Republican unanimity, Gage found himself increasingly isolated. Ever on the lookout for opportunities to exert leverage, Blue informed Wyman in September 1901 that 'It is rumoured in political circles that John Young of the Chronicle will prepare a manifesto for the purpose of attacking the Governor's policies. The manifesto will claim that plague has existed here and exists now, and that the Governor mismanaged quarantine to suit his own political motives or purposes.' In the aftermath of the 1902 Republican gubernatorial nomination, Glennan reported back to Wyman the local opinion that Gage had really lost the renomination because of his inflexibility concerning plague. Glennan observed that the *Chronicle* and the *Call* had both become 'hostile' to the retiring Governor. Pardee's nomination had in fact been pushed forward by the *Call*'s owner, Spreckles, whom Glennan described as Gage's principal

Republican enemy. Gage, he said, was understandably 'sore', and his friends were now lukewarm in supporting the Republican electoral campaign.[72]

Business again intervened decisively to shape local political decision-making about plague early in 1903 when, in consequence of the New Haven and Washington conferences, it again seemed probable that the other states would take measures which would throttle San Francisco's commerce. Wyman instructed Glennan to let it be known that outside confidence could only be restored if California acknowledged the presence of plague in Chinatown. The state representative at the Washington plague conference telegraphed Herrin to confirm that opinion. Herrin in turn, accompanied by his satellites the Mayor, the newspaper managers, and city business leaders, called on Pardee to thrash out a form of words which would be acceptable to all parties. The mercantile joint committee then drew up resolutions for Pardee and Schmitz to sign, which formally acknowledged the presence of plague and invited Public Health and Marine Hospital Service direction. In late 1907, again mobilized by apprehensions about quarantine, commercial associations intervened a third time in support of the anti-plague programmes. Business backed the Citizens' Health Committee and again supported Public Health and Marine Hospital Service direction of local health measures, in return for Wyman's confirmation that quarantine was unnecessary.[73] Blue noted that, perhaps influenced by this intervention, 'that portion of the San Francisco Press, chiefly the "Daily Chronicle," which has been antagonistic to us in its tone, has improved very greatly ... The Chronicle has gradually receded from its position, and while it is not enthusiastically in favor of the work, it is not opposing us as bitterly as formerly.' At the end of the plague eradication programme, businessmen rejoiced: not that the threat of plague had been lifted, but that 'the danger of quarantine has been eliminated'. Blue was congratulated for having shown 'the greatest possible consideration for our business welfare'.[74]

Business was blamed by outsiders during the plague epidemic of 1900–4 for 'dishonestly misrepresenting the facts and denying the existence of the plague in San Francisco.' During the second epidemic of 1907–8 as well, 'the general charge [was heard] that "the business interests" of San Francisco sought to suppress plague information for business purposes.'[75]

The earliest news blackout in 1900 had, however, been instigated not by businessmen or by their allies in either politics or the press, but by the city health authorities and the Marine Hospital Service. The decision to opt for 'secrecy' was initially taken by the City Board of Health because of the 'vicious attacks' by the local press, and was endorsed by Kinyoun and Wyman until they were able to confirm the diagnosis and devise an eradication programme that would be tolerated by all the contending parties.[76]

Wyman went even further in November 1900, and ordered the weekly *Public Health Reports* to stop publishing Kinyoun's reports from San Francisco. Plague disappeared from the official summaries of infectious disease in the United States. Kinyoun protested the deletions, noting that the press had concluded that Wyman no longer believed him, and that in consequence he was 'being disgraced and discredited'. Kinyoun did not know when he telegraphed news of the secret Sacramento conference in 1902 that White had, at the surgeon general's direction, already held secret meetings with all the newspaper managers to obtain their formal agreement that 'the facts are kept secret'. Wyman simultaneously urged the federal plague commission to withhold its report, arguing that 'it is considered very essential that it be confidential and no publication at present time.'[77]

The Surgeon General defended his position in a confidential letter to state health authorities. He conceded that plague reporting had been stopped in the *Public Health Reports* as a bargaining chip intended 'to bring about harmonious action' with all the interested parties in California. In order to achieve this, it had been necessary not to contradict publicly Gage's declaration that there was no plague. In return, the Marine Hospital Service had been able to thrash out a plan for co-operative action with Gage's commission. Wyman explained that in order to cement this agreement he 'felt convinced of the necessity of not giving out for publication all the facts in the case.' When the *Call* lashed out against the plague programme several months later, White in turn explained to Wyman that the newspaper 'was not a party to the agreement with the Department'. Wyman again resorted to secret undertakings to hold back the news late in 1902 as he maneouvred to engineer a federal takeover of plague prevention measures. His special representative, Glennan, was sent to meet with Gage, and won from the Governor an undertaking to 'fix newspapers [to] avoid publicity'. Glennan subsequently reported back that the 'newspapers here, by request, publish nothing'.[78]

Wyman exploited the resultant debt of gratitude owed to the Marine Hospital Service by Californian business organizations in order to ram through his objectives in 1903. The Surgeon General used local business-men to pressure state and city politicians to acknowledge plague and to invite federal intervention. Glennan reported that in meetings with key business leaders:

They all state frankly that this Service is the only one to help them, and they will secure State and city cooperation with us. But the form of acknowledgement stumps them. In the past three years, the plague question has become so complicated with State politics and rival commercial interests, that it is difficult to consider it separately. Pardee was elected by a small majority, and if he openly proclaims the existence of plague, it means his political death and a split in the Republican party. If pushed to extremes the Republican Committee will probably go to the President about it.[79]

The capitulation to federal demands in 1903 was largely stage managed by Glennan. The joint mercantile committee had initially been loath to budge beyond reference to 'alleged Plague', and it had 'required considerable care' by Glennan to 'induce ... them to come out in ... plain terms'. It was only with difficulty that he extracted the signatures of some business representatives because of their fear of knee-jerk quarantine. Once signed, the resolutions were rushed by a delegation to City Hall. Glennan recalled that 'The Mayor was taken by storm.'[80]

Local politicians could brag that they had saved the prestige of the city and the state. Business groups were gratified that they had staved off restrictive quarantines. However, the biggest winner was the Public Health and Marine Hospital Service. When representatives from the states met the federal agency in June 1903 to reconsider the plague situation in San Francisco, California toed Wyman's line. Pardee pledged that now 'there is no disposition to cover up or conceal anything', and that the local health authorities acted upon Blue's every wish. The conference resolved that in view of this 'harmonious co-operation' between the Public Health and Marine Hospital Service and the Californian health authorities, 'there is no need for quarantine restrictions of travel or traffic to or from that State.'[81]

Notes

[1] Banks, Read, 1906, title page.

[2] Irwin, 1906, pp. 6–7.

[3] Williams, 1951, p. 121. My own research of the service's annual reports and of the *Public Health Reports* puts the total closer to 150. Over 100 victims died from plague in Sydney also during 1900. See Curson, 1985.

[4] The position was renamed Surgeon General in 1902.

[5] United States Public Health Service, 1902, p. 16.

[6] Glennan to Wyman, 19 March 1903; Glennan to Wyman, 29 March 1903 (telegram), both in Public Health Service box, 551, NA.

[7] Blue to Wyman, 18 April 1903, United States Public Health Service, 1903a, p. 594 (24 April 1903). Glennan to Wyman, 4 May 1903, Public Health Service, box 541, NA.

[8] San Francisco Department of Public Health, 1896, p. 159.

[9] Deputy City Health Officer to Wyman, 16 February 1905, in United States Public Health Service, 1905, p. 345 (3 March 1905). United States Public Health Service, 1906, p. 162.

[10] *Examiner*, 22 March 1900, p. 3, Chinese quarter receiving a most thorough cleansing. ibid., 1 June 1900, p. 3, Board of Health called upon to provide for the quarantined inhabitants of Chinatown.

[11] Report of the chief sanitary inspector, 1 July 1900, in San Francisco Department of Public Health, 1901a, pp. 73, 74. *Examiner*, 4 July 1900, p. 9, Health Board has report on plague.

[12] Kinyoun to Wyman, 29 October 1900 and 6 December 1900, United States Public Health Service, 1902, pp. 494, 499. San Francisco Plague Commission, 1901, pp. 802–3. White to Wyman, 10 April 1901, Public Health Service, box 550, NA. Blue to Wyman, monthly reports in United States Public Health Service, 1903a, pp. 594, 773.

[13] *Chronicle*, 15 May 1903, p. 12, Urges removal of Chinatown. ibid., 6 November 1904, Sunday Supplement, p. 5, The people who lay for nickels in the streets of Chinatown.

[14] ibid., 1 July 1900, p. 11, Widen streets of Chinatown and purge place of its evils. ibid., 9 July 1900, p. 4, The reconstruction of Chinatown. San Francisco Department of Public Health, 1901b, pp. 18–9. *Examiner*, 2 December 1902, p. 8, Propose to cut two streets through heart of Chinatown. See the map of the proposed routes, dated 24 November 1902, Public Health Service, box 541, NA.

[15] California State Board of Health, 1906a, p. 82; ibid., 1906b, p. 36. San Francisco Chamber of Commerce, 1907, pp. 6, 45.

[16] San Francisco Department of Public Health, 1908, pp. 4, 13.

[17] United States Public Health Service, 1909a, p. 1722 (27 November 1908). San Francisco Department of Public Health, 1908, p. 2. Todd, 1909, p. 126.

[18] Mayor Taylor to President Roosevelt, 16 July 1908, enclosure in Blue to Wyman, 21 July 1908, Public Health Service, box 543, NA.

[19] The weekly statistics contained in the *Public Health Reports* suggest that 734 houses were demolished by the end of 1909. However, the Citizens' Health Committee reported that 1,713 houses were demolished during this period. See Todd, 1909, p. 141.

[20] ibid., p. 37. United States Public Health Service, 1909b, p. 13.

[21] Todd, 1909, p. 146. San Francisco Chamber of Commerce, 1909, pp. 6, 9.

[22] Glennan to Wyman, 14 January 1903, Public Health Service, box 541, NA.

[23] Todd, 1909, p. 30.

[24] Kinyoun to Wyman, 6 December 1900, United States Public Health Service, 1902, pp. 499–500.

[25] California State Board of Health, 1903, n.p. *Examiner*, 5 June 1900, p. 6, For the protection of the city.

[26] San Francisco Board of Supervisors, 1877, p. 11. See *Chronicle*, 9 March 1900 p. 12, Plague fake is exploded; *Bulletin*, 26 March 1902. p. 6, Removal of bubonic Health Board.

[27] *Chronicle*, 27 February 1903, p. 6, The rat-infection humbug. ibid., 17 November 1907, p. 28, A chimera to spare: it is neither bubonic nor plague, but an interesting myth. ibid., 20 April 1908, p. 6, The rat-catching farce. Blue to Wyman, 27 April 1908, Public Health Service, box 543, NA.

[28] Dr John M. Williamson to Mayor James D. Phelan, 30 June 1900, in San Francisco Department of Public Health, 1901a, p. 12. Williamson to Phelan, 30 June 1901, in San Francisco Department of Public Health, 1901b, pp. 2, 18.

[29] San Francisco Department of Public Health, 1908, p. 5. California State Board of Health, 1907a, p. 19; ibid.,1907b, p. 45; ibid., 1908, p. 84.

[30] Blue to Wyman, 30 November 1907, Public Health Service, box 543, NA.

[31] Young, 1915, p. 149; 1912, p. 807. *Examiner*, 27 April 1901, p. 1, Grand jury recommends the removal of police chief and rebukes Mayor Phelan.

[32] Young, 1915, p. 162.

[33] *Examiner*, 27 September 1901, p. 29, To the American people.

[34] *Bulletin*, 26 March 1902, p. 6, Removal of bubonic Health Board. Bean, 1972, p. 56.

[35] *Chronicle*, 6 July 1900, p. 14, Will fight to save Chinese quarter.

[36] White to Wyman, telegram, 7 October 1902, Public Health Service, box 549, NA.

[37] *Chronicle*, 10 March 1900 p. 7, Mayor Phelan puts himself on record.

[38] California State Board of Health, 1913, p. 11.

[39] *San Francisco Call*, 6 September 1901, State coin will pay for 'shadowing' work; ibid., 7 September 1901, What Ryfkogel thinks of Gage, both in an undated memo from Blue to Wyman, Public Health Service, box 541, NA. White to Wyman, personal letter, 7 March 1901, box 550. Glennan to Wyman, 21 October 1902, box 551. Blue to Wyman, 11 July 1901, personal letter, box 541.

[40] Glennan to Wyman, 8 December 1902, ibid., box 551. Kinyoun to Wyman, 10 October 1900, box 552. *Chronicle*, 29 December 1900, Falsified health reports, enclosure in Kinyoun to Wyman, 29 December 1900, box 552. *Chronicle*, 26 March 1902 p. 4, editorial.

[41] Mr Justice Harlan (1895), in *Hennington* v. *State of Georgia*, 163 U.S. 303, 304.

[42] Wyman, speech at the Chattanooga conference on quarantine and immigration, November 1905, printed in United States Public Health Service, 1906, p. 251.

[43] United States Public Health Service, 1904, p. 19. Snow, W.F., The policy of the State Board of Health, in California State Board of Health, 1909, p. 91.

44 *Examiner*, 17 June 1900, p. 15, Dr. Bazet wants nothing further to do with Gage. Dr H.M. Bracen in United States Public Health Service, 1903a, *Supplement*, p. 14 (6 February 1903).

45 Young, 1912, pp. 781–2.

46 White to Wyman, private letter, 19 March 1901, Public Health Service, box 550, NA. White to Wyman, 21 March 1901, United States Public Health Service, 1902, p. 541.

47 White to Wyman, telegram and letter, 12 December 1902, both in Public Health Service, box 549, NA. Glennan to Wyman, telegram, 14 December 1902, box 551.

48 White to Wyman, 29 May 1902 (telegram), 30 May 1902 (letter), both in ibid., box 549. Enclosure, Henry T. Gage to White, 28 May 1901, in White to Wyman, 29 May 1901, United States Public Health Service, 1902, p. 558. See Gage to Wyman, 24 June 1901, in ibid., p. 561. White to Wyman, 29 May 1901, Public Health Service, box 549, NA.

49 Little to the *San Francisco Bulletin*, 31 October 1902, in White to Wyman, telegram, 31 October 1902, ibid., box 549. Glennan to Wyman, telegram, 7 January 1903, box 551.

50 *Chronicle*, 7 February 1903 p. 14, Plain truth told about the bubonic plague fake.

51 United States Public Health Service, 1903a, *Supplement*, p. 19 (6 February 1903). Glennan to Governor Pardee, 8 January 1903; Glennan to Wyman, 11 January 1903, both in Public Health Service, box 551, NA.

52 United States Public Health Service, 1903a, pp. 200–1; Glennan to Wyman, 12 February 1903, in ibid., p. 274.

53 White to Wyman, personal letter, 26 February 1901, Public Health Service, box 550, NA. White to Wyman, personal letter, 7 March 1901, in ibid. (underlining in the original). *Chronicle*, 5 July 1900, p. 6, Reconstruction of Chinatown. ibid., 3 May 1900, p. 5, Health Board defies charter.

54 *Bulletin*, 26 March 1902, p. 6, Removal of bubonic Health Board'.

55 Kinyoun to Wyman, 6 December 1900 and 27 October 1900, both in United States Public Health Service, 1902, pp. 495, 492.

56 Glennan to Wyman, letter, 21 October 1902, Public Health Service, box 551, NA.

57 White to Wyman, 12 January 1902, ibid., box 549. *Examiner*, 28 March 1902, p. 14, Vicious acts of the old Board of Health. See the newspaper cuttings in White to Wyman, 26 March 1902, Public Health Service, box 549, NA.

58 Wyman in United States Public Health Service, 1903a, *Supplement*, p. 20 (6 February 1903).

59 Blue to Wyman, confidential letter, 5 November 1903, Public Health Service, box 541, NA.

60 California State Board of Health, 1907b, p. 45.

61 Kinyoun, 20 May 1900, in United States Public Health Service, 1901, p. 1260. White to Wyman, private letter, 10 May 1901, Public Health Service, box 550, NA. *Chronicle*, 23 May 1900, p. 6, Newspapers and the bubonic board. *Examiner*, 26 bMarch 1902, p. 1, Mayor Schmitz removes four members of Board of Health.

62 *Chronicle*, 22 March 1900, p. 5, Health Board brings calamity on this city. *Bulletin* editorial, 30 December 1900, enclosure in Kinyoun to Wyman, 29 December 1900, Public Health Service, box 552, NA.

63 San Francisco Chamber of Commerce, 1901, p. 66. White to Wyman, 11 June 1902 and 12 September 1902, both in Public Health Service, box 549, NA. *Chronicle*, 24 February 1903, p. 8, Plague fake disposed of.

64 Kinyoun to Wyman, 10 October 1900 and 29 December 1900, both in Public Health Service, box 552, NA.

65 Kinyoun, Bubonic plague, reprint from *Occidental Medical Times*, August 1901, p. 13, in ibid., box 552. Kinyoun to Wyman, 10 June 1900, box 552.

[66] Older, 1919, p. 25. *Examiner*, 16 October 1901, pp. 1, 6, Patronage, not principle, alienated the Republican press, says Wells.

[67] Kinyoun to Wyman, 10 October 1900, and telegram dated 12 October 1900, both in Public Health Service, box 552, NA. Older, 1919, pp. 23, 37.

[68] White to Wyman, coded telegram, 21 January 1901, Public Health Service, box 550, NA. Glennan to Wyman, 14 January 1903, in ibid., box 541.

[69] Blue to Wyman, personal letter, 25 July 1901, in ibid., box 541. White to Wyman, 12 September 1902, box 549.

[70] San Francisco Department of Public Health, 1901b, p. 2. Kinyoun to Wyman, 1 March 1901; Kinyoun, Bubonic plague, reprint from *Occidental Medical Times*, August 1901, p. 13, both in Public Health Service, box 552.

[71] Board of Trade of San Francisco, 1901, pp. 13–14. *Examiner*, 2 June 1900, p. 14, San Francisco merchants in mass-meeting aid the Health Board in quarantine work.

[72] Blue to Wyman, personal letter, 25 September 1901, Public Health Service, box 541, NA. Glennan to Wyman, 21 October 1902, box 551.

[73] San Francisco Department of Public Health, 1908, pp. 5–6; California State Board of Health, 1908, pp. 84–5. San Francisco Chamber of Commerce,1908, pp. 7–8; San Francisco Chamber of Commerce,1909, pp. 7–8.

[74] Blue, personal letter to Wyman, 11 May 1908, Public Health Service, box 543, NA. Merchants Exchange, 1908, p. 10. San Francisco Chamber of Commerce,1909, p. 9.

[75] King, L.M.; The record of the Merchants' Association in regard to bubonic plague in San Francisco, in *Merchants' Association Review*, 7 (79), p. 1 (March 1903), copy in Public Health Service, box 541, NA. Todd, 1909, p.31.

[76] Kinyoun to Wyman, telegram, 15 May 1900, in United States Public Health Service, 1901, p. 1255.

[77] Kinyoun to Wyman, telegram, 10 January 1901, Public Health Service, box 552, NA. White to Wyman, personal letter, 7 March 1901; and see his telegram to Wyman, 29 February 1901, both in box 550. Wyman to Professor Flexner, 2 March 1901, in United States Public Health Service, 1902, p. 523.

[78] Wyman, 15 March 1901, in ibid., p. 539. White to Wyman, 29 May 1901, Public Health Service, box 549. Glennan to Wyman, telegrams dated 16 October 1902 and 4 November 1902, ibid., box 551.

[79] Glennan to Wyman, confidential letter, 30 January 1903, ibid., box 541.

[80] Glennan to Wyman, 12 February 1903 (letter), 5 February 1903 (telegram), both in ibid., box 551.

[81] United States Public Health Service, 1903b, pp. 12, 24.

4

Indeterminacy: the Birmingham improvement scheme, 1875—1914

What was the purpose of the Birmingham improvement scheme? On first consideration, the scheme's objective seems straightforward. It was a project of 'slum clearance and rebuilding'. The scheme applied the 1875 Artisans and Labourers Dwellings Act in order to improve the quality of working-class housing in a notoriously insanitary district of the inner city. The City Corporation would buy up the entire 93-acre area, using its sweeping powers of compulsory purchase under the new Act. It would tear down the congested and dilapidated housing and redraw the streets and building allotments along more commodious lines. When leasing the replanned area the Corporation would ensure that the inhabitants were rehoused in comfortable homes. The scheme was thus a social reform package: 'it was undertaken by the Council without any thought of profit, and with the one desire to advance the health and morality of a large section of the population.'[1]

But if housing reform was such a pressing objective in 1875, why — with the completion of land purchases in 1881 — had the Corporation bought only 1,300 of the more than 3,000 working-class houses in the improvement area? Approximately 650 working-class dwellings had been demolished by the end of 1888, but not one new house had been built by the Corporation to replace them. Why, in 1914, were almost 200 of the houses which had been labelled as 'back slums' in 1875 still standing, and being rented to working people by the Corporation? Why, if the intention of the improvement scheme was indeed housing reform, had the planners from the very start envisaged the laying out of a broad new business thoroughfare through the resumed area as being the key component of their scheme? Why was the project always referred to by its promoters as the 'Street Improvement' scheme rather than as an artisans' and labourers' dwellings improvement scheme? Over 13,500 working people lived in the area through which the street was planned to run. Some 9,000 of these inhabitants were expected to be displaced, and an undertaking was given to set aside sufficient land for replacement housing to accommodate an equal number. No public housing

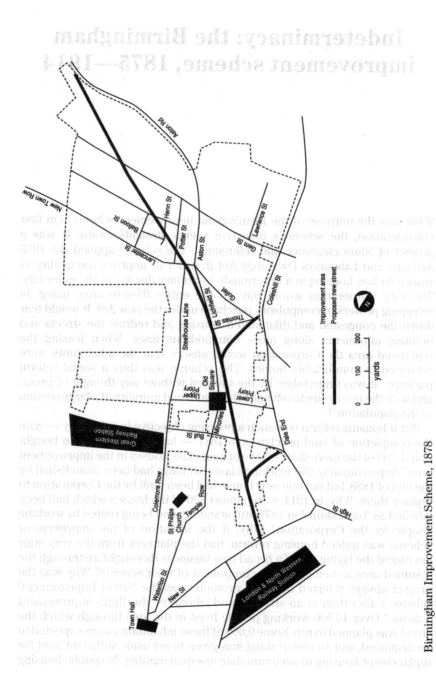

Birmingham Improvement Scheme, 1878

was in fact provided until the late 1880s and the 1890s, and no more was constructed before the First World War.

Other paradoxes abound. First, the Birmingham scheme has been frequently characterized as a pioneering housing reform by municipal government. The Home Secretary, Richard Cross, praised Birmingham for having 'set the lead' in applying the new Act, and as having begun one of the largest improvements in the nation.[2] Yet Liverpool had shown earlier interest in the new legislation, and Birmingham's scheme was modelled upon an improvement scheme begun in Glasgow almost a decade earlier. Second, and despite lurid depictions of Birmingham's improvement area as slumland, it was generally conceded that much of the resumed land in fact consisted of business premises rather than houses, and that other districts of the city had as bad or worse housing conditions and death rates from disease. Third, although land purchase for the scheme began immediately in 1875, and site clearing for the new roadway began in 1878, major construction work stalled in 1882. Thereafter the emphasis of the scheme switched from land resumption and remodelling to estate management of the properties that had been already purchased by the Corporation. The new Corporation Street had by 1882 been built for only half its planned length, sufficient to ease traffic flow in the business centre, but leaving untouched the most insanitary residential neighbourhood of all through which it was supposed to bore. The street was eventually completed in 1904. By 1909, with the completion of all subsidiary street works, the Corporation had still only purchased 45 of the 93 acres comprising the improvement area. Fourth, although the rationale used to justify the improvement scheme was its supposed benefit to the poor, members of the City Council and their officials consistently characterized those whom they had set out to help in negative and pessimistic terms. Working-class tenants were labelled as dirty, immoral, and unresponsive to housing improvements. Moreover, the City Council was antipathetic towards organized labour. Joseph Chamberlain spoke dismissively of 'those foolish people, the Trades Council of Birmingham'.[3]

The improvement scheme had begun amid crisis and uncertainty: environmental, administrative, and political. Birmingham's environmental problems were widely admitted. There were broadly two grounds for concern: the first aesthetic and functional, the second to do with quality of life. Joseph Chamberlain privately regarded Birmingham as 'one of the ugliest towns in England'. As modernizing industries decentralized to large new plants in the suburban periphery, as the scale of commerce extended, and the specialization of retailing intensified, the central city's jumble of ageing and poky shops, workshops and warehouses, traversed by a maze of narrow and congested streets, seemed more and more at variance with the requirements of a successful market-place metropolis. Chamberlain warned that Birmingham could 'be actually choked in its own growth, and stifled in its own prosperity.'[4]

Birmingham had long been known for the good drainage of its site and for the quality of its housing compared with other British cities. Rapid population growth and municipal regulatory inattention undid those attractions. At the 1868 social science conference in Birmingham, stinging criticisms were heard of 'the lamentable state of certain parts of the town', and in particular portions of the future improvement area. One source of concern was working-class back-to-back housing. Some 50,000 such houses were built in the inner city between the 1780s and the 1870s, when their further construction was banned. Many were clustered in courts — called 'pudding-bags' and 'villages' by their inhabitants — and were entered by narrow tunnels under the houses fronting the street. Back-to-backs had been pin-pointed as a health problem in 1840, at which time they accommodated approximately two-thirds of the city's population. Nearly a third of the population still lived in the 30,000 – 40,000 back-to-backs which none the less remained at the turn of the century, crowded into 'the central districts where numerous factories and works give employment to a large class of workmen who cannot afford, in many cases, to move into more healthful conditions in the suburbs.'[5] The other main source of concern was sewage disposal. In 1871 the city's first comprehensive survey of facilities for sewage disposal evoked appalled surprise at the 'enormous preponderance' of primitive, unregulated middens — 'huge[,] wet[, and] foetid' — and at the resulting contamination of the well water upon which a quarter of the city still depended. Late in 1874, a probing sanitary census of the city highlighted the extent to which proliferating problems of sewage and waste removal, together with a deterioration in the fabric of the inner city's housing stock, had undermined living conditions in the central wards of the city.[6]

The index of such environmental degradation was community ill health. Birmingham had traditionally basked in the reputation of being 'the most healthy of all the large towns'. However, by the 1870s Birmingham suffered 'the unenviable notoriety of having a higher death-rate ... than any of the large towns in the kingdom.' Many among the city's governors sought to ignore the worsening mortality statistics, but they could not shrug off the national criticism which accompanied them. Birmingham was now becoming characterized nationally as a pariah city: reeking, pestilential, and misgoverned.[7]

Administrative perplexities added to the sense of environmental crisis. Injunctions by country landowners to prevent river pollution from the city's sewage forced the Council in 1873 to overhaul their entire apparatus for waste disposal. These massive changes in, and costs upon, city waste disposal overlapped with a wider administrative revolution in municipal service provision in the wake of Chamberlain's election as Mayor in November 1873. Chamberlain's reform faction, propelled into office by the Liberal Association on an interventionist programme designed to restore Birmingham's position as the healthiest town in Britain, overturned the established parameters of municipal administration and budgeting.

Fiscal uncertainties accompanied this upheaval in local government administration. In 1874 and again in the following year, the city's budget estimates for capital works exceeded the maximum rate levies allowed by local statute. Chamberlain's appeal to ratepayers for authority to increase local taxes was decisively rejected by electors early in 1874. The Mayor complained that 'every day new duties are being imposed upon the Corporation' as a consequence of national legislation. He fretted, 'where the money is to come from for all this, I don't know. All our important towns are seeking for new sources of income.'[8] Birmingham's headaches were, however, exacerbated by local circumstances: by the snowballing costs of the court-imposed sewerage improvements, and by the Liberals' broader reform programme.

Intense political maneouvrings, played out in the elections for City Council, School Board, and Board of Guardians, intensified still further the sense of crisis. Political mobilization and polarization of a degree not hitherto seen in the city characterized electioneering in the early 1870s. As the old hegemony of the 'economist' faction withered, new alignments coalesced around the local party structures of Liberals and Conservatives. The volatility of local politics was fuelled further by the efforts of Chamberlainite radicals in the Liberal Association to use the preselection process for Liberal candidates to weed out old-style Whigs from local politics, a practice which was accused of 'shattering the old Liberal party'.[9] This feuding continued to colour municipal politics into the 1880s, when it was overshadowed by the outright split between Gladstonian Liberals and Chamberlain's Liberal Unionists. Still more contentiousness was introduced to local politics by working-class candidates who challenged the ability of any bourgeois representatives — Liberal or Conservative — to speak for working people.

It is historically tempting to argue, as Birmingham Liberals did, that the improvement scheme signified the imposition of order and direction upon the besetting indeterminacies of big-city living. They argued that the making of Corporation Street capped a series of reform initiatives which were making Birmingham the best-governed city in the world. In reality, however, the improvement scheme ended as it had begun: in crisis and uncertainty. Environmentally, the still nebulous concerns of housing reformers in the 1870s had by 1914 been replaced by a preoccupation by city administrators, the city press, and private reforms groups with the intractable nature of what they all now called the city's 'slum problem'. On the one hand, this resulted in a much sharper focus of attention upon inner-city living conditions, and in particular upon that 'bugbear of housing reformers in Birmingham', the back-to-back house. On the other hand, it had produced an additional anxiety that 'new slums' were proliferating as the result of jerry-building in the suburbs.[10] Worries about ill health gave urgency to discourse about slums. Some 6,000 middens still existed in the city in the late 1890s. Concerns about Birmingham's death rate compared to other cities intensified after the turn of the century. Almost a quarter of Birmingham's houses remained unsewered in the early 1900s. Most of these relied on an unsatisfactory dry-earth pan system, which had been introduced as a holding operation in 1873, and which was still in use on the eve of the First World War.[11] Administratively, concerns were frequently aired about the proliferating bureaucracy of city government, and about the uncertain seas of metropolitan governance upon which they had been launched with the creation of Greater Birmingham in 1911. Fiscally, the early twentieth century was characterized by the preoccupation of electors and policy-makers with crushing rates. Politically, too, these were years of turmoil occasioned by the rise of the Independent Labour Party and the subsuming of the once dominant Liberal Unionists within local Conservative politics.

Street Building, 1875–1888

The Cross Act received royal assent in June 1875. Chamberlain moved immediately to have the statute implemented in Birmingham, explaining that it sought to substitute 'good & wholesome dwellings for some of the terrible rookeries in which the poor now live'.[12] By the end of July a new standing committee — the Improvement Committee — had been formed to prepare schemes for the resumption and rebuilding of insanitary areas. Two official representations by the Medical Officer of Health, encompassing an area of 93 acres in the central city districts of St Mary's Ward and Market Hall Ward, were lodged in October and November 1875, and a scheme to resume and remodel the district passed Council without opposition. Pending Parliamentary enabling legislation, a private non-profit Improvement Trust was initiated by Chamberlain and his allies, which began buying properties early in the new year. Birmingham formally petitioned the Local Government Board in January 1876 for a provisional order to undertake the scheme. This was granted in June, enabling the Corporation to take over from the Trust negotiations for property purchase. A confirming Bill was enacted in August, authorizing the Corporation to borrow up to £1,000,000 to complete the scheme. The City Council imposed an annual levy of £20,000 from the rates to top up the income expected to be generated by leasing, in order to meet repayments and interest. Construction work on Corporation Street began at New Street in August 1878.

'A Grand Street'[13]

The building of Corporation Street was hailed by Birmingham Liberals as 'the most remarkable and most effective improvement of all'. Joseph Chamberlain firmly established the parameters of public knowledge concerning the unfolding project in four widely publicized speeches before the Birmingham City Council. Three were delivered during initial consideration of the scheme in 1875, and the fourth was presented during 1878 in a statesman-like review of the scheme's subsequent progress. Chamberlain predicted that this 'gigantic scheme of improvement ... would alter the character of ... the worst part of the town' and 'give comfortable dwellings to 40,000 of the population'. It was widely anticipated that the scheme 'will sweep away a whole district of the very worst and lowest streets in Birmingham', and provide instead homes suitable 'for honest and respectable work people'.[14]

Notwithstanding the rhetoric of social reform, Chamberlain and his allies had from the outset calculated that the undertaking 'was not to be merely' a scheme of sanitary and housing improvement to benefit the working classes, but a 'great town improvement' designed to give impetus to the gradual remodelling of the central city core by private enterprise. Construction of the New Street and Snow Hill railway stations during the 1850s had already resulted in the clearance of many supposed slums. The process had continued in the 1860s with the demolition of more houses, small workshops, and shops in the neighbourhood of Colmore Row, and during the 1870s additional 'slums' were torn down as part of street-widening works along Ann Street and Colmore Row and the building of the city's Council House. Chamberlain and his colleagues now eyed a large strip of land in the heart of the city, lying between the two central railway stations and stretching from the principal thoroughfares of New Street, High Street, Dale End, and Colemore Row towards the busy suburban arterial Aston Road. Within this area, Chamberlain speculated, they might

run a great street as broad as a Parisian boulevard from the middle of New Street to Aston Road. We might throw open a street such as Birmingham has not got, and is now stifling for the want of; for our streets are too narrow for an important and growing town like this. We might demolish the houses on either side of this street, and of such cross streets as it may be found necessary to make, and let or sell the new frontages for such improved rents as they will bear, and then build working men's houses behind.

Such an undertaking, Chamberlain calculated, would be a boon for retailing. It would also facilitate traffic flow within the city centre, and between it and suburban Aston, and link the Great Western with the London and North Western railway stations by tunnel, thus complementing expansion programmes by both railway companies. By such means he sought to make Birmingham 'the metropolis of the Midland Counties'.[15]

Chamberlain frankly acknowledged the 'twofold aspect of the Scheme', explaining that it 'was intended to combine a great town improvement with the reconstruction of an unhealthy area.'[16] Municipal land purchase for street improvements had hitherto been constrained by the legal requirement to pay compensation for compulsory land sale, and immediately to resell surplus lands along the new street frontages, as Birmingham had discovered to its cost during the widening of New Street in the late 1860s. Now, by linking their work to sanitary reform, the Cross Act's compulsory purchase powers could be used to escape the crushing compensation penalties that normally attached to land-resumption schemes. The Act also gave access to low-interest Treasury loans. Moreover, it enabled them to retain the freehold to 'large slices of property', and thus to benefit from the leasehold revenue 'which would come to the Corporation in turning poor property into first-class property'.[17]

The trick was to use the Cross Act in order to choose an area of depressed property values and low rates adjacent to the city business core, which could be quickly turned around into prime real estate. It was conceded after the scheme's commencement that the land selected by the Corporation in fact lay 'in the best part of the town, and would be constantly improving in value.' Chamberlain, it transpired, had 'never intended' to purchase all 93 acres within the improvement area. Rather, by nominating a sufficiently large area over which to exercise a 'power of choice', it was planned to drive down purchase prices. In these calculations, 'the key to the whole situation' was not the unhealthy area nominated in the Medical Officer of Health's representations, but the properties lying closest to the business core. By beginning the street-making scheme here, in the area running between New and Bull Streets, the improvements would inflate the values of the shabby properties to the north-east which the Corporation had snapped up at rock-bottom prices at the beginning of the scheme.[18]

There was in fact little originality in Birmingham's vaunted improvement proposal. A similar but smaller-scale plan had been shelved in the early 1870s because of the high cost of resuming land. Chamberlain resurrected that plan when the Cross Bill seemed to make such projects financially possible. However, the Corporation of Liverpool had been quicker to recognize the Bill's potential to be applied comprehensively to urban renewal if its rehousing obligations could be watered down in Parliament. Liverpool was also more decisive in securing amendment of the Bill with this end in mind. Long before Chamberlain's espousal of town improvement, the term had gained national currency to describe the responsibilities and to measure the performance of municipalities in providing and modernizing public facilities and services.

Chamberlain's espousal of 'sanitary reform ... [as] a hobby of mine'[19] similarly drew upon a well-established national discourse about urban ill health and possible palliatives. In January 1874 Chamberlain organized a large sanitary conference in Birmingham, which he billed as the first ever national sanitary conference in Britain. He used the occasion to assert the interrelationship between city ill health, bad housing, and urban poverty, and later in the year announced that he was devoting his special attention to the subject of providing decent housing for the poor. Yet this subject had already achieved national publicity when the Charity Organization Society began to investigate the issue early in 1873. The Charity Organization Society floated the idea that Glasgow's Improvement Trust, established in 1866, might provide a blueprint for national action. Chamberlain adopted the idea, and invited the Trust's chairman to his sanitary conference in Birmingham as a keynote speaker.

Although Chamberlain's ideas were not novel, his achievement was to grasp more fully than any other politician in Britain the electoral value of the image of the modern city, and to capitalize upon city improvement as a potent symbol of modernity and progress. To this end he embarked on 'all kinds of schemes' for the improvement of the city, all of them designed with an eye to the 'sense of the importance & dignity of municipal life which I am so anxious to emphasize.' Chamberlain claimed in speaking engagements across the country that the 'dignity ... and importance' of municipal institutions was exemplified by Birmingham, where the improvement scheme and other municipal initiatives had promoted 'progress, improvement, and advance in every direction'. So successful was his advocacy that Gladstone, visiting the city in 1877, characterized Birmingham 'as being ... the centre ... of the Municipal life of the country.'[20]

Chamberlain used city improvement as a springboard into national politics which would distinguish him from the social reformism of Disraelian conservatism, and from moderates in the Liberal Party. Chamberlain sought to forge a new Radical faction within the Liberal movement, and to assert his leadership over it. He had by 1874 packaged a loose collection of popular social reform issues into a coherent critique of the condition of British society which, by the mid-1880s, he had further matured into the 'unauthorized programme' of radical social reform, which he publicized everywhere as the best means of overcoming the great cleavages of wealth and poverty in contemporary society.[21] These objectives had become even more urgent following Chamberlain's election to Parliament as a representative for Birmingham in June 1876. In quest of a Cabinet position in the next Liberal ministry, he accused the Liberal leadership of 'groping blindly in the dark' for policies which had credibility with working-class voters. Chamberlain argued that visionary social policies were needed to regain office, and that the radical programme of 'the municipal Liberals of Birmingham' provided the necessary blueprint. He proffered the improvement scheme as the most visible statement of Liberal radicalism, and was delighted that the scheme earned 'the unstinted praise of the entire press of the country', and established 'his fame ... as a radical reformer'.[22]

When Chamberlain spoke at a Council banquet late in 1876 to celebrate his election to Parliament, the retiring Mayor reiterated that the 'great scheme of improvement' was the crowning symbol of 'Radical' Birmingham. Chamberlain resigned from the City Council in May 1880 after the Liberal Party's victory in the national elections and his subsequent appointment to Cabinet. A memorial fountain and public square were ceremonially opened in October in his honour, and at a special Council meeting Chamberlain was applauded for his authorship of the scheme, and for having steered it to a stage at which 'its practicability [had been fully] established, and its ultimate success assured.'[23]

The measuring stick used by Chamberlain's municipal successors to gauge the extent of that success was highlighted in 1882, with the release of a progress report by the Improvement Committee. The occasion made the opportunity for a major vindication of the scheme by Chamberlain's brother Richard, who was himself Mayor in 1879–80 and chairman of the Improvement Committee. Echoing his brother's words in 1875, Richard Chamberlain drew attention to the 'vast amount' of insanitary houses which had been cleared away by the street works, and to the 'new and stately buildings' which were now being erected along its length. He gloated that as a result 'Birmingham was becoming more and more the metropolis of the midland Counties.'[24] As Richard Chamberlain's oratory made plainer than ever before, sanitary reform was consistently subordinated by the scheme's planners to urban renewal. In 1882, with street building stalled at Aston Street and the slums largely untouched, the *Birmingham Daily Mail* expressed satisfaction that the city now possessed 'a beautiful broad thoroughfare, with splendid buildings and every prospect of it becoming the equal of some of the finest streets in Europe.' Sanitary reform was regarded as merely a by-product of such urban renewal, and was in any case interpreted narrowly to mean nothing more than slum clearance. Increasingly, Liberals insisted that building 'such a noble street in the centre of the town' was 'in itself a great sanitary measure', because it rolled back 'back slums' and weeded out 'hotbeds of disease'.[25]

The national debate on housing and poverty that spilled over from London in the early 1880s in the wake of G.R. Sims' 'Horrible London' articles in the *Daily News* and Andrew Mearns' *The Bitter Cry of Outcast London* was used by Birmingham Liberals to consolidate further the public face of the improvement scheme. Joseph Chamberlain sought to encapsulate the whole subject of housing reform in an article for the *Fortnightly Review*, which presented the Birmingham improvement scheme as the most important of all the municipal schemes to date.[26] Meanwhile, responding to the now 'fashionable amusement' of 'slumming' in London, the Birmingham City Council set up an Artisans' Dwellings Inquiry Committee to review local conditions. The Committee concluded in 1884 that 'no town in England could boast of better arrangements for the housing of the poor', and commended the Improvement Committee for having already removed or repaired 'much of the worst property in the town'. Liberals crowed that their opponents, whose imaginations had been 'stimulated by the revelations of "Horrible London"', would be 'disappointed because there were no black spots in Birmingham.'[27]

The decade closed amid a chorus of municipal self-congratulation. In 1888 a special meeting of Council granted the freedom of the borough to Joseph Chamberlain. Tributes rained upon Chamberlain for 'the policy of improvement which you inaugurated'. Later in the same year the Council, citing the magnitude of its municipal improvements, Birmingham's status as the largest provincial city in England, and the jubilee of its municipal incorporation, petitioned to be named a City. At another special meeting of Council early in 1889 the Queen's charter was read granting Birmingham 'the rank and dignity of a City'. The simultaneous tabling of the Improvement Committee's annual report was made an occasion to underline this achievement by triumphant review of a decade's achievement by the grandest improvement project of all, the construction of Corporation Street.[28]

Notwithstanding the breezy confidence with which the improvement scheme was publicly reviewed by its proponents, the project's focus had from the start been clouded by criticism and uncertainty. Conservatives complained during the 1875 municipal elections that a sizeable portion of the proposed roadway traversed areas which lay outside the intent of the

Cross Act. By the 1880 elections Conservative opinion had so hardened that the scheme was dismissed by them as nothing more than 'a gigantic land speculation'. It was hinted that Corporation Street was the result of a deal struck between the Council and the railways to provide better access to the station termini 'at the expense of the ratepayers'.[29]

More damaging criticism resulted from tensions within the Liberal movement between Whig traditionalists and Chamberlain radicals. Former Liberal Alderman Henry Hawkes, who had resigned in 1875 to become Borough Coroner, launched a stinging attack on the improvement scheme when he was invited to address the annual dinner of the Birmingham Landlords' and Ratepayers' Mutual Protection Association in 1878. There was, he said, no relationship at all between the supposedly insanitary areas contained within the scheme, and the actual areas of highest mortality with which he dealt as coroner. The scheme had simply been contrived in order to obtain land without paying for compulsory purchase. Joseph Chamberlain's long speech that year reviewing the scheme, seemingly so statesman-like, was in fact a desperate effort at damage control in case the scheme 'should suffer in public estimation' as a result of Hawke's comments. During the 1878 and subsequent municipal elections, Conservative and working-class opponents of the Liberal Association repeated Hawkes' accusations that the powers of the Cross Act 'had been entirely misappropriated'. Hawkes gave them more ammunition when he ridiculed the scheme again in 1882 and 1886.[30]

Birmingham Liberals were sensitive to Hawkes's criticisms for two main reasons. First, they recognized that he had a point. Much of the improvement area was not more dilapidated and insanitary than other districts of the city. The Medical Officer of Health had not himself initiated, but had been requested to draw up, the official representations of the supposedly insanitary area. Yet even the area of worst housing in the district he so obligingly condemned in 1875 had been passed over by him as altogether tolerable when he had inspected it in 1873 in response to residents' protests at its insanitary condition.[31] The second area of Liberal concern was that Hawkes's comments might reinforce misgivings about the scheme that had already been expressed by the Local Government Board. The Board held the power to wreck the scheme. Already, in 1876, it had seemed that they were about to do so.

In March 1876 the Local Government Board inspector, John Thornhill Harrison, held a formal inquiry into the proposed scheme. Harrison was unimpressed by representations of the entire improvement area as insanitary. The inspector instead divided the proposed improvement area into three. One portion, the land along the proposed site of Corporation Street between Bull Street and Aston Road, was in Harrison's opinion 'notoriously unhealthy' and was a correct subject for redevelopment under the Cross Act. However, he concluded that the neighbourhood where the Council proposed to begin street-works, from New Street to Bull Street, was not an insanitary district and should not have been included in the official representation. The third portion of the improvement area, through which it was intended to build abutting streets linking Corporation Street to the Great Western Railway on one side, and to the intersection of High Street and Dale End on the other, was also judged by Harrison to have been incorrectly included in the official representation as insanitary areas. Harrison conceded that there was no reason why a scheme to improve worker housing should not also answer the needs of a growing town. He therefore recommended that both of the contentious areas be allowed to remain in the improvement scheme. However, in the case of what he called 'the improvement portion' of Corporation Street between New and Bull Streets, Harrison proposed that the land could only be acquired compulsorily under the less attractive terms offered by the Lands Clauses Act, which governed municipal street improvements. In the case of the abutting lands he recommended that there should be no provision at all for compulsory purchase.[32]

Harrison's suggestions caused consternation. It seemed that if the land between New and Bull Streets — the centrepiece of Chamberlain's original calculations — could only be purchased under the same terms as in 'an ordinary town improvement scheme, the whole thing falls to the ground.' Chamberlain called on the President of the Local Government Board, remonstrating that he had received repeated Conservative assurances that the land in question would be included in the compulsory powers sought by the City Council. The Mayor returned to Birmingham crowing that Sclater Booth 'has promised to throw over the Commissioner & give me all I want! Hooray for the Tories!' However, John Lambert, Secretary of the Board, backed Harrison. He warned that the scheme 'partakes too largely of the character of a Street improvement', emphasizing that they 'ought not to debar the owners from compensation for compulsory purchase.' Harrison's recommendations were subsequently incorporated in the provisional order which was granted by the Board in June 1876, and, despite a Council deputation to London, were retained in the confirming Act passed in August.[33]

Lambert again cautioned in 1877 that the scheme 'partakes more of a Towns improvement Scheme, than of a proceeding contemplated by the Artisans and Labourers Dwellings Act.' His concern was confirmed when Harrison reviewed the scheme in April 1882. Harrison accepted that the building of Corporation Street had been successful as an aid to the commercial redevelopment of the city centre, and in a narrow sense as a sanitary reform as well. He was concerned, however, that the scheme fell down as a wider social reform package. Harrison pointed out that the Corporation had only purchased some 44 of the 93 acres originally included in the improvement area, and that this 'selection ... has been largely determined with reference to the street Improvements which they desired to carry out.' He worried that little of the purchased land had been remodelled. Harrison concluded somberly that the 'non-purchased and non-improved parts of the Area tell very plainly that the Scheme has been carried out too much as a great Town improvement.' The London-based *Charity Organisation Review* publicized those concerns in 1884, repeating

The Gullet, off Lichfield Street, Birmingham, c. 1882–84

criticisms that the 'poor people have been allowed to go on rotting, while the Improvement Committee spent £1,500,000 in pulling down dwellings and buying valuable properties without erecting a single artisan's dwelling on the site.'[34]

'A millstone of liabilities' [35]

Considered even as a town improvement, many in Birmingham contended that the scheme had tarnished edges. Local shopkeepers voiced frustration that the redevelopment had depreciated property values and that evictions were draining away their clientele. Conservatives sought to gain political mileage by asserting that the enormous debt run up by the scheme 'would be impossible to shake ... from their shoulders.' Local Conservatives gained a powerful ally in the Conservative Chancellor of Exchequer, Sir Stafford Northcote, who accused Birmingham of extravagantly spending money borrowed for sanitary reform 'in embellishing and improving the town, in creating new streets, and making magnificent boulevards.'[36] Conservative criticisms were fuelled when, in 1879, 1883, and 1886, auctions to lease new street allotments failed to attract the expected bidding.

Liberal leaders, anxious to wrest back the initiative in opinion-making concerning the scheme, decided that Richard Chamberlain should imitate his brother's performance of 1878 and present a major speech in justification of the scheme before the full Council. Chamberlain's eloquent speech in May 1882 was thus an attempt to put a brave face upon the long list of setbacks to the improvement scheme.[37] Liberals blamed their woes on three causes: a downturn in the local economy, the Treasury, and the Local Government Board. Joseph Chamberlain had already conceded when he answered Hawkes's criticisms in 1878 that the beginning of the scheme had corresponded with a collapse in the Midlands iron industry upon which the city's economy depended. Liberal spokesmen throughout the 1880s blamed the depression for hampering efforts to let properties in the improvement area, and for collapsing property values, thus cancelling the rate increases that had been expected to accrue from the scheme. The Treasury was simultaneously criticized for exacerbating these financial worries. The scheme's financial viability had been premised upon the Corporation's ability under the Cross Act to insulate ratepayers from the scheme's true cost by 'borrowing money cheaply'[38] from the Treasury at 3.5 per cent interest, repayable over 60 years, rather than upon the money market at up to 5 per cent interest. When the Treasury demurred, the scheme was almost wrecked. It was only saved by declining interest rates in the private money market.

The City Council had embarked upon the scheme with a low-interest, short-term loan of £500,000 from the Bank of England, pending the expected longer-term arrangement with the Public Works Loans Commissioners for a Treasury loan. In September 1876, however, the Commissioners announced that under their fixed lending terms the maximum loan period was only 50 years, repayable at 5 per cent interest, and that the 3.5 per cent rate was fixed to an even shorter repayment period of only 30 years. The scheme's promoters reacted with 'amazement and chagrin'. Chamberlain remonstrated that he had reached a 'tacit understanding' with the Disraeli Government that Birmingham would be offered the most liberal terms under the Cross Act. He sought a compromise agreement to repay the loan at 3.5 per cent interest over 50 years, first with the Commissioners, and then directly with the Treasury. In December, however, the Treasury confirmed that they could not lend at 'so low a rate'.[39]

The City Council unsuccessfully sought to realize its preferred terms by raising a £1-million loan on the private money market. A crisis loomed. The Bank of England's temporary loan was soon to expire and additional loans were needed to continue property purchases. The Council shored up its position by arranging additional short-term funding from the Bank of England. Chamberlain simultaneously appealed to the President of the Local Government Board to approve a compromise deal for long-term borrowings from the Public Works Loan Commissioners to repay the bank. He proposed to finance the improvement scheme over 60 years as in the original plan, to be financed in part by a Treasury loan at 3.5 per cent and repayable over 30 years. As this was paid off, he proposed to refinance the scheme by periodical borrowings from the private money market so as to extend repayments over 60 years. He also requested permission to increase the Corporation's credit ceiling to £1,500,000 in order to continue property purchases. Both applications were accepted.

Squeezed by the Treasury's reluctant terms, the Corporation juggled loans, overdrafts, and interest rates to keep the scheme afloat. The Local Government Board worried that Birmingham had become a prisoner to the vagaries of fluctuating interest rates in the short-term money market, and that the continuing local depression might at any time prompt investors to call for the immediate return of their money, which the city might not be able to meet. To avoid this eventuality, the Board authorized the refinancing of all Birmingham's debt by the raising of debentures. The Corporation's second venture into the London money market, early 1881, was a success, raising £2 million in long-term debentures at the unexpectedly low rate of 3.5 per cent. The loan was used in part to pay off some of the Public Works Loan Commissioners' advances. However, the Commissioners thereupon refused to advance further loan instalments under the terms of the agreement in 1879. A Council deputation called fruitlessly on the Local Government Board to intercede with the Commissioners. Late in 1882 the Improvement Committee had to return, cap in hand, to the Commissioners for an additional loan after the scheme's borrowing ceiling had been raised yet again, to £1,600,000. In yet another blow, the Commissioners would only lend under higher rates of interest that had been fixed by the Public Works Loans Act of 1879. A further source of worry emerged in the mid-1880s with the growing reliance upon the fluctuating interest rates of the short-term money market as the fixed-interest loans from the Treasury were repaid. These financial uncertainties were finally clarified late in the decade. In

1887, a long-term stock offer at 3 per cent interest was successfully filled on the London money market, enabling all Treasury and short-term loans to be paid off early in 1888.

Municipal planners in Birmingham had little cause to thank the Local Government Board for this easing of the financial pressures on the improvement scheme. The Board's decisions had twice significantly inflated the scheme's cost. By endorsing Harrison's recommendation that all the properties between New and Bull Streets be obtained under the provisions of the Lands Clauses Act rather than the Cross Act, the Board considerably increased the cost of land purchase. The Council sought to minimize the effects of the Board's ruling by offering generous terms for private settlement, knowing that going to arbitration under the Lands Clauses Act could result in costly awards in compensation for compulsory purchase and disturbance of trade.

The ill effects flowing from Harrison's inquiry were compounded by the official arbiter whom the Board appointed to determine compulsory purchase prices for those properties where agreements had not been reached. The first battle between the City Council and the Board on this score occurred late in 1878 over the terms of the arbiter's appointment. The Corporation wanted the arbiter's jurisdiction confined to properties specified by them. When the Board demurred, the Town Clerk complained that the Board had all along known that the 'essence' of the scheme was the ability to choose those properties in the improvement area that they wanted to purchase, rather than having to take the whole area. Birmingham won that point. The City Council next sought to ensure that the terms of the arbiter's jurisdiction did not enable him to award compensation to leaseholders and tenants as well as to property owners. The Cross Act had been drafted with the intention of achieving the immediate purchase and total clearance of improvement areas. The Birmingham Corporation now contended that by 'working the Scheme gradually', they intended to purchase only selected freeholdings which could be bought at a good price, and to let their leases run out 'with as little disturbance as is practicable' in order to avoid compensation. They remonstrated with the Board that it 'would be fatal to its success and financially disastrous' if they were now forced 'to pay for a great mass of property and interest which they do not desire to purchase'.[40]

The official arbiter, Sir Henry Hunt, was appointed by the Board in the middle of 1879. His actions realized the Corporation's worst fears. Hunt announced that the City was obliged to purchase and immediately clear all the land within the improvement area that had been scheduled for compulsory purchase, and that in consequence he was bound to award compensation for disturbance of trade to all leaseholders and tenants as well as to freeholders. The arbiter later recalled that the Board's instruction to him not to give compensation for disturbance to trade 'did not commend itself to my sense of justice'. A legal challenge to Hunt's jurisdiction and a deputation to the Local Government Board were both futile. Anticipating that Hunt's interpretations would 'greatly increase the cost of the Scheme', the Improvement Committee frantically sought to hammer out private settlements before Hunt's awards were formally announced in March 1880, and thereafter challenged some of Hunt's valuations in court. When the first court case was decided in favour of the Corporation early in 1881, most of the remaining cases were settled privately. The overall effect of Hunt's ruling, however, was to inflate still further the scheme's cost.[41]

Liberals had always boasted that the improvement scheme would not cost ratepayers a farthing. Joseph Chamberlain contended that even the £20,000 annual levy from the rates was really balanced by the profits made by the municipalization of the gas works. When annual interest repayments and other expenditures quickly exceeded receipts from rents and grants in aid from rates, the Improvement Committee nevertheless felt constrained to abide by the 'general understanding' that the ratepayers would not have to contribute more than £20,000 a year. The Committee therefore set up an overdraft account in December 1880 to carry forward the deficiency, and as costs continued to exceed revenue, the Committee allowed the annual deficits to accumulate, thus adding to the overall interest burden.[42]

The Improvement Committee grasped for other ways to balance their books. They sought to maximize rent collection from Corporation properties in the improvement area. In so doing, the scheme's focus changed from an undertaking in urban renewal to one in estate management. In 1887 the chairman of the Improvement Committee emphasized that it was important not to 'meddle' with Corporation properties in the improvement area as the rents they brought in just covered the interest on borrowings. The Committee simultaneously sought to reduce expenditure. This was achieved in part by economizing on house repairs and by cutting salaries. The debt crisis was also responsible for winding down street making. In 1881 the Improvement Committee recommended against embarking on building the second half of Corporation Street. Liberals thereafter repeatedly cautioned against proceeding with costly street building. When a Labour Councillor asked in 1888 when Corporation Street would be built through the insanitary area to Aston Road, he was told that there was no intention of going on with the scheme in the foreseeable future.[43]

The Council had in the meantime sought to ride out the financial crisis by applying to the Local Government Board in 1886 to raise their credit ceiling yet again by another £100,000, to £1,700,000. This, it was calculated, would be sufficient to cover the annual deficiency until 1893, when income from property and grants in aid from the rates would at last balance the books. However, the Board rejected the application late in the year, and when it was renewed, rejected it again early the next year. The Improvement Committee, desperate to sway the Board, wrung from the full Council an undertaking to increase the annual rate contribution to £25,000. In a frank admission of their predicament to their colleagues, the Committee reported that they had already overdrawn their credit limit by £29,000. Moreover they acknowledged that the annual deficiencies had become 'very much greater than was originally contemplated' and had accumulated a high-interest overdraft of almost £96,000. Application to the Board was renewed a third time in May 1887, and was pressed upon the reluctant Board for the remainder of the year. Local Government Board officials privately complained that the undertaking had become an 'expensive' one, but conceded that the Corporation was so heavily in debt that if they refused to sanction the new loan the city would be placed in 'an extremely awkward position'.[44] Finally, after more intense lobbying, and a commitment by the Improvement Committee not to apply for any more loans, sanction to increase the credit limit was granted in December.

'... a piece of deception from beginning to end'[45]

Late in 1876 the *Birmingham Daily Mail* reviewed the first year of operation of the improvement scheme. The newspaper cautioned that whereas the Corporation had spent freely to buy properties lying along the route of Corporation Street, there had been to date 'just the least danger that the Town Council might not have been so alive to the necessity for building up as they evidently were to the necessity for pulling down.' The *Mail* reminded its readers that the Cross Act had been 'intended not only to sweep away rookeries' but to supply decent working-class housing in their place.[46] The Improvement Committee had indeed been slow to formulate any clear plan to provide working-class housing in the improvement area. Harrison's inquiry early in 1876 had been told that although all the new street frontages would be reserved for shops and warehouses, almost all the rear allotments would be used for new artisan housing. Moreover, the Corporation pledged that new houses for working people would be built on a separate site at Summer Lane before any evictions began in the improvement area. Although street building began as planned in 1878, efforts to rehouse the evicted working people were beset with uncertainty and delay.

The delay was caused in part by uncertainty as to who was actually going to build the proposed new houses. Notwithstanding widespread expectation that the Corporation was about to accept house building 'as a municipal duty', Liberals scotched the idea. Chamberlain had suggested to Harrison that the Corporation might itself build the necessary houses. At other times however, Chamberlain argued that the Council's responsibilities stopped with the demolition of insanitary housing as they laid out the new streets. In 1878, responding to Hawkes, Chamberlain declared that 'We are not going to build a single house.' In 1884 he assured the Royal Commission into the Housing of the Working Classes that 'the re-construction and re-housing of the poor may be safely left to private enterprise.' Other Liberal speakers clamoured that 'it was no part of the duty of the Corporation to erect artisans' dwellings.' That was a responsibility, they said, for private philanthropists to copy from the likes of George Peabody and Sir Sydney Waterlow in London.[47] Notwithstanding the expectations that it would demolish and rebuild, the Improvement Committee late in 1876 tentatively embarked upon an alternative policy of containment and estate management, directing the repair of insanitary houses owned by the Corporation in order to make them tenantable for working people.

Considerable confusion also prevailed over what should be built. Some within the Liberal movement advocated experimental blocks of tenements built on the 'flat system' as in Glasgow and London, because they were cheaper to build than self-contained houses and could therefore be let at lower rents. Other Liberals doubted that flats were financially viable, and objected that it was not in any case the habit of Birmingham working people to live 'in apartments and in flats'. The Improvement Committee reached the same conclusion after visiting Glasgow, Edinburgh, and London, and prepared plans for two-storey 'cottages' laid out in 'open terraces' as guidelines for potential private developers of the Summer Lane site. So unresolved was the committee on basic principles, however, that when no developers took up their plans, they proposed new plans in 1878 which substituted flats.[48]

Ambiguity extended also to the question of who should be built for and where. Deliberations in the Improvement Committee focused almost exclusively upon housing provision for artisans, not 'for the lower grade of the Working Classes'. When Liberal Alderman William Cook suggested that the Committee also consider the needs of labourers, his proposal languished until it was finally discharged early in 1888. The full Council was lacklustre about anyone providing new housing in the central city. The Improvement Committee conceded that the Corporation was obliged by the Cross Act to rehouse an equal number of working people to those displaced. However, they looked with unconcealed admiration at the efforts of the Improvement Trusts in Glasgow and Edinburgh to disperse population so as to reduce densities within their improvement schemes. Liberal politicians listened benignly to the labour movement's demands for more tram lines and cheaper fares so as to enable working people to escape the 'misery' of the inner city and live instead in the suburbs.[49]

The Council's low interest in the rehousing goal of the Cross Act was highlighted by the sites chosen for replacement housing. The Summer Lane site lay a mile beyond the main improvement area so that the housing obligation would not impede commercial redevelopment of the cleared land. It was consequently too far away from the city centre to be attractive to speculative house builders, or practical for displaced workers. The site was unsuccessfully offered for lease at auction in 1879. Those few allotments which were subsequently leased were dismissed by Henry Hawkes as being occupied by 'master tradesmen and other middle-class residents'.[50] In 1883 the Corporation obtained permission from the Local Government Board to sell a large part of the site and to substitute another area closer to the city centre for artisans' housing. Early in 1884, the remaining land at Summer Lane was belatedly leased for the construction of working-class housing. However, no private developers could be found to build on the replacement site, in Ryder Street between Old Cross and Gem Streets.

The delay over rehousing became increasingly a source of notoriety as, from the 1878 municipal elections onwards, Conservatives sniped at the Liberal Association for having deceived the working classes and perverted the intentions of the Cross Act. Conservatives assailed Joseph Chamberlain during the 1880 general elections for having lied on the rehousing question, capitalizing upon remarks by Hawkes during a coroner's inquest that despite the improvement scheme 'Thousands of people live in no better dwellings.'[51]

In 1882 these criticisms of municipal housing policy took an alarming new turn when the Local Government Board took up the issue and threatened to withhold sanction for further borrowing. Harrison, when he reviewed the scheme in 1882, reported that nothing had been done either to rehouse those working-class tenants who had been evicted by the demolitions, or to improve the condition of the housing stock — about one-third of the total — within the improvement area that had not been bought by the Corporation. The Board conceded that they could not push the matter far because Parliament had passed amendments in 1879 and again in 1882 which were designed to 'relax' the Cross Act's rehousing obligations.[52] The Board none the less demanded an explanation from the Corporation, and delayed for three months after receiving Harrison's report before sanctioning Birmingham's request to extend its loan ceiling.

Birmingham Liberals, stung by the mounting attacks, began to put together a coherent rationalization for their inaction. They remonstrated that working-class houses which had been purchased by the Corporation and whose sites were not needed for street making were being rehabilitated by the Improvement Committee all the same. Insanitary courts were being made habitable by knocking down houses to let in fresh air and light, by removing middens and laying sewers and water mains. The Health Committee was simultaneously using its powers under the Public Health Act to order the demolition or repair of insanitary housing in the improvement area that had not been purchased by the Corporation. As a result of the two committees' work, housing conditions in area had been 'very materially improved in character'[53] and the death rate in the district had been greatly reduced.

These Liberal responses slowly evolved into a shadowy but coherent policy. First outlined publicly by Joseph and Richard Chamberlain in their speeches to Council in June 1878 and May 1882, the policy was consolidated in 1884 by the report of the Artisans' Dwellings Inquiry Committee. The policy called for a cautious programme of containment by repairing houses in the city centre, pending a lasting resolution of the housing crisis by private enterprise. Liberals contended that, in the short term, housing reform was already being accomplished as the result of an over-supply of cheap rental accommodation within the city in consequence of speculative house building in the suburbs and the consequent drift of working people from the centre. In the longer term, they said, private-market estate development around the city's periphery would complete the housing reform.

Liberals argued that because the long-term resolution of slum housing depended upon residential decentralization to the suburbs, it would be 'idiotic' to build new working-class houses in the city centre. Rather, the most useful housing policy was to obtain concessional working-class fares on the trams and trains in order to help working people to commute between suburban homes and city work-places. Liberals conceded that high land prices made multi-storey flats in the city centre the only business-like way of providing new houses. However, they ruled out any such local government undertaking on the grounds that multi-storey flats were 'not adapted to the English workman, who prefered a self-contained dwelling.' A Liberal Unionist speaker drew applause at an election meeting in St Mary's ward when he asserted that the bulk of artisans did not want back houses built in blocks behind Corporation Street, but suburban cottages 'with a bit of garden and the opportunity of keeping a pig'.[54]

Radical Conservatives countered that relying on private-market supply of low-income housing was to avoid the responsibilities imposed on City Councils by Disraelian reform in the 1870s, and that 'claptrap' talk of facilitating cheap travel to the suburbs was simply 'cheap philanthropy'. Moreover, after the Liberal split in 1886 over Irish Home Rule, labour candidates sponsored by the Birmingham Trades Council and the Social Democratic Federation savagely attacked the Liberal Unionist majority in Council for having duped working people in order to use the improvement scheme merely to aid big business. Even before the Liberal split, sharp disagreements had existed behind the façade of party unity about the details of housing containment in the city centre. By the mid-1880s the Improve-ment Committee, responding to criticisms from all quarters about the insanitary condition of many of the houses in the improvement area, began to think more seriously about an experiment in flat building. Their calculations were given urgency by growing national interest in the subject of public housing in the wake of *The Bitter Cry*. Significantly, their proposal was unveiled in the middle of 1885, on the eve of a general election during which the Conservative leader, Lord Salisbury, had 'caused the whole nation to consider the question of the "housing of the poor".'[55]

The proposal, for the Corporation to build and operate an experimental four-storey block of 23 flats, brought into the open the simmering ambiguities, inconsistencies, and disagreements which had all along characterized Liberal housing policy. The Improvement Committee hoped to cater 'for workmen of the better class, whose employment necessitates their living within easy reach of their work, and whose earnings will enable them to pay the moderate rental.' They also sought to appease local traders whose businesses had been hurt by the scheme's disruption of the area.[56] By advocating the house-building experiment the committee chairman, Richard Chamberlain, contradicted the common-sense opinions of most of his Council colleagues. He cautioned that although there were large numbers of vacant houses in the city's outskirts, the supply of cheap rental houses in the centre was only very small. Yet it was here, he said, that demand was concentrated, because many working people were still obliged to live in the centre owing to the cost and time of tram and bus travel. Chamberlain urged that in order for the policy of containment to work, it was necessary for the City Council to build some houses in the centre as a holding operation. The proposal for municipal house building was thrown out by both Unionist and Gladstonian Liberals. The object of the improvement scheme, they said, had already been realized with the clearing and beautification of the improvement area. It was not proper for the Corporation to build houses. Working men should save and become their own landlords. Conservatives joined the Liberals in discounting Chamberlain's arguments. They all agreed that the prolonged depression, as well as threatening to bankrupt the whole improvement scheme, had produced a glut of cheap rental houses. The suburbs were easily accessible. Continuing decentralization of the population was the way of the future, as city centres were given over more and more to business.[57]

Home building, 1889–1901

The 1890s were represented by the City Council as a period of financial consolidation for the improvement scheme. Corporation rental properties generated an ever increasing income, the number of empty building allotments dwindled, and property rates steadily inflated. In 1895 the first small annual reduction in rate relief to the scheme was possible. These achievements were capped by the leasing of the last allotment in Corporation Street early in 1900. As a city improvement, the scheme could thus be said by some to have been successfully concluded. Yet in the opinion of others the scheme had still not, after a quarter of a century, effectively begun as an undertaking in comprehensive housing reform. The building of Corporation Street remained stalled at Aston Street. Although some 900 working-class houses had been demolished, only 100 had been erected by private enterprise in their place. The Improvement Committee dwelt instead on the efficient management of the rental properties on its books, and on the profitable leasing of the cleared allotments. In November 1899 the Committee's name was changed to the Estates Committee, in tacit recognition of the scheme's changing emphasis from street building to estate management.

Yet if the street improvement was not, with hindsight, seen in 1901 as having been a direct instrument of slum clearance in the ways anticipated in 1875, the turn of the century was none the less represented by Liberal leaders in both the Unionist and Gladstonian camps as the conclusion of an ultimately more effective housing policy of cautious containment which had first taken shape during the 1870s and 1880s. That evolving policy, first specified by the speeches of the Chamberlains in 1878 and 1882, and by the report of the Artisans Dwellings Inquiry Committee in 1884, was extended during the 1890s as the result of close collaboration between the Gladstonian-dominated Improvement and Health Committees. The former Committee embarked upon a wide-ranging programme for 'the opening out and reconstruction of unhealthy areas'.[58] In May 1894 a second small improvement area of about an acre between Milk Street and the Great Western Railway viaduct was represented as a congested and insanitary area, cleared, and offered to private developers for artisan housing. In February 1898 a third insanitary area of three acres, containing 223 back-to-back houses, was identified but action was deferred pending completion of the Milk Street scheme. A fourth area, comprising 16 acres in the St Laurence parish, opposite the Aston Road boundary of the main improvement scheme, was represented by the Medical Officer of Health late in 1901. Meanwhile, the Health Committee's use of the 1890 Housing of the Working Classes Act to order the closing and repair of insanitary houses was hailed as an outstanding example of Gladstonian reformism.

Both Committees had simultaneously initiated three experiments in municipal house building. In 1889 the Corporation built a two-storey block of 22 houses along Ryder Street, on the old Gem Street site that had been reserved by the Local Government Board for new working-class housing. Another 81 terrace houses were built between 1891 and 1893 in nearby Lawrence Street. Between 1898 and 1900 the Corporation built four two-storey terraces of flats and more terrace houses in the Milk Street improvement area. The Manager of the improvement area could confidently assert that as a result of this collaborative approach to housing policy, the 'Labouring men of Birmingham are being catered for in the manner of accommodation on a more liberal basis than almost any other Town or City.'[59]

In July 1900 William Cook, chairman of the Health Committee, fore-shadowed yet another initiative. Administering the policy of containment by ordering the piecemeal repair or demolition of insanitary houses had convinced his Committee that another 'great improvement' project was needed in order to clear away the remaining older housing stock in the inner city. To embark on this, however, without simultaneously providing replacement housing 'would be to carry out an un-housing scheme, ... and be a hardship to the very class whom it is most desired to help.' The Committee therefore proposed to use the Council's authority under part three of the Housing of the Working Classes Act in order to buy land at Bordesley Green, about three miles from the city centre, and build a municipal suburb there. Once this was done, the Corporation could proceed to 'sweep away' the remaining slums in the central city. Council approved the concept. In June 1901, having purchased the Bordesley Green site, the Health Commit-tee sought formal authority to build the estate. Cook simultaneously proposed, in conjunction with the Estates Committee, that two four-storey blocks of flats be built at Potter Street in the original improvement area, for those working people who were unable to live in the suburbs. It was only by adopting the flat system, the Health Committee argued, that the borough could achieve 'the solution of the Housing problem in the centre of the City'. The Committee none the less emphasized, echoing Richard Chamberlain's argument in 1885, that municipal flat building served merely as a temporary holding operation. The inexorable trend of modern city living was outwards. The Committee predicted that building affordable rental cottages on the city's periphery, linked to the centre by cheap and frequent trams and trains, 'will be one of the most important factors solving the difficulties connected with such central insanitary areas.'[60]

In a stinging rebuff to Cook, both proposals were thrown out by the full Council in a cliff-hanging vote. The Council resolved instead to establish a new housing committee and to transfer housing responsibilities to it from the Estates and Health Committees. This outcome was the culmination of mounting public criticisms and internal dissension during the 1890s. These criticisms came to a head during 1901, when the 'housing problem' became the central topic of local political debate, amid a chorus of accusations that Birmingham, 'the first provincial municipality who obtained powers to improve Slum-Land', had done less than any great city to resolve the slum problem. The claim was sensationalized by the Conservative *Daily Gazette* when it began publishing James Cuming Walters' *Scenes in Slum-Land* in March in order to discredit the Liberal Health Committee. That objective was simultaneously pursued by the Unionist and Conservative Party machines.[61]

The three figures most intimately identified with current municipal housing and improvement policies stood condemned. Dr Alfred Hill, the Medical Officer of Health since 1872, was presented as an ageing incompetent. Gladstonian Alderman Dr Alfred Barratt, who had helped Joseph Chamberlain launch the improvement scheme and who had sat on the Improvement Committee since its inception, was accused in Unionist ward meetings of being the owner of 'one of the lowest courts' in slumland. Cook, who had sat on both Committees and been chairman of the Health Committee for 25 years, was unfairly abused as a landlord with a vested interest in opposing municipal house building. Cook and Hill sued for libel. The October municipal elections were convulsed by Birmingham's perceived slum crisis, which was now widely blamed on Cook's 'stick-in-the-mud system' of housing reform.[62]

The events of 1901 exposed as illusory the seeming consensus and clarity of purpose which had cloaked municipal improvement and housing administration during the 1890s. Housing issues were shown instead to be deeply polarized between the competing viewpoints and agendas of acrimonious groups. In the wake of the Liberal split in 1886, separate Unionist and Gladstonian party organizations and obligations cut across the previous broad Liberal consensus and complicated policy-making. Collaboration between the Health and Improvement Committees eroded as the latter became dominated by Unionists, and as the Health Committee was increasingly targeted for politically motivated attacks by Unionists and Conservatives in the Council chamber and in the daily press. The increasingly assertive and independent stance adopted by the labour movement in local politics further upset the older political equations. Austen Chamberlain's defeat in 1889 by the president of the Birmingham Trades Council, running as a Gladstonian candidate, was a great shock to Unionists, who campaigned thereafter in ever closer alliance with the Conservatives. The favourite target for both Unionists and Conservatives was the Gladstonian Health Committee, which they identified as a mouthpiece for the radical housing proposals of the Trades Council, the Social Democratic Federation, and the Independent Labour Party.

Behind the contrived façade of apparent consistency and consolidation, housing policy initiatives originated as *ad hoc* adjustments to the more insistent demands and criticisms which were generated by the combative nature of local politics. With critics of the improvement scheme still assailing it as 'a gigantic failure' which teetered on the brink of bankruptcy,[63] decision-making by the Improvement Committee was inseparably linked to considerations of debt management. In the main, this meant containment rather than new initiatives. Suggestions in 1892 and 1894 that the Committee undertake large-scale schemes for worker housing were scotched in view of the politically unendurable extra rate burden such initiatives would entail. The Ryder and Milk Street houses were both 'built from necessity, not from choice', because of undertakings to the Local Government Board to provide some replacement housing for that torn down by both improvement schemes.[64] Municipal house building at Ryder and Lawrence Streets were undertaken in large part as exercises in pragmatic 'estate improvement',[65] designed to arrest the depopulation caused by the improvement scheme, and the prejudicial effect this was having on the letting value of Corporation-owned houses and the leasing of new allotments. The decision to build at Lawrence Street was also undertaken to address the 'constant complaint' by local shopkeepers at the depopulation caused by the scheme.[66] The Birmingham Ratepayers' Union had publicized these complaints since the late 1880s, and during the 1890s it won a string of electoral victories, especially in St Mary's ward, which it claimed had been 'laid waste' by the Improvement Committee.[67]

The Health Committee's trumpeted housing initiatives in July 1900 — and in particular its recognition of the necessary fit between clearing old houses and building new ones — occurred in defensive reaction to the negative publicity generated by the practice of containment during the 1890s. Delegates to a housing conference organized by the Birmingham Trades Council in 1899 were told that Birmingham working people were overcrowded 'in dirty and unhealthy slums' because of a chronic under-supply of affordable rental houses which had been exacerbated by 'the grand improvement' scheme. Independent Labour Party candidates in the municipal elections of 1901 complained that the 'great Improvement Scheme, no doubt, effected an improvement in the centre of the city, but it resulted in the ... unhousing of about 5,000 people. To meet this the Council only provided for a few hundreds, and were in that way responsible for the creation of slums.' The Medical Officer of Health's disclosures about inner-city mortality rates and housing conditions in his annual reports of 1899 and 1900 were called scandalous by the labour movement, Liberal Unionists, and Conservatives. The Birmingham Board of Guardians weighed in, drawing the Local Government Board's attention to the 'urgent and pressing need' for public housing to overcome the 'extreme overcrowding and consequent misery' caused by the Health Committee condemning insanitary dwellings without providing replacement accommodation.[68]

The Potter Street afterthought to the Bordesley Green scheme occurred after an embarrassing series of public rebukes delivered by Birmingham church leaders in the wake of Walters' disclosures in the *Gazette*. Nonconformist and Anglican clergy established a ginger group, the Sanitary Aid Committee, to publicize and help ameliorate 'the terrible condition of the poor of Birmingham'. The official representation of the St Laurence parish as an unhealthy area was a product of its pressure. The Sanitary Council's secretary, the Reverend Thomas Bass, in whose parish *Scenes in Slum-Land* was largely set, in April sent a copy of the book to the Local Government Board. Bass was scathing of the Health Committee's policy of 'tinkering and patching of old property', and demanded that the Board prod the City Council into action to remove the slums. Acting on the Board's advice, in early June Bass organized a group of ratepayers to lodge an official complaint about the sanitary condition of the St Laurence parish district adjoining the main improvement area, thereby requiring the medical officer to undertake an official representation of the district. Hill's confidential report was leaked by the Unionists as part of their attack on the Health Committee in the October municipal elections. The report's corroborative depiction of slumland 'caused some sensation', and assured the appointment of a new housing committee after the elections.[69]

The inevitable consequence of these *ad hoc* responses to the contingencies of electoral pressure was an abiding indeterminacy of principle, and volatility in programme outcomes. The majority of electors and their representatives, regardless of party affiliation, continued to cling to the apparently common-sense viewpoint of the 1880s that lasting housing reform was best left to the market-place. They asserted that speculative house building in the suburbs had a trickle-down effect as artisans abandoned the inner-city housing market for the new accommodation on the city's periphery. The existing supply of houses in the centre was thus more than equal to meet demand, especially as this demand weakened in consequence of the replacement of inner-city housing by warehouses, shops, and offices. It appeared axiomatic that 'Ground in the centre of the city must tend to increase in value, and the result must necessarily be to drive the labouring population to the outskirts.'[70]

Such thinking was encouraged by the labour movement's consistent representation of inner-city housing as irredeemable slums which needed to be swept away by the Corporation and their inhabitants relocated in low-density public housing estates 'in the outlying districts of the City'. During the 1899 and 1900 municipal elections the Trades Hall Council sent circulars to all candidates asking if they would vote to provide low-rental housing in the suburbs, and published a list of preferred candidates on the basis of the answers received. Gladstonians embraced the labour movement's agenda in the hope of winning quick electoral returns. They advocated pressuring tram and rail companies to provide cheap transport, and suggested that the Council might even buy land and build detached garden cottages in the suburbs. Liberal Unionists shied away from the latter proposal, but conceded to electors that by municipalizing the trams working people could be encouraged to own their own suburban cottages with a 'bit of garden'.[71]

The logic of such thinking was shattered by Cook in the early 1900s. His proposals for municipal housing in Potter Street and Bordesley Green were couched in explicit acknowledgement that an intractable housing crisis existed in the city centre, which was reflected in increasing rents, crowding, and ill health. He conceded that these outcomes had been exacerbated by the Improvement and Health Committees. These admissions undermined the credibility of the policy of short-term containment in the inner city, upon which the logic of suburban resettlement had all along been based. In so doing, Cook exploded the loose Liberal consensus on housing policy which had endured since the late 1870s.

The Improvement and Health Committees had long been aware of the limitations of containment as a holding operation in the inner city. The former committee had acknowledged in 1891 that Corporation-owned houses were getting beyond repair, and were already 'falling about their ears'. The Health Committee knew from their policing of the Housing of the Working Classes Act and the Public Health Act that 'there is much small house property in the City that requires almost constant attention to keep it in a habitable condition.' Accumulating evidence by the early 1890s of an increasing short supply of low-rental accommodation in the inner city further exposed the fallacy of containment. A joint investigation of labourers' housing by the Health and Improvement Committees in 1898 confirmed that there was indeed a 'scarcity' of such housing. However it was not until the Health Committee undertook a comprehensive survey of the housing market in 1900 that the bulk of Gladstonian Liberals were convinced that private enterprise was 'unequal' to the task of supplying the demand for cheaper houses.[72]

By now it was clear to all that as a business undertaking in the city centre, housing provision — because of the costs of land purchase, construction, and maintenance — could never bear the low returns attendant upon working-class rentals. Suggestions that the Corporation undertake the task were none the less still fiercely resisted by a majority of Councillors, regardless of party affiliation, who clung to the old objection in principle to the idea of a public authority 'competing' with private entrepreneurs. Moreover, the prospect that the Council might mask its costs by drawing subsidies from the rates in order to offer rents below what the private market could profitably sustain was condemned as an inequitable impost upon all ratepayers for the special benefit of 'a particular class'. Unionists objected that subsidized housing 'would, in effect, be a pension scheme under pretence of being a housing undertaking.' Even Gladstonians balked at the prospect of providing 'almshouses wholesale.'[73]

Municipal house building stalled largely because of this insistence that investments in houses 'be made remunerative'. The Ryder and Lawrence Streets schemes were both designed to be financially self-supporting, but they consequently charged such high rents that they were widely admitted to be of limited effectiveness as blueprints for new houses that working people could afford. The Improvement Committee had in 1889 considered building a multi-storey block of flats in order to cut building costs and thus lower the rents. However the matter was deferred in the wake of Ryder Street's financial success. It was not until the Milk Street improvement scheme was launched in 1894 that the Committee again seriously suggested building flats. This time they cautiously suggested a small rate subsidy to lower the rents further, but the idea was damned as a 'Socialistic enterprise' and the whole housing scheme was dropped. The Committee resubmitted the proposal in 1897, this time without any provision for rent relief. The proposal was again thrown out, in large part because of opposition from Cook, who argued that without rate relief the rents would be so high as to make the whole exercise in house building 'useless'. It was only after intense pressure from the Local Government Board that the Council in 1898 agreed to build flats at Milk Street and to subsidize their operations for five years.[74]

Cook — the man savaged in 1901 for causing the housing problem — had conceded more readily than anyone else that Birmingham's experiments in municipal housing 'did not touch the fringe of the question' of how to provide good housing for the labouring poor.[75] Yet the building of subsidized multi-storey flats, which he saw as a partial answer to the problem, was resisted by the City Council because of the opposition of organized labour. The labour movement, committed to achieving public housing in the suburbs rather than in the city centre, condemned the Ryder and Lawrence Streets terraces as 'more after the style of workhouses' than home-places. Labour leaders were even more uncompromising in their opposition to flats. The Milk Street flat scheme was damned by them as 'dangerous to morality, the comfort, and the convenience' of tenants.[76] Their opposition was responsible for the Improvement Committee dropping the original idea of building four-storey flats at Milk Street, and adopting instead plans for low-rise flats. The Labour movement's hostility to inner-city flat living predictably gained the support of their electoral partners, the Gladstonian Liberals, who contended that Birmingham workmen would never consent to live in the 'barrack-like boxes of dwellings, superimposed in layers one upon another', that were to be found in Glasgow, Edinburgh, Liverpool, and London. Unionists likewise condemned Glasgow flats as 'an eyesore and a disgrace', and contended that the 'prejudice' of Birmingham working people made flat building unviable.[77]

Radical Conservatives rejected the whole tenor of housing debate as it had been set by Liberal, Unionist, and Labour speakers. The debate had, they said, been skewed by 'slavish subservience' to the Birmingham Trades Hall and the Independent Labour Party, which represented only 'the fairly well to do and prosperous artizans of the trade union and friendly society stamp', and who regarded the semi-skilled as 'dirt to be trampled upon and ignored'. Conservatives argued correctly that discussion of housing needs in Birmingham had consequently always revolved around the provision of artisan housing rather than addressing the different needs of the 'humbler' labouring classes.[78] Yet as the *Daily Gazette* pointed out, there had never been a housing shortage in the rental range affordable by artisans, because the private market supplied housing where a viable market demand existed. The municipal low-rise, self-contained houses, designed to over-come labour movement hostility to high-rise flats, thus duplicated what the market had already provided, and were in too high a rental bracket to compete against the low-rent back-to-backs where the labouring poor lived. The suburban Bordesley Green scheme was yet another unnecessary 'sop' to the artisans, because the trade-union movement wanted 'self-contained residences built for them in salubrious suburbs at the public expense'. One working-class candidate for the Conservatives and Unionists asserted that 'a residence at Bordesley Green was as impractical as a villa on the Riviera' for low-wage working people.[79]

Conservatives insisted that the 'slum problem must be grappled with in the slums.' In 1898 a working-class Conservative candidate conceded that although the Council had provided reasonably well for the housing needs of artisans, it had failed to address the needs of labourers. Many small houses had, he said, been removed by the improvement scheme, but they had not been replaced with others at the same rent so that families had been driven to share accommodation. Conservatives reasoned that instead of compet-ing with private enterprise to provide working-class accommodation in the suburbs, the City Council should throw its energies into schemes like Potter Street in the city centre, where the high price of land prevented private enterprise from providing cheap housing to those 'whose poverty compels them to live in foul dens close to the centre of the city.' The only way this could be done was by building multi-storey flats.[80]

Amid this sea of indeterminacy, Joseph Chamberlain and the 1875 improvement scheme ironically came to be upheld by all contestants as measuring sticks against which to emphasize the present inadequacies and inconsistencies of their opponents. Radical Conservatives asserted in 1901 that Birmingham was a quarter of a century behind current municipal housing practice because Joseph Chamberlain's original intention to sweep away the slums and rehouse their occupants had been forgotten: the 'present condition of slum-land was because there had been no continuity of the wise policy instituted by Mr. Chamberlain in 1875.' During the 1891 municipal elections one Social Democratic Federation candidate similarly recalled happier times when Joseph Chamberlain was still 'really a friend of the working classes'. Labour representatives complained in 1901 that housing reform in Birmingham had been at a standstill since the heroic days when Corporation Street 'was thrust through a part of the city containing some of the worst rookeries that could be imagined'.[81]

Practical housing, 1902–1914[82]

The City Council decided early in 1903 to continue building Corporation Street to Aston Road. The street's whole length was opened in December 1904. The Corporation was still negotiating to complete the leasing of the new street frontages at the outbreak of the First World War. Total expenditure for the whole scheme, including house building, came close to

£1,750,000. Yet as one Conservative Councillor, forgetting his party's initial scepticism, pointed out in 1909, the scheme's heavy cost was offset by an already large and increasing annual income. The scheme would, he said, become 'a magnificent asset' to the city. In 1912 the Finance Committee reported that the total rate subsidy to date had averaged slightly under the £20,000 per year anticipated by Joseph Chamberlain in 1875.[83]

The completion of Corporation Street caused the demolition of 172 working-class houses, and the eviction of some 850 residents. No additional municipal housing was built to accommodate them. Upon the completion of minor street works in 1909, the Corporation remained landowner of 485 working-class houses in the improvement area. One-third of these were new buildings. The remainder were old, some of them back-to-back dwellings in courts whose only access was through tunnel entries. By 1914, 191 of these older houses remained. The estate manager conceded that rental policy was not decided 'quite on philanthropic lines'. The Corporation, he said, 'did not like housing the poor and undesirable', but preferred to maximize the income-earning capacity of the estate. Houses were rented pending the negotiation of building leases for their sites.[84]

The appointment of the new Housing Committee, chaired by Liberal Unionist John Nettlefold, had resulted in a decisive switch away from the provision of new municipal housing. Nettlefold moved quickly in 1902 to consolidate his victory over Cook's policies, winning Council approval to lease the land at Bordesley Green rather than build there, and to reject the Potter Street flat proposal. He also won support for the principle of piecemeal housing repairs instead of the additional large-scale improvement schemes Cook had foreshadowed. Rather than launching a new improvement scheme in the St Laurence parish area, the Committee sought to apply 'firm but friendly pressure upon the property owners' to repair or demolish their properties. The Committee also purchased scattered properties with the object 'of improving the slums' by demolishing front and rear houses in order to transform 'obscure courts ... into open and airy terraces'.[85]

In March 1904 the Council approved the application of these policies throughout the city. Evolving housing policy was further systematized at Nettlefold's instigation in 1906. As one Unionist committee member explained, they had hitherto concentrated on 'driving out disease and death from the slums', but now 'they also wanted to acquire powers to prevent the formation of similar slums in the suburbs.' Borrowing from Germany, the Council endorsed town extension planning and municipal land purchase in order to control future growth around the city's periphery, and called for national town planning legislation to enforce town extension plans and to enable comprehensive municipal land purchase. In 1907, in what was hailed by Nettlefold as the first application of these principles in England, the Bordesley Green site was leased to a Birmingham Friendly and Building Society for working-class, owner-occupier housing 'in accordance with garden city ideas'. The Housing Committee took advantage of the 1909 Housing and Town Planning Act to launch two town planning schemes in the immediate pre-war years. Nettlefold proclaimed that Birmingham was in 'the van' of slum reform and town planning innovation in Britain.[86]

Midway through 1913, the Council appointed a special committee to inquire into 'the housing conditions of the poorer parts of the City', and advise on Council policy-making. The committee was chaired by the rising star of local politics, Neville Chamberlain. It also included Liberal housing reformer, George Cadbury, and Independent Labour Party Councillor George Shann. The committee's report, presented in October 1914, vindicated the old policy of containment in the city centre, and in so doing upheld Nettlefold's practice of 'patching' in preference to large-scale municipal slum clearance and housing provision. The resolution of Birmingham's slum problem, the committee concluded, lay in the 'constant migration of the working classes from the centre to the suburbs', which should be facilitated and controlled by municipal planning and land purchase. As better-paid working people left for new suburban homes, they vacated inner-city houses for those classes 'a little below them', and so, incrementally, 'each class moved up step by step.'[87]

Despite this semblance of consolidation and achievement, municipal housing policy in Birmingham had continued to be characterized by indecision and contradiction, amid crisis talk about deteriorating living conditions and a collapsing housing market. Such alarmist reaction resulted in part from the slumland sensationalism which had been entrenched in local housing debate by Walters in 1901. Walters' radical conservatism was perpetuated by Bass, who constantly sought to publicize the 'awful revelations of the slums of Birmingham'. Labour and Liberal politicians repeatedly sought electoral mileage by asserting that under Unionist and Conservative guardianship Birmingham had acquired 'one of the worst names with regard to slums among the cities of this country'. The alarm about Birmingham's housing crisis was also grounded in an emerging consensus that the intractable core of the city's slum problem consisted of the over 40,000 back-to-back houses and 6,000 courts which, by 1914, still remained after 40 years of vaunted housing reform. The 1914 inquiry's confirmation that house building was failing to keep pace with the growth of population simultaneously questioned the supposed palliative of 'the operation of the ordinary law of supply and demand' upon which the policy of containment had always relied.[88]

The confusing multiplicity of opinion as to appropriate policy responses was heightened by the erosion of the long Unionist 'ascendancy' as new political alignments formed and imposed altering parameters upon municipal debate.[89] The watershed in this unravelling of Unionist power was the annexation of suburban municipalities to form the boundaries of Greater Birmingham in 1911. The new Council elected that year was very different from the old. Not only was it greatly enlarged, but two-thirds of the Councillors were newcomers. For the first time, the Unionists were junior partners in the Unionist-Conservative alliance which had endured since the Home Rule split in 1886. The volatility of local politics was increased by the Independent Labour Party, which emerged from a string of electoral successes early in the century as a major new player in municipal government. The entry of significant numbers of labour representatives into the City Council transformed hitherto common-sense assumptions into contested terrain. When Nettlefold suggested in 1903 that slums were largely perpetuated by the habits of the poor, the Independent Labour Party countered with lectures and photographic displays on housing and concluded that anyone who sought to reduce so complex a problem to the drinking habits of tenants was 'either a knavish liar or a fool. (Applause)'. Labour politicians popularized the alternative idea that 'Capitalism ... was responsible for the slums', and that the slow pace of municipal housing reform was because the Council was stacked with speculators, jerry-builders and slumlords. Unionists, striving to retain electoral support among working people, were forced increasingly on to the back foot as they denied that 'Socialists were the only people anxious to do away with the slums.'[90]

As the insistent delivery of alternative viewpoints clouded more and more what was common-sense opinion in housing policy, Council decision-making became ever more confused, contested, and *ad hoc*. Nettlefold, the dominant voice early in the twentieth century after his eclipse of Cook, found himself in turn isolated as the new political alignments in Council sorted themselves out. He lost the chairmanship of the Housing Committee in 1909, and his Council seat in 1911. In the same year his creation, the Housing Committee, was absorbed into a new Health and Housing Committee. Both policy initiatives in the city centre — the continuation of Corporation Street and Nettlefold's policy of rehabilitating the existing inner-city housing stock — had in fact begun as half-hearted concessions to pressure by the Local Government Board in response to lobbying by local critics of Council inaction.

The decision in 1903 to complete Corporation Street had been forced by the intervention of the Local Government Board, after the Council had the previous year decisively defeated a recommendation from the Estates Committee to continue the street. Bass had thereupon requested the Board to force the Council to continue the task of 'slum reform' by completing the street through the original insanitary district to Aston Road. The 1875 scheme had been approved and funded, he said, in order quickly to 'clear out these slums', but the Corporation had instead made themselves 'Slum owners, with public funds'.[91] The Board undertook a damning review of the scheme's progress, which was widely publicized by Bass in the local press. The Council nevertheless again voted not to continue street building, and sent a deputation to London to suggest a five-year postponement. It was only when this ploy was unsuccessful that the Estates Committee was instructed to prepare plans to complete Corporation Street.

The Board's intervention exposed the complicated motives and competing interests shaping Corporation policy. The *Daily Gazette* continued to point to the hypocrisy of representing the 'great improvement scheme' as a slum clearance measure when in fact the death rate in the as yet untouched insanitary area was now higher than it had been in 1875.[92] Businesses with leaseholds in Corporation Street demanded that the street be continued in order to honour municipal undertakings to do so when they signed their leases. The City Council as a whole argued that the district was no longer a slum because of their work of piecemeal repair and demolition in the area. Conveniently noting the accumulated evidence of an under-supply of low-cost rental accommodation in the city centre, Councillors belatedly cautioned that further street making would accentuate the housing difficulties of the poor. Behind these rationalizations, the majority of Councillors sought to kill the scheme because of the additional expenditure it would entail, and because many existing shops and offices in Corporation Street were still unoccupied.

The official representation of part of Bass's St Laurence parish as an unhealthy area presented another dilemma for Council. The Medical Officer of Health reported that another full-blown improvement scheme was needed. His conclusion had been prompted only in part by Bass's lobbying of the Local Government Board. Hill had also been 'spurred into action' by the efforts of Nettlefold and other Unionists to discredit Cook's Health Committee. Unionist politicians, sensing that 'the Housing ticket was the Thing to go for' in the 1901 municipal elections, took up Bass's calls without realizing 'the vast extent of the machinery they, for electioneering purposes, were setting in motion'. With the Local Government Board now awaiting a Council response, Nettlefold had to act upon an official representation in which he did not fully believe. He approached the Board's president to find a way out of the problem, and an inspector was sent to give advice. The inspector confirmed that most of the represented area was not irredeemably insanitary, and could be rehabilitated without large-scale resumptions and rebuilding. Nettlefold's vaunted reform initiatives were in fact copied from the inspector's suggestions. Further irony, the solution Nettlefold grasped for in fact merely formalized *ad hoc* practices which the Improvement Committee had cautiously pursued since the 1870s, and which had been carried on with greater vigour outside the main improvement area during the 1890s by Cook's Health Committee.[93]

The logic of Nettlefold's policy of 'ending or mending ... existing slums' was immediately contested. Radical Conservatives led the attack. Bass, supported by the *Daily Gazette*, damned the policy as 'one of tinkering, whitewash, and patching'.[94] Bass periodically queried the Local Government Board as to the adequacy of the Housing Committee's actions, and orchestrated public meetings, newspaper exposés, and challenges by Conservative allies in Council. The labour movement took up Bass's allegations, and savaged Nettlefold for not initiating large-scale clearance schemes to replace back-to-back housing. The criticisms carried conviction because they seemed so well grounded in common sense. Cook had already conceded in response to Walters at the turn of the century that comprehensive slum clearance was needed, and yet Nettlefold, the man who had led the attacks on Cook for tinkering, was now pursuing the same discredited policy.

Other common-sense judgements, however, supported the Housing Committee's programme. Notwithstanding the allegations of tinkering, reports by the Local Government Board in 1904 and by the Medical Officer of Health in 1912 and 1913 demonstrated that a substantial amount of demolition and repairs had taken place in the St Laurence parish improvement area.[95] Nettlefold acknowledged public demands that Birmingham's slums be cleared away. However he contended that experience in Liverpool, Glasgow, and London had shown that to buy up and reconstruct unhealthy areas was so prohibitively expensive as to be limited to a few showcase schemes which helped only a few. Wider housing reform, he said, could only be achieved by requiring owners to repair at their own expense. It was, he acknowledged, 'not a very showy way of doing it, but it was more business-like and more effective.' Nettlefold cautioned that the Council could not in any case demolish quickly and on any scale without creating a 'house famine'.[96] The plea was disingenuous, as it had been Cook's own argument when savaged by Nettlefold at the turn of the century, and had been used by Joseph Chamberlain in response to Hawkes in 1878.

Conservative critics of the Housing Committee demanded that the Corporation build Liverpool-style flats to replace the back-to-backs. The labour movement, still resentful that Cook's attempts to initiate large-scale municipal housing had been defeated by Nettlefold's 'plots', took up Bass's concerns that rents in the courts improved by the Housing Committee had been increased beyond the means of working people. Responding to this hostile clamour, Nettlefold conceded that municipal house building seemed the obvious policy to pursue, but contended that Liverpool had spent large sums building flats without ever managing to house more than a few. Moreover, he maintained that the experience of Birmingham's three housing schemes had shown that municipal house building acted as a disincentive to private home building and was beyond the means of the working people who had been evicted in order to build them. He damned municipal housing as 'a form of rate-aided charity', and claimed that the 'increased rates necessitated by municipal house building will press most heavily on the large class just above "the poverty line".' In common with labour spokesmen, Nettlefold characterized municipal flats as barracks which perpetuated congestion. The only lasting solution to the housing crisis in the city centre, he said, was decentralization of the population to the suburbs. In the interim, the City Council should repair the existing terraces of back-to-backs.[97]

Here was the ultimate irony. The Council's supposedly revitalized housing policy, as annunciated by Nettlefold, amounted to no more than a reassertion of the old principle of inner-city containment as a holding operation until private enterprise met the housing demand created by the 'general and ever-increasing exodus of working men' to the outskirts of the city in the wake of the decentralization of industry. Yet, further irony, much of the labour movement's hostility to Nettlefold stemmed from his opposition to the Bordesley Green scheme and hence, they reasoned, his hostility to municipal encouragement of decentralized working-class housing. Labour spokesmen continued to argue, as they had throughout the

1890s, that housing containment in the centre was not working because private enterprise was failing to satisfy the demand by working people for affordable housing away from the city centre. To demolish houses in the city centre and inflate the rents of the remainder by forcing costly repairs without simultaneously providing municipal cottages in the suburbs served only to exacerbate the 'slum question'. By 1904, the Independent Labour Party and Trades Council had begun to refer to German town-planning initiatives and the need for municipal land purchase and estate development to anticipate the speculators and jerry-builders. In 1913 Independent Labour Party Councillor George Shann demanded comprehensive municipal action to provide decentralized working-class housing on garden-city lines.[98]

The labour movement's vilification of Nettlefold obscured his sincere efforts to encourage decentralization of the population. He was active in the Garden City Association, and chairman of the town planning committee of the Association of Municipal Corporations. Nettlefold had opposed Cook's Bordesley Green scheme on the principle of municipal housing, not municipal encouragement of decentralization. He argued that the motor for suburbanization had to be private enterprise. Nettlefold believed local government should remove impediments to the 'natural' functioning of the market 'law of supply and demand'. During his chairmanship the Housing Committee sought to stimulate the supply of private housing by loosening building by-laws so as to reduce building costs, and by advocating road improvement and a tram system, all to encourage the 'exodus to the suburbs'. Nettlefold's attention became taken up more and more with attempting to demonstrate the commercial viability of working-class suburban housing estates laid out on practical town-planning principles. He became chairman of Harborne Tenants Ltd., which in 1908 set out to build a 'garden suburb' at Harborne that would show a healthy return to investors and yet offer house rents within the means of the poorer classes. Housing had to be made to pay, he said. Yet it was 'no good building castles unless people can afford to live in them'.[99]

Nettlefold's advocacy of practical housing and town planning was endorsed by Neville Chamberlain and other prominent Unionists. He also won the support of many one-time opponents. Liberals were impressed by his championship of city planning as a means of protecting national fitness. George Cadbury saw in his policies a means of multiplying the Bourneville experiment around Birmingham in order to empty the inner-city back-to-backs and simultaneously guard against the creation of 'fresh slums' in the suburbs. Nettlefold also began to earn the respect of radical Conservatives. The *Daily Gazette*, which once had demanded his resignation, supported his arguments and published his speeches. In 1911 Bass chaired a large meeting which thanked Nettlefold for his leadership of town planning experiments which were designed to drain the population from the city's 'squalid areas' and to prevent the growth of 'future slumlands'. However, Nettlefold was opposed by small business and property interests in the city centre, which attacked the Housing Committee for having 'put the screw on' small landowners, whose properties had been 'turned inside out' or demolished at its orders. He was also attacked by the suburban building industry, which feared that town planning regulations would have the effect of 'practically stopping the building trade'.[100]

In an ironical twist of fortunes, Nettlefold was challenged during the 1906 municipal elections by the Conservative–Unionist alliance. Municipal land purchase was called a 'suicidal' policy that would increase rates. Town planning was labelled wrong in principle, because it represented 'an interference with the liberty of the subject'. It was in any case 'practically impossible to expect the Council to be able to provide garden cities around Birmingham.' Nettlefold retained his seat, but lost it in 1911 when he was again opposed by the Unionist machine. Unionists complained that he was in 'too much of a hurry', and had come to the Housing Committee with 'proposals that really took one's breath away'. They clamoured that housing policy in the city centre had been hampered by Nettlefold's 'attitude of extreme aggression' towards landowners, and that his application of town planning principles was hindering private enterprise development in the suburbs. Nettlefold and Cadbury were accused of having produced 'arcadian retreats' at Harborne and Bourneville that could be afforded only by better-paid working people and the middle classes. Unionists sneered that there 'was a considerable danger lest town planning should develop into a class movement by the creation of suburbs of smug respectability for the aristocracy of labour.' The old Conservative argument against Cook was now used against Nettlefold, the man who had led the charge against the Liberal leader at the turn of the century.[101]

The attainment of practical housing for working people seemed, in 1914, even more perplexing an undertaking than it had in 1875, and perhaps more so even than in 1901. Observers could recognize elements of common sense in all the contending blueprints for housing reform. However, they could equally well grasp the limitations and contradictions in each which were highlighted by the partisan sniping that coloured municipal politics. It was inevitable that, in a spatially diverse and socially unequal society like Birmingham, common-sense opinion was not easily shared.

Amid the sea of indeterminacy which this contentiousness produced, the 1875 improvement scheme stood out, increasingly mythologized in the recollection, for the apparent clarity of its purpose and unambiguity of its early achievement. The Independent Labour Party fastened on the imagined achievements of Birmingham radicalism under Joseph Chamberlain in order to assert the Unionists' subsequent repudiation of social reform.[102] Unionists themselves nostalgically recalled 'the reputation achieved forty years ago for good government.' Neville Chamberlain, impatient for Birmingham again to set an example for the whole country, recalled 'the golden days of Birmingham' in the 1870s. The centrepiece of that era, he said, was 'the great improvement scheme which drove Corporation Street through a mass of slums.' It was, he said, the 'first great town-planning scheme' in the second city of the empire.[103] Even Conservatives like Bass now perpetuated the illusion that the scheme's origins were grounded in disinterested slum reform, and that the construction of 'magnificent buildings' along Corporation Street was an adequate measure of its achievement. The *Daily Gazette*, once the improvement scheme's implacable foe, urged in 1902 that the extension of Corporation Street would be 'one of the best public improvements'.[104]

Notes

1 Garvin, 1935, p. 194. *Daily Post*, 6 March 1878, p. 4, leader. See Bunce, 1885, chapter 14; Vince, 1902, chapter 16; see also Briggs, 1952, pp. 16–22, 77–87; and the sceptical assessment of the scheme in Smith, 1979, p. 224.
2 *Daily Post*, 18 October 1875, p. 7, The Home Secretary on the Artisans' Dwellings Act. ibid., 7 October 1876, p. 3, Mr. Cross on working men's dwellings. In 1893 it was claimed that 'Birmingham has set municipal example to other cities', Workmen's Cottages, 1893, p. 191.
3 Joseph Chamberlain to John Bunce, 6 December 1880, in Chamberlain Papers, JC5/8, UBA; and Chamberlain to Jesse Collings, 10 April 1876, in ibid., JC5/16.
4 Joseph Chamberlain to Sir Charles Dilke, 6 September 1872, in ibid., JC5/7. Borough of Birmingham, 1875b, p. 29.
5 *The Builder*, 17 October 1868, pp. 757–8, leader; and 10 October 1868, pp. 751–2, Condition of Birmingham; also Edgar, 1869, pp. 476–7, 506. *BPP*, 1840, question 1273, p. 72. Report by John Thornhill Harrison, 19 February 1874, and memorandum by Robert Rawlingson, 4 March 1874, in MH 12, No. 13321, BPRO. Robert A. Slaney, R.A., Report on the state of Birmingham and other towns, *BPP*, 1845, p. 2. Sutcliffe, A., A century of flats in Birmingham 1875–1973, in Sutcliffe, 1974, pp. 181–2. *BPP*, 1908, p. 86.
6 Report of the Birmingham Sewage Inquiry Committee, 1871, in BCL. Report by Dr Buchanan and Mr Netten Radcliffe, Systems in use in various northern towns for dealing with excrement, in *BPP*, 1870, p. 130. Report of the Sanitary Committee, BCCP, 26 February 1875.
7 See the comments by Liverpool's sanitary pioneer, Dr W.H. Duncan, in *BPP*, 1844, Appendix, p. 22. *The Lancet*, 7 February 1874, p. 215. See ibid., 25 January 1873, p. 148, Sanitation at Birmingham; and *The Builder*, 7 November 1874, p. 932, The sanitary state of Birmingham.
8 Press cutting of a speech by Chamberlain, dated 13 April 1874, Chamberlain Papers, JC4/1, UBA.
9 *Daily Post*, 22 October 1873, p. 5, Birmingham School Board election; and 27 October 1873, p. 7, The municipal elections.
10 City of Birmingham, 1914, p. 3. The term 'new slums' was widely used by housing reformers, politicians, and journalists.
11 See BCCHC, 12 July 1898. *BPP*, 1908, p. 81. BCC to LGB, 15 July 1912, in HLG 1 'O' Files, Box 142, No. 856.101.01, BPRO.
12 Borough of Birmingham, 1875a, p. 81.
13 Joseph Chamberlain, minutes of evidence before the LGB inquiry, in John Thornhill Harrison to Sclater Booth, 13 May 1876, MH 12, No. 13324, BPRO.
14 Bunce, 1885, volume 2, p. xxiv. See the speeches in Borough of Birmingham, 1875a; Borough of Birmingham, 1875b; Borough of Birmingham, 1878. *Daily Mail*, 25 November 1875, p. 2, Mr. Joseph Chamberlain at Sheffield. Public address by Chamberlain in undated newspaper cutting (January 1876), Joseph Chamberlain Papers, JC4/5, pp. 16–17, UBA. *Daily Post*, 2 October 1875, p. 5, Birmingham and

the Artisans' Dwellings Act. ibid., 23 November 1876, p. 5, Visit of the Home Secretary to Birmingham.

[15] Birmingham Liberal Association, 1879, p. 5. Borough of Birmingham, 1875a, p. 83. Borough of Birmingham,1875b, p. 30.

[16] ibid., p. 18. Chamberlain, J., 1883, p. 770. Chamberlain claimed a significant part of the credit for securing amendments to Cross's draft bill which had 'somewhat enlarged' its scope with this end in view; Borough of Birmingham, 1878, p. 12. Chamberlain ensured that this object was stated even more explicitly in the special enabling legislation which confirmed the Local Government Board's provisional authorization of the scheme.

[17] Richard Chamberlain, in *Daily Post*, 24 May 1882, p. 5, Birmingham Town Council.

[18] *Daily Gazette*, 15 December 1880, p. 6, Birmingham Town council. BCCIC, 19 December 1883. Chamberlain, 1883, p. 770. Borough of Birmingham, 1878, p. 21.

[19] Press cutting of a speech at the Severn Street Ragged School in Birmingham, dated 30 November 1874, Joseph Chamberlain Papers, JC4/1, UBA.

[20] Speech at Hull, 5 August 1885, in Boyd, 1914, volume 1, p. 170. Chamberlain to Jesse Collings, 12 September 1875, Joseph Chamberlain Papers, JC5/16, UBA. Press cutting of an address to the Leeds Liberal Association, 10 January 1877 , in JC 4/5, p. 77. BCCP, 5 June 1877.

[21] See Chamberlain to John Morley, 10 August 1873, Joseph Chamberlain Papers, JC5/7; Chamberlain, J., 1874, pp. 405–29; Chamberlain's speech at Hull, 5 August 1885, in Boyd, 1914, volume 1, pp. 167–70.

[22] Chamberlain, 1877, pp. 126–34. Heath, 1876, p. 5.

[23] Boyd, 1914, volume 1, p. 72. BCCP, 26 October 1880.

[24] *Daily Post*, 24 May 1882, p. 4, leader. ibid., 8 March 1882, p. 5, Birmingham Town Council.

[25] *Daily Mail*, 24 May 1882, p. 2, leader. *Daily Post*, 3 October 1881, p. 8, The municipal elections. BCCIC, September 1882. *Daily Post*, 29 October 1878, p. 5, The municipal elections.

[26] Chamberlain, 1883, pp. 761–76; and see Harris, Chamberlain, 1883, pp. 587–600. See also the editorial leaders in *Daily Mail*, 26 November 1883, p. 2; *Daily Post*, 27 November 1883, p. 4; and *Daily Gazette*, 27 November 1883, p. 4.

[27] Sir Walter Foster, quoted in *Daily Post*, 12 October 1886, p. 5, The municipal elections. Report of the Artisans' Dwellings Inquiry Committee, p. 28, in BCCP, 3 June 1884. *Daily Post*, 25 June 1884, p. 7, Birmingham Town Council.

[28] BCCP, 28 March 1888, 4 December 1888, 5 February 1889.

[29] *Daily Post*, 26 October 1880, p. 8, The municipal elections. *Property Advertiser*, 1 August 1881, in Osborne, 1907, n.p.

[30] Hawkes, 1878. *JC5/8*, Chamberlain to John Bunce, 5 June 1878, Joseph Chamberlain Papers, *JC 5/8*, UBA. *Daily Gazette*, 29 October 1878, p. 5, The municipal elections.

[31] See Hill's testimony in John Thornhill Harrison to Sclater Booth, 13 May 1876, MH 12, No. 13324, BPRO. See Hill's earlier report in BCCP, 15 April 1873.

[32] Harrison to Sclater Booth, 13 May 1876, in MH 12, No. 13324, BPRO.

[33] *Daily Mail*, 29 March 1876, p. 2, leader. Chamberlain to Jesse Collings, 10 April 1876, Joseph Chamberlain papers, JC5/16, UBA. Birmingham Town Clerk to John Lambert, 9 June 1876, in MH 12, No. 13324, BPRO. Memorandum by Lambert to Sclater Booth, 26 May 1876, attached to Thornhill Harrison to Sclater Booth, 13 May 1876, in MH 12, No. 13324.

[34] Memorandum by Lambert to Sclater Booth, 2 August 1877, in Birmingham Town Clerk to LGB, 5 July 1877, MH 12, No. 13327. Harrison to John Dodeson, 15 June 1882, in M.H. 12, No. 13341. *Charity Organisation Review*, 13 (517), 1884, p. 42.

[35] Editorial in *Birmingham Daily Times*, 12 April 1886, in Osborne, 1907, n.p.

[36] *Daily Post*, 21 October 1876, p. 8, The municipal elections. *Daily Gazette*, 26 October 1878, p. 5, The municipal elections. See also Chamberlain, pp. 614, 754, and Northcotte, pp. 603–7, 673, in *BPD*, 1878–9, volume 249.

[37] Improvement Committee Report, BCCP, 23 May 1882.

[38] Borough of Birmingham,1875b, p. 19.

[39] *Daily Post*, 4 July 1877, p. 4, editorial. BCCIC, 13 December 1876. Letter by the Secretary of the Treasury, 21 December 1876, in ibid., 22 December 1876.

[40] Birmingham Town Clerk to LGB, 18 October 1878, in MH 12, No. 13329, BPRO. Chamberlain to Sclater Booth, 30 April 1879, BCCIC, 14 May 1879. ibid., 12 November 1879.

[41] Hunt in *BPP*, 1882, question 220, p. 15. BCCIC, 14 January 1880.

[42] Chamberlain to Jesse Collings, 12 September 1875, Joseph Chamberlain Papers, JC5/16, UBA. William Cook in *Daily Post*, 17 February 1886, p. 7, Birmingham Town Council.

[43] ibid., 16 February 1887, p. 7; and 8 February 1888, p. 7.

[44] Improvement Committee Report, BCCP, 15 February 1887. Memorandum by Hugh Owen to President Ritchie, 26 September 1887, and attached file, bundled with Birmingham Town Clerk to LGB, 8 July 1887, in MH 12, No. 13356, BPRO.

[45] *Daily Post*, 29 October 1880, p. 5, The municipal elections.

[46] *Daily Mail*, 14 November 1876, p. 2, leader.

[47] ibid. Evidence by Chamberlain and William Martin to the LGB inquiry, in John Thornhill Harrison to Sclater Booth, 13 May 1876, MH 12, No. 13324, BPRO. Borough of Birmingham, 1878, p. 17. Chamberlain in *BPP*, 1884–5, question 12,356, p. 443. *Daily Post*, 30 October 1879, p. 8, The municipal elections. See Heath, 1876, p. 12.

[48] *Daily Mail*, 14 November 1876, p. 2, leader. *Daily Post*, 30 October 1879, p. 8, The municipal elections. Improvement Committee Report, BCCP, 1 May 1877. BCCIC, 14 March 1877 and 22 June 1877. Improvement Committee Report, BCCP, 13 November 1877. Memorandum by Lambert, 2 August 1877, attached to Birmingham Town Clerk to the LGB, 5 July 1877, MH 12, No. 13327, BPRO.

[49] BCCIC, 17 November 1886, 8 December 1886, 8 February 1888. *Daily Gazette*, 25 October 1886, p. 3, The municipal elections.

[50] Henry Hawkes, Improvement scheme, in *Daily Mail*, 22 May 1882, p. 3.

[51] BCCHC, 21 April 1880.

[52] *BPP*, 1880, p.civ.

[53] BCCIC, 27 September 1882.

[54] *Daily Post*, 20 October 1883, p. 5, The municipal elections. Report of Artisans' Dwellings Inquiry Committee, p. 36, in BCCP, 3 June 1884. *Daily Post*, 13 October 1883, p. 5, The municipal elections.

[55] *Daily Gazette*, 25 June 1884, p. 4, editorial. ibid., 2 June 1885, p. 4, leader.

[56] BCCIC, 13 May 1885; Improvement Committee Report, BCCP, 2 June 1885.

[57] *Daily Post*, 3 June 1885, p. 7, Birmingham Town Council; and see *Daily Mail*, 16 May 1885, p. 2, leader. *Daily Post*, 1 June 1885, p. 4, leader. *Daily Gazette*, 2 June 1885, p. 4, leader; *Daily Post*, 17 October 1887, p. 7, The municipal elections (Councillor Lancaster).

[58] Medical Officer of Health to the Improvement Committee, BCCIC, 9 February 1898.

[59] ibid., 11 November 1896.

[60] Health Committee Report, 31 July 1900, in City of Birmingham, 1900, p. 627. *Daily Post*, 26 October 1900, p. 10, The municipal elections. Health Committee Report, 18 June 1901, City of Birmingham, 1901, pp. 540–1.

[61] See *ibid.*, pp. 198, 573–4; and *Daily Gazette*, 19 June 1901, p. 5, The housing problem in Birmingham. ibid., 27 February 1901, p. 4, editorial; 15 April 1901, p. 6, Correspondence (Councillor Lovesey); 6 March 1901, p. 4, leader.

[62] ibid., 25 April 1901, p. 4, leader; 19 June 1901, p. 4, editorial.

[63] H. Viney to the LGB, 12 November 1895, enclosing a cutting from the *Birmingham Telegraph* entitled The Birmingham City Council's affairs, MH 12, No. 13371, BPRO.

[64] *Daily Post*, 6 January 1897, p. 8, The City Council. ibid., 3 July 1889, p. 4, editorial.

[65] ibid., 3 May 1893, p. 4, Birmingham City Council (Cook).

[66] ibid., 25 February 1891, p. 7, The City Council.

[67] ibid., 22 October 1895, p. 8, The municipal elections.

[68] ibid., 9 October 1899, p. 8, The housing of the working classes: conference in Birmingham. ibid., 18 October 1901, p. 10, The municipal elections. Health Committee report, 31 July 1900, in City of Birmingham, 1900, pp. 631–2. See Fallows and Hughes, 1905.

[69] Health Committee report, 30 July 1901, in City of Birmingham, 1901, p. 627. The Reverend Thomas Bass to the LGB, 15 April and 26 November 1901; Dr Alfred Hill to the LGB, 9 November 1901, all in HLG 1 'O' Files, Box 142, No. 856.101.01, BPRO. Review of the Reverend Thomas J. Bass in *Edgbastonia*, 1904, 24 (272), p. 4. See Bass, 1898; 1903.

[70] *Daily Mail*, 5 January 1897, p. 2, leader.

[71] Arthur Eades, secretary of the Birmingham Trades Hall Council, to the Town Clerk, 4 December 1899, in City of Birmingham, 1900, p. 93. *Daily Post*, 12 October 1898, p. 9, The municipal elections.

[72] ibid., 25 February 1891, p. 7, The City Council. Health Committee Report, BCCP, 26 July 1898. BCCIC, 12 July 1898. *Daily Post*, 28 July 1900, p. 6.

[73] ibid., 2 May 1894, p. 6, The City Council; 6 January 1897, p. 4, editorial; 28 July 1900, p. 6; 1 August 1900, p. 3, Birmingham City Council.

[74] Birmingham Town Clerk to the LGB, 29 June 1891, together with attachments, in MH 12, No. 13364, BPRO. *Daily Mail*, 1 May 1894, p. 2, leader; and see BCCIC, 9 May 1894. *Daily Post*, 6 January 1897, p. 8, The City Council.

[75] ibid., 4 May 1898, p. 9, Birmingham City Council. See also Cook's statements in ibid., 4 May 1892, p. 7, The City Council; 3 May 1893, p. 4, Birmingham City Council; 28 October 1893, p. 5, The municipal elections.

[76] ibid., 21 October 1893, p. 5, The municipal elections; 27 July 1898, p. 3, Birmingham City Council.

[77] ibid., 27 July 1898, p. 4, leader; 21 October 1893, p. 5, The municipal elections; 24 October 1900, p. 9, The municipal elections.

[78] *Daily Gazette*, 13 February 1901, p. 4, editorial; 6 February 1901, p. 4, leader; 7 March and 8 February 1901, p. 4, editorials.

[79] ibid., 27 July 1898, p. 4; 13 June 1901, p. 4, leaders. *Daily Post*, 29 October 1901, p. 9, The municipal elections. See ibid., 31 October 1900, p. 9; also 19 June 1901, p. 6.

[80] *Daily Gazette*, 6 February 1901, p. 4, editorial. *Daily Post*, 22 October 1898, p. 7, The municipal elections. *Daily Gazette*, 6 February 1901, p. 4, editorial.

[81] ibid., 19 June 1901, p. 6, The housing problem in Birmingham; see ibid., 15 April 1901, p. 6, Correspondence; and 20 April 1901, p. 4, St Martin's Conservatives and the slum articles. *Daily Post*, 23 October 1891, p. 5; 23 October 1901, p. 9, The municipal elections.

[82] The phrase is taken from the title to Nettlefold, 1908b and Nettlefold, 1910.

[83] ibid., 22 October 1909, p. 3, Birmingham municipal elections. Finance Committee Report, 3 December 1912, City of Birmingham, 1913, pp. 90–1.

[84] City of Birmingham, 1914, Appendix, questions 607–8, p. 52.

85 Housing Committee reports, 6 January 1903, City of Birmingham, 1903a, pp. 111–12; and 29 March 1904, City of Birmingham, 1904, pp. 273.

86 *Daily Post*, 16 October 1906, p. 12, Dudderston Ward Unionists. Nettlefold, 1911, p. 11. Housing Committee Report, 15 January 1907, City of Birmingham, 1907, p. 100. Nettlefold, 1908a, pp. 6, 17.

87 City of Birmingham, 1913, p. 455. City of Birmingham, 1914, pp. 5, 17. Neville Chamberlain in *Daily Post*, 30 October 1914, p. 3, Housing reform conference.

88 Bass to the LGB, 27 March 1902, in HLG 1, box 146, folder 856.7041.04, BPRO. *Daily Post*, 31 October 1908, p. 14, The municipal elections; 13 October 1914, p. 6, leader.

89 ibid., 3 November 1913, p. 6, editorial.

90 ibid., 29 October 1903, p. 11, Municipal elections; 25 October 1907, p. 5, Birmingham municipal elections; 24 October 1907, p. 5, Municipal elections.

91 Bass to the LGB, 27 May 1902, in HLG 1, box 142, No. 856.101.01; 26 July and 29 October 1902, box 146, folder 856.7041.04, BPRO.

92 *Daily Gazette*, 25 September 1902, in Bass to the LGB, 26 September 1902, in HLG 1, box 146, folder 856.7041.04, BPRO.

93 Inspector Bicknell to the LGB Chief Engineer, 15 February 1902, in HLG 1 'O' Files, Box 142, No. 856.101.01, BPRO. Housing Committee Report, 4 March 1902, City of Birmingham, 1902, p. 236. Nettlefold to Walter Long, 5, 15, and 25 February 1902, in HLG 1 'O' Files, Box 142, No. 856.101.01, BPRO.

94 Nettlefold, 1906, p. 23. Bass to the LGB, 18 April 1903, in HLG 1, box 146, folder 856.7041.04, BPRO.

95 See Meade-King, report to the LGB Chief Engineering Inspector, 15 November 1904, HLG 1 'O' Files, box 142, No. 856.101.01, BPRO.

96 Speech to Christian Social Union, 9 October 1911, in Nettlefold, 1911, p. 23. *Daily Post*, 30 October 1903, p. 11, Municipal elections.

97 Councillor John Fallows to the LGB, 6 November 1902, in HLG 1, box 146, folder 856.7041.04, BPRO. Nettlefold in *Daily Post*, 21 October 1903, p. 4, Birmingham City Council; and 30 October 1903, p. 11, Municipal elections. Housing Committee Report, City of Birmingham, 1903a, pp. 804–5. Nettlefold, 1914, pp. 156, 248–51.

98 Housing Committee Report, City of Birmingham, 1903a, pp. 800–7. *Daily Post*, 17 October 1906, p. 4, The municipal elections; 16 October 1913 p. 13, Selly Oak ward.

99 Nettlefold, 1905, pp. 11, 13–4. *Daily Post*, 21 October 1903, p. 4, Birmingham City Council. Nettlefold, 1911, pp. 9–10.

100 Cadbury in the *Daily Post*, 31 October 1906, p. 12, Municipal elections. Bass to the LGB, 24 October 1911, in HLG 4, box 283, folder 856.508.1, BPRO. *Daily Post*, 24 October 1908, p. 6, Birmingham municipal elections; ibid., 29 October 1912, p. 11; 17 October 1912, p. 5.

101 ibid., 12 October 1906, p. 12, The municipal elections; ibid., 27 October 1906, p. 13; 31 October 1906, p. 12. ibid., 31 October 1911, p. 11, Municipal elections; ibid., 28 October 1911, p. 14; 24 October 1911, p. 6, Greater Birmingham.

102 ibid., 6 October 1905, p. 11, Municipal elections; 16 October 1907, p. 3, Birmingham municipal elections.

103 ibid., 29 October 1908, p. 5, The municipal elections; ibid., 19 October 1911, p. 4; ibid., 13 March 1913, newspaper cuttings volume 1, in the Neville Chamberlain Papers, NC 15/14, UBA.

104 Bass to the LGB, 27 May 1902, in HLG 1, box 142, No. 856.101.01, BPRO. *Daily Gazette*, 25 September 1902, in Bass to the LGB, 26 September 1902, in HLG 1, box 146, folder 856.7041.04, BPRO.

5

Contingency: Municipal Slum Clearance in Sydney, 1879 – 1900

Buildings 'unfit for human habitation'

In 1884 an inner-Sydney working woman, egged on by neighbours, stood on her doorstep and shouted abuse at the municipal officials inspecting their homes. The chief target of her spleen was the City Council — which she labelled 'a den of thieves' — and its chief sanitary inspector, Richard Seymour, whom she called 'the evil one himself'.[1] The woman and her neighbours were acting out their pooled resentment at their powerlessness in the face of high-handed and intrusive policies pursued by the bourgeois state.

The Sydney City Council had been established in 1842. Municipal government extended piecemeal to the suburbs as well from the late 1850s. The City Council, as constituted under a redrafted Corporation Act in 1879, consisted of 24 aldermen charged — after British precedent — with responsibility for the 'good rule and government' of the city. Each December they elected one of their number as Mayor for the new year.

Elections for one-third of the Council took place every November. Electors had always been restricted to male property holders. This electorate was even more strictly limited to ratepayers under the Act of 1879, which disenfranchised many thousands of tenants who had previously been included on the municipal rolls. It was not until 1888 that the vote was restored to the lessees of rateable properties, and in 1900 it was extended to lodgers. Women remained unfranchised. Yet male ratepayers — depending upon the amount of property they owned — had been able to vote up to four times in each ward since 1879. Any elector was eligible to stand for office, but the Council's daytime sittings and the absence of payment for office holders generally limited participation in local government to wealthy and leisured men.

Alban Riley was typical of this loose governing class. Riley, who later became Mayor of Sydney, was commended to voters in 1885 as having been 'successful in business, and [with] the leisure which he has fairly won, and the experience and qualities of mind and character which he has gained and

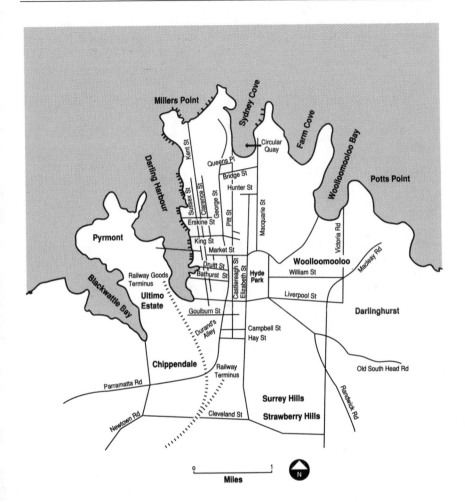

Sydney, 1880

developed he is willing to devote to the city's interests.' Inevitably, the city's interests were synonymous in Riley's eyes with the unimpeded market-place development of Sydney. Municipal politics was in consequence dismissed even by many qualified electors as a closed preserve mono-polized by property and business interests:

It has represented not much more than a small clique of retired capitalists residing in suburban villas or touring in Europe, and governing the premier municipality of New South Wales in the sole interest of their own few pairs of breeches' pockets, to the utter disregard of the hundred thousand other persons whose lives and whose businesses were affected by such government.[2]

Some aldermen undoubtedly responded to the challenge of big city government venally, others with sincerity. All of them, however, given the restricted nature of municipal politics, interpreted the tasks of governance broadly, as did Riley. The common sense of the businessman determined public policy-making; other viewpoints were unaired in Council. The Sydney Town Hall therefore stood as a remote and unresponsive institution in the eyes of the neighbourhood women in 1884 who stigmatized the Council as 'a den of thieves'. Its extravagances were supported by taxes which they paid for indirectly in their rents, without their having in return any say in the shaping of municipal policy or means of reply to the daily administration of municipal regulations.

It was through the Council's sanitary and building staff that working-class tenants most regularly encountered municipal administration, hence the vitriol reserved by the woman in 1884 for Richard Seymour, the chief Inspector of Nuisances between 1863 and 1896. Working-class children did live longer, and the material lives of working-class families did improve, as a consequence of municipal service provision and sanitary regulation. However, working-class families were also the last to be relieved from the backlogs and omissions in municipal sanitary administration, and the first to be targeted and prosecuted by municipal officials. Seymour was the Council officer who was immediately responsible for the intrusive and sometimes hurtful application of bourgeois-defined public health 'nuisances' and their imagined palliatives.

The post and responsibilities of Inspector of Nuisances were copied from the local city statutes in the mother country. Seymour oversaw the routine policing of public health regulations, and patrolled the city daily to enforce the cleaning of private yards and alleyways and the emptying of cesspools. He regularly prosecuted the occupants of dwellings and common lodging-houses for keeping 'filthy premises' in contravention of municipal sanitary by-laws. Two sub-inspectors worked for Seymour in the early 1880s. By 1901 the municipal sanitary department employed ten principal inspectors of nuisances.

An ever widening interpretation of nuisance abatement by this growing department was achieved through the trouble-shooting activities of the City Health Officer, a part-time post that had been created in 1857 upon the model of legislation in London. The gradual consolidation of the machinery of preventive medicine in Sydney was a chance achievement. It relied less upon statutory blueprint than upon the personal commitment of the three pioneering doctors who successively held the post of Health Officer between 1857 and 1888. These officials, guided by the example of Dr John Simon in England, chose not to confine themselves to the narrow statutory definitions of their office, but to range 'somewhat at large' across the challenges of public health administration in a big city.[3]

The health officers, in increasingly systematic house-to-house inspections across the city, began to apply the term 'unfit for human habitation' to dwellings which they considered should be demolished because of their insanitary or dilapidated condition. The term had no legal basis in colonial legislation. Rather, it was borrowed by the health officers from the 1851 legislative framework with which Simon had worked in the City of London.

Sydney health officers sought to build the principle into their own administration of preventive medicine. George Dansey, City Health Officer from 1870 to 1888, could by the mid-1870s point to some measure of success in this effort. He reported that the sanitary department had, by a vigorous policy of prosecuting owners and tenants for violations of sanitary regulations, been able to pressure the owners of buildings 'unfit for human habitation' to demolish and rebuild. In 1874 Seymour, too, expressed satisfaction 'that on the expiry of existing leases many rookeries which now deface and disgrace the City will be demolished to make way for a better class of buildings. These desirable results are in a great measure due to the action taken against tenants and owners in the Police Courts.'[4]

This increasing regulatory interest in the city's building stock — notwithstanding the primitive nature of local building regulations — was further sustained by a third municipal official, the City Architect and Building Surveyor. The post had been an ill-defined one under Sydney's original Building Act of 1837, but revised legislation in 1879 required the appointment of a qualified surveyor as City Building Surveyor to oversee all new building permits and to order the repair or demolition of ruinous and dangerous buildings. The small staff of inspectors which gradually accumulated around the Building Surveyor was amalgamated with the City Surveyor's Department in 1900, but continued none the less to possess semi-autonomous departmental status within the city bureaucracy.

Throughout the nineteenth century, the City Council possessed no free-wheeling statutory authority to demolish 'slums'. Authority on paper only had existed in both the Building Act of 1837 and the 1850 City Corporation Act to obtain demolition orders from magistrates to deal with 'ruinous' or 'dangerous' buildings. The wording related only to structural defects, however, and thus did not apply to the sanitary shortcomings which defined buildings as 'slums' in the eyes of municipal health inspectors. The same clause was nevertheless retained in the revised Corporation Act of 1879. Indeed, the Colonial Secretary emphasized that it 'was not intended to give any corporate body power to knock down old buildings.'[5]

A similar clause, providing for the repair or demolition of buildings 'in a ruinous state and dangerous to the public', also appeared in a revised building Bill which the Council submitted to Parliament in 1877. The Bill had been drafted by the City Building Surveyor in consultation with the City Health Officer, who had repeatedly urged redrafting of the 1837 Building Act so as to imitate legislative innovations in Britain and so enforce minimum sanitary standards in new houses. The Health Officer's pet subject became the Bill's focus. Introduced to Parliament as the City of Sydney Improvement Bill, the improvements envisioned consisted only of planning controls by the Building Surveyor and City Health Officer over new building construction, and did not extend to comprehensive clearance powers over existing buildings. Instead, a single clause modelled on the British Public Health Act of 1875 gave legal substance to the health officers' long habit of labelling insanitary dwellings 'unfit for human habitation'. Such dwellings would henceforth have to be vacated until they were satisfactorily repaired.[6]

This seemed a minor provision. By contrast, the proposed reforms over new building construction went too far for many architects, builders, and developers, who campaigned to convince Parliament that under the proposed legislation the municipal officials would 'be made autocrats'.[7] The Bill was referred to a select committee, which recommended that an independent Improvement Board consisting of an architect, a builder, a doctor, and two other members should be appointed by government to hear appeals against proposed municipal by-laws and against decisions made by municipal inspectors. The committee also suggested that the clause relating to ruinous and dangerous buildings be modified to enable the Building Surveyor rather than the courts to enforce repair and demolition orders issued by the new Improvement Board. This, it was hoped, would allow near-immediate action against dilapidated or dangerous structures by cutting away the lengthy judicial process that was still required to be gone through in applying the similar clause against ruinous or dangerous buildings in the Corporation Act. However the committee gave no consideration to the wider question of demolishing property on general sanitary grounds. Thus amended, the Improvement Act was passed in 1879.

It was not until the belated passage of the colony's first comprehensive Public Health Act in 1896 that the City Council was empowered to order the demolition of buildings which they had condemned as being 'unfit for human habitation'. This new authority, however, was largely illusory. Every condemned building had first to be reported to a full meeting of the Council; not until the Council's next meeting, at least a fortnight thereafter, could the building be condemned. After another fifteen days, if this order had been ignored, a magistrate's closing order might be sought, but no penalties could be imposed, and another week had to be allowed for the building to be vacated. The tenants' moving expenses were to be paid by the Council. At the next meeting of the Council, a demolition order could be approved, but the owner then had one month in which to file objections. Only after three months was the Council empowered to carry out the work. At any stage, if the owner agreed to carry out the Council's directions but then failed to do so, the whole legal process had to start again from the beginning. The Building Surveyor complained that the procedure was so 'slow, tedious and bristling with legal difficulties, that to actually demolish any insanitary dwelling under the Public Health Act, a period of about six months must elapse.'[8] Moreover, the cost to the Council of applying the clause on any scale was plainly prohibitive.

It is a paradox, given the effective absence of any statutory framework for municipal schemes of urban renewal, that the City Council condemned approximately 4,000 buildings between 1880 and 1901, and that, at their orders, well over half of these buildings were demolished. This unlikely development was the outcome of an elaborate web of unrepeatable connections between chance happenings. The programme began late in 1879 shortly after the passing of the Improvement Act, when Thomas Sapsford, just appointed as City Building Surveyor, sought to take advantage of the statute's expeditious procedure for referring examples of 'ruinous and dangerous' buildings to the new Improvement Board which could order repairs or demolition. The Council's own programme was launched independently of the Improvement Board early in 1880, using the new power in the Improvement Act for the Mayor, Building Surveyor, Health Officer, and Inspector of Nuisances jointly to inspect and issue closing orders against insanitary buildings which they condemned as being unfit for human habitation. The addresses of offending buildings were accumulated by the three Council officials during their routine inspections, and the pooled list became the basis for periodic reinspections with the Mayor. These tours did not confine themselves to ordering the vacation and repair of insanitary buildings as the Act had authorized, but ambitiously sought to bluff landlords into pulling down their properties.[9]

Ad hoc adjustments, prompted by contingent circumstance, periodically modified municipal practice. In 1885 the Mayor, Thomas Playfair, in order to expedite matters, directed that if buildings condemned as unfit for human habitation had not begun to be demolished within a week they were to be referred to the Improvement Board, which alone appeared to have the legal authority to enforce demolition orders. Even the Board's powers, it soon transpired, were not in practice as full as had been anticipated: its chairman admitted later in the year that 'the Improvement Board had not the power which it was evidently the purpose of its promoters to give it. It had not the power to deal with houses simply because they were in an insanitary condition.' Playfair's experiment was consequently short-lived, and the number of cases referred to the Board dwindled. Health officials continued to prepare lists of buildings for inspection by mayoral tours, but within the Council bureaucracy concern mounted at the accumulating number of condemned and recondemned properties over which proceedings were stalemated because the orders to repair or pull down were being ignored. The issue was given another twist in 1888 when the City Auditors pointed out that the City Council had lost some £35,000 since the end of 1882 in non-collected rates on condemned buildings, and that closing orders were now costing £8,000 annually in lost rates.[10]

Inspection tours with the Mayor ceased in 1890 as the municipal slum clearance programme entered another phase. Thereafter, the City Building Surveyor alone issued repair and demolition orders, citing as his authority the clause in the Improvement Act against 'ruinous and dangerous' buildings. Whenever his directions were disregarded, he referred the cases on to the Improvement Board. This mechanism had the drawback of being confined to structures which were demonstrably unsound, whereas the clause against buildings 'unfit for human habitation' could be applied more loosely to any buildings deemed to be in insanitary condition. Yet it had the advantage of quick referral if necessary to the Improvement Board, whose demolition and repair orders in these instances at least were legally unquestionable.

Fresh difficulties arose, however, when Parliament rejected the Board's budget estimates for 1895, and the Government failed to fill a vacancy on the Board. Paralysed, the Improvement Board ceased to function early in 1896.

With the Board defunct, no machinery remained to enforce municipal orders under the Improvement Act against ruinous and dangerous buildings or to prosecute offenders, so the clause became inoperative. When owners disregarded his directions, the City Building Surveyor sought court orders by resorting to the clause relating to 'ruinous or dangerous' buildings in the 1879 Corporation Act, but this long drawn-out procedure was, he complained, an 'ineffectual and tardy method'. As another tactic, mayoral inspection tours to condemn buildings as unfit for human habitation under the Improvement Act resumed tentatively in 1898. But without an Improvement Board for property owners to appeal to against the decisions made during these tours, Council officials feared costly litigation if they sought to enforce repairs or demolition work upon owners who ignored the condemnation notices. With the Improvement Act now 'practically useless', the Building Surveyor turned in 1900 to the cumbersome procedure laid down in the Public Health Act of 1896 for condemning houses 'unfit for human habitation'.[11]

By the turn of the century, the City Council had none the less sustained a slum clearance programme over 20 years. During those two decades a sixth of the city's 1880 housing stock had been condemned. Taken together, demolitions carried out at the Council's orders outnumbered the remaining building stock in each of the city's five inner wards. Municipal activity was greatest around the beginning and the end of this two-decade period: during a smallpox epidemic in 1881, and an outbreak of the bubonic plague in 1900. In a flurry of activity, over 300 buildings were condemned as unfit for human habitation during the first year of the programme, and some 450 more were condemned during 1881, approximately three-quarters of which were demolished. Although this momentum was not sustained, activity continued at a high level to the end of 1883, some 1,300 buildings having by then been condemned since the start of the mayoral tours. The number of closing orders declined thereafter, although tours were regularly held into the middle of the decade. The total number of buildings condemned by the end of 1887 was 1,726, of which 1,576 had been demolished. The frequency of mayoral tours dwindled considerably from 1886, although a spate of notices were issued again during the last such inspections in 1889. This higher level of activity persisted beyond the cessation of the mayoral tours until the end of 1892, by means of the clause against ruinous and dangerous buildings. From the late 1880s, however, policy had moved away from seeking the demolition of buildings to securing their repair, and throughout the 1890s regulatory activity focused on achieving specific repairs to properties: the repair or removal of walls, water closets, balconies, awnings and street signs. Even these reduced goals were pursued cautiously after 1892, although activity built up again from 1896. During the bubonic plague in 1900, 146 buildings were pulled down at the Council's orders, out of a total of approximately 425 buildings which were certified as being unfit for human habitation. This was the highest number of buildings condemned since the smallpox alarms in 1881 at the commencement of the municipal drive against the 'slums'.

City 'improvement'

Notwithstanding the fluctuating levels of municipal commitment, the altering strategies, and the switch in overall direction of municipal effort from demolition to repair, local government officials had sustained an urban renewal programme that was both long-lasting and large-scale. The overriding Council objective to facilitate orderly market-place development is easily recognizable. But it is less evident how the Council was able to pursue this goal so successfully when for most of these years there was no legal authority for it to do so.

The municipal 'improvement' crusade against the slums was represented very much as a preventive public health measure. As in Birmingham and San Francisco, however, bourgeois sanitation and market-place considerations went hand in hand: Council officials emphasized at the start of their programme that the condemned buildings 'were utterly useless, and were so filthy that in case of an epidemic they would become hotbeds for the generation and spread of the pestilence.' The smallpox epidemic of 1881, which greatly stimulated the mayoral inspections of insanitary buildings, underlined the vulnerability of the market-place city to disease: public transport services were disrupted, emergency services totted up large bills for both City Council and colonial legislature, and, most importantly, quarantine restrictions threw the city's maritime trade into chaos.[12]

The City Council's crack-down on old and insanitary buildings sought always to accord with the ongoing commercial redevelopment of the central city into a specialized business district. As one newspaper editorial noted late in 1883, 'Civic condemnations of property may be made in the light of the fact that large and handsome structures are going up on all hands, throwing small and old buildings completely into the shade. Acting under a feeling of this sort, the authorities may condemn buildings now which they would not have condemned three years ago.'[13] By weeding out obsolete and low-rated premises, the City Council hoped to stimulate the property market's redefining of legitimate uses for central city land.

The *Herald* drew attention to a municipal survey of demolitions and construction work during 1880 and 1881 as

a record of [the] good practical work performed by the MAYOR and his officers since the City Improvement Act came into operation. It also serves as an indication of the private enterprise which is daily replacing old tumble-down buildings with substantial structures more in accord with the requirements of the community, and better calculated to accommodate and promote the trade of a city which we are told on very excellent authority will become the chief commercial centre of Australia.

At the end of the decade a guidebook reviewed the effect of this conjunction between private and state urban-renewal strategies. The guide noted that 'the older portions of the town [were being] pulled down to make way for factories and warehouses of modern design and great capacity; while some of the worst tenements in the lower localities, through the efforts of the corporation, are being rapidly swept away.'[14]

But how could the City Council embark upon such 'improvements', still less sustain them, without clear statutory authority? The answer lies in part in the ongoing public discussion since the mid-1870s of slum-derived health problems and of the redevelopment powers needed to abolish them. By the end of the decade this had created a climate of opinion in which many laypeople and experts alike believed that the ambiguously named Improvement Act intentionally gave the City Council those powers.

City *improvement* was an expression learnt from the mother country. There, in large and widely publicized undertakings such as the Birmingham and Glasgow Improvement Schemes, it meant radical projects of inner-city slum clearance. These blueprints were greeted enthusiastically by politicians and journalists in Sydney. In 1877, a parliamentary committee on overcrowding had recommended that similar schemes were needed 'to buy up unhealthy tenements and crowded areas so as to open up broad thoroughfares in closely packed quarters of the city.' Richard Cross's 1875 Artisans' and Labourers' Dwellings Improvement Act was hailed in Sydney as in British cities for facilitating that object. The *Herald* responded to the local report on city overcrowding by urging the enactment of a measure 'more or less similar in principle to Mr CROSS's Act, to provide for the compulsory purchase of areas which are so overcrowded with unhealthy tenements as to be a source of public danger, in order that they may be swept clean and thrown open to the light and air, and become sites of buildings worthy of human habitation.'[15]

Local opinion in Sydney conflated the colonial and British Improvement Acts. The misconception was strengthened by Parliament which, in amending the Improvement Bill, had reviewed the proposed clause against insanitary buildings and had considered whether 'Mr Crosse's [*sic*] principle might be incorporated in this bill.' The *Daily Telegraph* voiced the resultant beliefs of many when it commented at the start of the mayoral tours: 'Some active steps are at last being taken under the City Improvement Act which gives the City Council power to cause the removal of buildings which are unfit for human habitation.'[16]

That this belief persisted, however, was contingent upon the opinions of the assortment of individuals who each year occupied the positions of Mayor, aldermen, and their officials. It was their opinions which determined local government practice. Richard Seymour, for example, in carrying out his duties exhibited a distaste for working-class households and an intolerance of Chinese immigrants in the inner city. George Dansey, the City Health Officer, naïvely hoped that commercial redevelopment would force inner-city residents out to find better housing in the suburbs. Thomas Sapsford, the City Building Surveyor from 1879 to 1885, regarded bourgeois morality as the benchmark for both good health and civilized behaviour, and interpreted the Improvement Act as governing both: 'The intention of the Act was to a certain extent to prevent immorality as well as to preserve the health of the Citizens and beautify the City, and if dens are ... permitted to exist for the accommodation of infamy in the very heart of the City good health cannot possibly prevail.'[17]

To the eyes of these local government officials, a clear gulf existed between city and slum, slum-dweller and citizen. Moreover, both Sapsford and his replacement, George McRae, disregarded the social implications of urban renewal and concentrated instead upon the straightforward replacement of 'unsightly tenements', 'hovels and rookeries', with 'handsome and stately buildings, the architectural features of which constitute a lasting ornament to the city.' The City Surveyor carried their thinking through to more grandiose proposals for city improvement, lobbying throughout the 1880s and 1890s for the entire demolition of an assortment of 'slum' neighbourhoods, so as to 'transform these areas into some of the handsomest portions of the city.'[18] A succession of mayors and municipal inspectors sought to redesign to their taste the aesthetic continuity of the city's streetscapes by weeding out advertising signs, awnings, and balconies which to their eyes appeared jarringly vulgar, irregular, or decrepit.

In self-consciously framing and advertising uniform improvement policies out of these quirks of individual preference, the City Council and their officials sought to project a set of connected images about the essential features of efficient city governance. In so doing they reacted to the conflicts and resulting indeterminacies of big-city living by asserting the underpinning culture they believed to be appropriate to full citizenship in a modern city. They gave definition to what they regarded as modern, logical, and progressive in the terms of that culture. And in projecting their statements of what constituted a modern city, they sought also to be seen to be governing effectively within the terms of modern city culture.

Communication and endorsement of municipal improvement strategies were in turn contingent upon the city press. Sydney's three main daily newspapers in the last quarter of the nineteenth century were the *Evening News*, the *Daily Telegraph*, and the *Sydney Morning Herald*. The *Evening News* was Sydney's largest-circulation newspaper. It claimed a distribution twice that of its nearest competitor. The newspaper had been established as the colony's first penny paper in 1867. It carried a heady mix of city news and human interest stories. The *Daily Telegraph*, founded only in July 1879, overtook the *Sydney Morning Herald* in the late 1880s as Sydney's second-largest volume newspaper. Despite being the city's only penny morning newspaper, it struggled initially to find a secure market footing, and was baled out by Melbourne financiers. The *Daily Telegraph* faced another crisis in 1882 when its founding editor quit, and its Victorian backers signalled that they, too, had had enough. A new company was floated, and new editorial department chiefs were appointed to oversee the framing of big-circulation news. The *Sydney Morning Herald*, launched in 1841, had for almost 30 years been the city's only morning paper. Although outpaced in sales in the 1880s by the *Daily Telegraph*, it continued to be regarded as Sydney's 'quality' newspaper. Until 1893 its price was double that of its competitors, and it was two to three times their size. Its advertising columns dwarfed those of its competitors.

Vying with one another for circulation, the daily newspapers quickly grasped the dramatic potential of the City Council's initiative. Banner headlines in the *Evening News* gave public notice of the first mayoral inspection tour in 1880:

Through The City Styes And Stews

A Mayoral Visit

Nests Of Vice And Fever.[19]

During the early 1880s sensational newspaper stories of slumland discovery and purification decisively influenced community perception of municipal improvement policy. However, whereas the Council's programme persisted through different phases over two decades, media coverage fluctuated wildly between the newspapers and over time, and struggled after the early 1880s to retain its initial spectacular impact. Popular journalism used the mayoral tours as the vehicles for its own dramatizations of the modern city, and as the tours were increasingly enmeshed within the internal bureaucratic routines of the Building Surveyor's department, media interest waned.

The ongoing municipal improvement programme addressed different, although frequently overlapping, strands of discourse and responded to different agendas. Four of these contingent elements were, first, the ongoing negotiation of Council policy in concert with the flows and eddies of community electoral debate; second, the exchanges between Council and landowners; third, the narrow compass of autonomy for experimentation and innovation which bureaucratic practice gave municipal officials; and fourth, the rivalry that quickly grew up between the Council and the Improvement Board.

Electors

Council programmes were debated, amended, endorsed, or rejected in the city's annual contests for local office. In these forums were negotiated the qualities and tasks electors regarded as appropriate for the administrators of a modern city.

Business excellence, it was generally conceded, equipped men for municipal office: the 'City Council should be constituted of the very pick of the city's commercial and professional experts.' Candidates vied to fit that image: 'the experience he had gained during 20 years of active business life would enable him, now that he had leisure at his command, to discharge his duties as their representative in a manner which would merit their entire approval'. It followed that local government was firmly asserted to be but an adjunct to private enterprise: 'There was nothing so much misunderstood at the present time as the rights of such bodies as the City Council, or the right they should have as between the citizens and private enterprise. No one could charge him with wanting to interfere in any way with private enterprise. ("Hear, hear").'[20] Municipal endeavour was consequently defined to accord with the premises of market-place culture: 'there was a general desire for aldermen who were more in touch with the progressive spirit of the times. Brisbane Ward was the commercial centre of Sydney, and should take the lead in working out those reforms which ... would help to make Sydney the metropolis of Australia'.[21] The other face of Brisbane ward — site of the city's biggest concentration of dwellings with four rooms or less — was never mentioned.

City improvement — meaning the economical provision of services and facilities to property holders — dominated municipal electioneering. Candidates debated the provision of water and sewerage services, the durability of wood blocks and tar for street paving, the virtues of electricity and gas for public lighting, the provision of garbage incinerators. The horizons of such public policy-making collapsed inwards as discussion of improvement strategies was constantly overshadowed by parochial squabbling over the allocation of these amenities. The clamour for local improvements was qualified, moreover, by jealous demands for rigorous accounting. *Economy* and *extravagance* were key words for any participant in municipal politics: it was the duty of Council to see 'that the ratepayers' money should not be fooled away.' Protests were frequently aired that 'the hard-earned money of the ratepayers had been wasted in a scandalous manner.'[22] The necessity for cost cutting was constantly reiterated. Every year electoral debate centred on the level of the property assessment, water and sewerage rates, and upon the necessity for their reduction.

The parameters of Council responsibility which were set by electoral discourse left little scope for engagement in broader consideration of improvement strategies. The *Daily Telegraph* dramatized a scene during one of the mayoral inspection tours in which the City Health Officer drew attention to the drainage problems caused by decaying sandstone guttering, and said that the gutters should be replaced with harder bluestone: "'And why isn't it done?" queried a reporter. "Oh," replied another official, "If an alderman was to vote for such a thing it would be called ruinous extravagance, and at the next election he would be sure of being returned — to private life."' General public health issues were little canvassed. Candidates periodically called for more public baths, and on rare instances for city parks or playgrounds. Slum clearance was rarely mentioned. The broader issue of urban renewal was couched in terms of the priorities of the urban market-place, to mean redevelopment of the harbour foreshores 'for the purpose of wharves, warehouses, railways, &c.' One candidate claimed that 'slum' clearance really entailed pouring money 'to improve ... the ... main streets of the city, whilst the back slums had been neglected.'[23]

Concern was voiced periodically at the consequences of the municipal renewal programme for the tenants of condemned properties. Recognition stirred of the plight facing the lessees of small businesses:

To men of moderate means engaged in storekeeping the destruction of their premises means in many cases positive ruin. They lose their connection, which is very often entirely local; they have to sacrifice their stock, and in all probability are unable to obtain suitable premises to resume their business in. In the meantime, their goods being bought on credit they have to meet their obligations, with no chance of providing for them.

Some entrepreneurs were quick to recognize and capitalize upon the pressures placed on working-class tenants as well:

During the past 12 or 18 months some 1500 or 1600 houses in Sydney have been condemned under the City Improvement Act as unfit for habitation. Most of these houses have been tenanted by working men whose work was in the city. Now they have to move further out, and many are buying land and putting up their own dwellings. Others, however, cannot do this. Hence the great demand in and around the city for building allotments and small residences. We call attention to our great sale of 124 allotments on the Golden Grove Estate next Saturday afternoon; when we shall sell capital building plots for railway employees, mechanics, workmen, and others. The builder and capitalist will also find this a good opportunity to purchase.[24]

Philanthropists were slower to respond to the Council's slum clearance programme. It was not until 1884, in the wake of the local interest generated by publication in Britain of *The Bitter Cry of Outcast London*, that newspaper tales of slumland crusades at home suggested in passing that housing projects for low-income families should be tried along the lines of the philanthropic housing companies in London. Riley commented during his campaign for Council office in the following year that 'some valuable sites in the city were occupied by mere hovels, and he thought that in the near future the corporation might very well raise a special loan and buy up many of those places and erect model homes for poor people.'[25]

Such suggestions solicited the interest of listeners to discussions that had proceeded intermittently in Sydney since the late 1850s: how best to improve working-class housing conditions in the inner city. Riley again demonstrated his engagement in this debate when, as Mayor, he concluded an inspection tour in 1887 by announcing to reporters 'his intention of bringing before Parliament the desirability of erecting houses in the city for the working classes which would be comfortable and healthy, and which could be let at a very low rental.' Participants in the debate now belatedly recognized that municipal urban renewal had exacerbated housing problems, because the labour market was so structured that many working people clung to home-places in the central city. The palliatives which they offered for these problems, however, were still governed by the rules of the market-place. Central-city real estate was priced high because 'the owner of city land considers how much it is worth per foot. If its value be a thousand pounds, he holds that it ought to yield him the return which a thousand pounds well invested should bring in.' Advocates of housing schemes for the working classes therefore sought to demonstrate that 'the thing [could] be done on a commercial basis with a satisfactory prospect of receiving fair returns.'[26]

It was a futile effort. Riley called a citizens' meeting in December 'to invite the co-operation of gentlemen of capital and of philanthropic instincts' in launching a public company to build and operate '"artisans" model dwellings within the city limits'.[27] His initiative exposed the fragility and unreality of the discourse of housing reform: a sub-committee was formed, more meetings were called, estimates were prepared and building plans debated, but neither capitalists nor the citizens generally responded to these moves, and few reformers were prepared to countenance schemes sponsored by the state rather than private enterprise.

Given the community's unresponsiveness to the social costs of urban renewal, and the absence of sustained policy debate about city improvement issues in their broader sense, the stimulus behind the Council's slum clearance programme depended in large measure upon the personal interests and political calculations of the individual elected by the aldermen each year to the office of Mayor. Riley's championship of philanthropic capitalism in housing reform is a good example. It was inevitable, owing to the nature of municipal office and the prevailing canons of electoral debate, that each Mayor equated progress, improvement, and modernity with the dicta of business and the market-place.

The mayoral inspections were launched and energetically pursued through 1880 by Mayor John Fowler, whose public reputation and stature within the City Chamber benefited enormously thereby. In the press he was hailed as 'one of the most influential ... [and] practical of the city fathers' and 'a leader in good works'. In Council he was credited by his colleagues with having 'initiated the system of inspecting and condemning the rookeries of the city', and a resolution was passed expressing 'thanks ... for his valuable and efficient services to the city.' Fowler's successors likewise earned community 'credit' for throwing themselves into the mayoral inspections.[28] Thomas Playfair, however, who held office in 1885, was less enthusiastic about interfering with private property, and subsequently direct mayoral engagement in slum clearance began to dwindle. Riley was censured for posturing, rather than taking definite action. Mayoral tours ceased altogether in 1890 when Sydney Burdekin, a millionaire property owner, was elected Mayor.

Landlords

In 1886 the new Mayor, alderman John Young, had announced his intention 'during his mayoral year to make a clean sweep of the abominable dens of the city. It is a surprising fact that not a few buildings in the very heart of the city that were condemned two years ago are still standing. Mayor Young intends that his condemnations shall be carried out.'[29] Young's pledge, and its sequel, help to explain mayoral disengagement from urban renewal after the mid-1880s. In so doing they direct attention to the second contingent element in the dramatic exchanges which were shaping municipal policy: the interplay between the Council and the owners of property. The slum problem, as we have seen, barely figured in the municipal agenda debated at ward meetings during election times. Mayors consequently grew frustrated, as Playfair's experiment in 1885 demonstrated, at the drain on their time caused by the fruitless reinspection of already condemned properties as more and more property owners resisted the condemnation orders. They turned the problem over to their officials.

Young's efforts to make a 'clean sweep' turned the slum question briefly into a major political issue which rebounded against the Mayor. Property owners and their allies in Council challenged Young's authority. His successors prudently chose to distance themselves from further political fallout: mayoral tours were replaced by the bureaucratic routines of the City Building Surveyor's office. Young was criticized in Council for 'overdoing the condemnations', and it was alleged that 'favoritism' was evident in the uneven manner in which the notices were enforced. These criticisms reflected resentments that were building up among some property owners in reaction to Young's campaign. Robert Chadwick, owner of a 15-house tenement row called 'Tin Row' that had been condemned by Young, formed a Ratepayers' Association in 1886 to oppose the Council's programme. A deputation headed by Chadwick presented Young with a petition signed by 670 ratepayers, which protested against the operation of the Improvement Act. The deputation complained of 'arbitrary' actions and 'abuses' by Council officials, and Chadwick spoke of the hardships experienced by his evicted tenants.[30]

Notwithstanding Chadwick's carefully considered ploy to capture a passing issue of current media interest, it was the perceived wrongs to landlords, and not to their tenants, which generated debate and mobilized action sufficient to influence the direction of the municipal urban renewal programme. Indignant owners sometimes resorted to newspaper letters to challenge condemnation notices and 'damaging' press descriptions of their properties. Others initiated appeals to the Improvement Board against the Council notices. Often these appeals merely sought either to demonstrate that the premises in question were not so bad as to be 'unfit for human habitation', or to request that the order be amended to permit repairs in place of demolition. Other appeals were aggressively conducted, contending that 'the decision of the Mayor was harsh, arbitrary and unnecessary', that his inspectors were 'possessed of "over official smartness"', and that the Council programme had to be corrected so as 'to do as little injury as possible to the owners of property.'[31]

Landlords succeeded through these widely publicized appeals in arousing community disquiet that the Council's powers were indeed excessive. In 1882 and again the following year, suburban municipalities shied away from adopting the Improvement Act because its reputation in Sydney as being 'arbitrary in some respects is the opinion of a large section of the public'. More importantly, appeals to the Improvement Board helped to expose the tenuous legal foundations of the Council's urban renewal programme. Legal argument was put to the Board and repeated in newspaper commentaries that the Council's orders to demolish buildings within 14 days 'was an unjustifiable exercise of authority', as the Legislature had 'never contemplated that the mere fact of a place being in an unclean state should be sufficient ground to order it to be pulled down.' The *Daily Telegraph*'s coverage of the inspection tours noted for the first time in January 1881 that although 'no previous order of condemnation has been disregarded, the Mayor has not the power to compel owners to raze their properties. All that can be done under the Act ... is to serve a notice for the premises to be vacated within seven days, and, in the event of non-compliance, a heavy penalty can be imposed for each day that they are occupied over that time.'[32]

Municipal sensitivity to adverse public comment, and the vulnerability to court challenge of any notice that implied that buildings 'unfit for human habitation' must be demolished, thereafter impeded rigorous pursuit of the slum clearance objective. Mayoral inspections became taken up with the tedious task of reinspecting premises that had been previously condemned but were still standing, as Council officials sought to intimidate the owners to comply with their orders rather than prosecute and risk an embarrassing defeat in court. Owners increasingly took advantage of this indecision. Some landlords simply boarded up their properties, thereby complying with the letter of the law but calling the Council's bluff regarding the instruction to demolish. Others procrastinated or openly defied the Council's notices, continuing to tenant their properties and calculating that the Council would not press the matter further. Indeed, it was not until May 1882 that the Council mounted its first prosecution for failure to vacate a condemned building. Although successful, only minimal penalties were imposed by the magistrate. There were few subsequent court prosecutions.

Inspectors

The butts of property holders' agitation were the municipal officials who prepared the lists of insanitary buildings. The *Herald* was clearly perturbed by the criticisms, and although sympathetic to the goal of city improvement, cautioned that 'the rebuilding should be the outcome of a specific law, not of a strong-handed administration.'[33] This contentious discretionary authority by the Council's executive officers to shape policy as they sought to interpret and translate legislative enactments into workable bureaucratic routines constitutes the third contingent element that shaped the municipal urban renewal programme.

Building Surveyor, Health Officer, and Inspector of Nuisances held a complementary view of their function in policing building regulations: urban-renewal policy was to be an adjunct to the commercial redevelopment boom in the property market which was rebuilding the city centre. As Sapsford commented to the Improvement Board during an appeal case on buildings condemned in Rowe Street and Abercrombie Lane, the 'officers of the Council had taken a broad view of the question in condemning these buildings. Had they been situated in the skirts of the City they might have been repaired, but looking to their position they had felt themselves justified ... in condemning them, influenced by a hope that it would tend to the improvement of the City at large.'[34]

It was Sapsford who had set in train the entire programme of urban renewal. The new Building Surveyor, swayed by community discussion of the need for comprehensive slum clearance powers, mistakenly believed —

Queen's Place, off George and Pitt Streets, Sydney, c.1875

together with many others in Sydney — that the Improvement Act's vague provisions against old and insanitary buildings gave a general licence 'to cause the removal of buildings which are unfit for human habitation'. As we have seen, Sapsford had immediately begun to refer such buildings to the Improvement Board for them to issue demolition orders. Technical flaws in the wording of the Board's authority to condemn 'ruinous *and* dangerous' buildings, together with legal opinion that the clause did not in any case cover buildings condemned on sanitary grounds alone, quickly undercut the Board's authority. Sapsford turned instead to the Improvement Act's clause relating to buildings 'unfit for human habitation'. In conjunction with Dansey and Seymour he submitted reports to the Council listing dwellings in neighbourhoods that had been made notorious by community discussion of slum-generated ill-health during the 1870s. The three officials recommended that the 'tenements ... be demolished or repaired.' Legal opinion sought by the Council confirmed that insanitary buildings could be ordered to be pulled down if they were jointly inspected and condemned by the Mayor in the company of his three officials, and in May 1880 the first mayoral tour gave effect to this advice.[35]

Notwithstanding the initial general perception that the mayoral inspections were '[b]acked by very large legal powers', the municipal bureaucracy quickly realized the uncertain extent of their authority, and the consequent need to build into their initiative what could be deemed to have been 'no doubt' the 'intention of the Act' as well as the letter of the law if a programme of urban renewal was to be sustained. Corporation officials were making policy; the performance of the mayoral tours sought to define a new reality. The wording of the notices sent to the owners of condemned property strongly implied, without actually asserting, that the buildings had to be immediately demolished. In consequence many owners, 'believing that a continued occupation of the premises condemned would cause their compulsory demolition, anticipated the order by removing the objectionable building.'[36]

Council inspectors actively perpetuated this illusion in negotiations with property owners. Newspaper descriptions of the mayoral tours remarked upon the 'great alteration' to inner-city streetscapes as landlords responded to or sought to forestall municipal condemnation notices. As the inspectors well knew, to condemn and order the vacation of buildings halted the investment returns on the owners' capital. In 1899 the City Building Surveyor noted that 'in spite of not being invested with proper powers, I have by using tact and discretion, managed to get nearly all buildings requiring repairs or demolition, attended to, and that without conflict with the owners.' Officials used the example of condemned buildings that had been demolished by their owners in order to exert pressure on neighbouring landlords to take 'the hint' and do the same, thereby 'swelling the already large number of compulsory demolitions'. In the meantime the Building Surveyor periodically drafted amendments to the Improvement Act and lobbied constantly within the municipal bureaucracy and City Council for new legislation in order to strengthen local government jurisdiction over new and existing buildings. [37]

Bureaucratic initiative was, however, severely constrained by the electorally defined parameters of municipal responsibility. The Building Surveyor's frustration at the low priority aldermen gave to his urgings for legislative reform shows through clearly in his annual report for 1900: 'apparently the Council did not see their way clear to carry out what I so strenuously advocated.' Electoral discourse often targeted municipal officials for criticism, and the Council was always touchy about the performance and accountability of its expanding bureaucracy. Aldermen stormed that the bureaucracy, from the Town Clerk downwards, treated members of the Council with 'contempt ... as so many mere marionettes': poor 'dummy figures moved by wires and operated upon by the intelligent will of the wire-pullers.'[38]

Mayors periodically expressed dissatisfaction that condemnation orders were not being sufficiently enforced by their officials. In 1890 the sanitary inspectorate was shaken by a probing review of its slum-clearance programme initiated by the Mayor, who complained that buildings condemned years previously were still standing, and that 'the council was paying their officers large salaries for doing nothing.'[39] Sapsford had been severely reprimanded for exceeding his authority in consequence of his 1879 experiment at referring insanitary buildings to the Improvement Board rather than to the City Council. The tendency for the Building Surveyor during the mid-1880s independently to collaborate with the Board in achieving the demolition of old buildings abruptly ceased when aldermen again took exception to a City Corporation official undertaking work for an outside authority. The official was censured yet again in 1892 for working too closely with the Board.

The Board

Relations with the Improvement Board constituted a fourth contingent element in the Council's unfolding urban renewal programme. The Board had been established by Parliament solely as an appeal tribunal for the building trade; consideration had then been focused upon building permits for new works, and not upon demolition of the old. Discussion before the select committee reviewing the Improvement Bill had, however, raised the broader question of establishing in Sydney a strong new metropolitan organization of local government upon the lines of the London Metropolitan Board of Works, and media commentary linked the creation of such a body with the enactment of broad powers for city improvement upon the London model. The new Board's registrar suggested erroneously that the Sydney statute was based directly on the London legislation which had created the Metropolitan Board of Works. It was widely anticipated that the Board was a nascent government board of health and works, and that the City Building Surveyor was to be its executive officer. This was certainly the interpretation of the appointees to the Improvement Board, and they quickly prepared amendments to ensure that 'the intentions of the Legislature' in these respects were more fully realized.[40] Their ambitions over subsequent years focused upon the winning of comprehensive powers for slum clearance and urban renewal.

Problems soon emerged with the Board's strategy. In government eyes the Improvement Act 'had been introduced by a private member ... and consequently was not in any sense a Government measure.' The Board was regarded by them as a tribunal of private citizens who worked part time for the benefit of the building trade, and which was financed by fees paid by appellants to it. Government therefore resisted the Board's claim to belong to the regular state bureaucracy. The Colonial Secretary insisted that 'he did not consider this in any sense a Government Board, or the Government in any way responsible for the Board's proceedings.' Legal opinion obtained by the Board countered that 'the "City of Sydney Improvement Board" is a Government Board, the opinion of the Colonial Secretary notwithstanding.'[41]

Ad hoc problem-solving by the Government appeared for a time to confirm the lawyer's opinion: it stepped in to pay for private office space in 1879 when the Board was refused accommodation by the City Council, and subsequently transferred the Board to rooms in its own state office buildings; it allowed career civil servants to undertake the Board's secretarial and clerical needs; and it provided a small annual budget to cover these administrative costs when the Board's fees proved inadequate. Government budget papers thereafter listed the Board as a branch within the Colonial Secretary's Department, and the annual reports which the Board sent unsolicited to that department began to be printed in the parliamentary papers. Parliamentarians began to assume that the Board was indeed a part of the civil service. With the onset of the Great Depression of the 1890s, however, the pressing need for economies quickly confirmed the low priority which senior politicians had always attached to the Board. In 1893 the Board's registrar was transferred to a regular civil service posting when Parliament cut his salary from the Board's budget, and the elimination of the remainder of its budget in the following year forced the Board to vacate its civil service office. Government inaction in filling a vacancy caused by the death of one Board member in 1894 left the Board's decisions without legal force.

To compound the Board's problems, it had soon become evident that the Improvement Board could not, after all, depend on the City Building Surveyor to act as its executive officer. Sapsford's early reprimand by the City Council demonstrated that the Building Surveyor took his orders from the Council chamber and not the Board. The Building Surveyor was instructed not to report insanitary buildings to the Board, or carry out its orders without Council authorization. The Board was disappointed when in 1880 and again in 1888 the legal advice it sought concluded that there were no clear ways of 'compelling' the City Building Surveyor to enforce its orders.[42] In 1889 the Board unsuccessfully sought to initiate a writ against the city official before the Supreme Court to test that opinion. Thereafter the Board sought to circumvent the Building Surveyor by instigating private citizens to lodge complaints with it about dilapidated buildings. The experiment was of limited utility because it had long ago been demonstrated, when the City Building Surveyor did refer insanitary buildings to the Board, that it could not in any case issue demolition orders unless the properties were in a state of near collapse.

Even the Board's relevance as an appeal court was increasingly thrown into doubt. Parliament's expectation that the Board would be needed to adjudicate disputes over building permits was rarely fulfilled because the City Council interpreted building regulations generously. When the Board began hearing appeals in 1880 against condemnation notices issued by Council, both Sapsford and the City Solicitor queried the extent of its jurisdiction to do so. Early in the following year defending counsel, too, joined in this attack by questioning the Board's habit of ordering repairs in place of municipal demolition orders, and asserting that it had jurisdiction merely to uphold or reject the Council's notices. A ticking time bomb had been set which was eventually exploded by the pugnacious Robert Chadwick in 1888.

Chadwick had appealed to the Board in August 1886, as the Council was preparing to prosecute him for ignoring its closing order. After a prolonged hearing his case was upheld, subject to him carrying out renovations ordered by the Board. The tenements remained occupied and unrepaired, and in 1887 they were again condemned by the Council. Chadwick appealed to the Board against this fresh notice in March 1888. When challenged with not having carried out the repairs ordered in 1886, his lawyer countered that the previous ruling had been illegal as the Board had power only to determine whether the condemned buildings were unfit for human habitation. Board members were flummoxed, and a deputation was hurriedly sent to the Colonial Secretary to urge an immediate amendment of the Act. Chadwick's appeal was none the less thrown out by the Board, and Chadwick turned to the Equity Court to restrain the Council. In August 1888, however, the court decided for the Council, finding that the Improvement Act in fact contained no provision for appeals on buildings ordered 'unfit for human habitation'. It seemed to all that the Improvement Board's ability to arbitrate in matters of slum clearance policy was at an end.

Members of the Improvement Board used their annual report later in the year to press for legislative reforms which would reassert their authority as an appeal tribunal. The Board had vigorously lobbied governments ever since 1879 for legislative amendments to give them fuller powers to shape urban renewal policies in Sydney. The matter of appeals was only one plank in their campaign. They sought also to repeal the City Council's jurisdiction over building regulation and urban renewal, making the City Building Surveyor responsible to the Board alone and giving the Board clear authority to order the repair or demolition of insanitary buildings. Amending legislation was prepared by the Board and introduced to Parliament by the Colonial Secretary in 1880, but it was not taken beyond its first reading. Redrafted amendments were again urged upon the Colonial Secretary by deputations from the Board throughout the later 1880s and early 1890s. A

Government amending Bill was eventually prepared in 1892 but was never introduced to Parliament. The issue was overshadowed by parliamentary tumult surrounding the disintegration of traditional political alignments in New South Wales during these years and the forging of new alliances based upon protectionism versus free trade.

Although Parliament was preoccupied with other issues, the original drafters of the Improvement Act did not treat the Board's proposed amendments to the law so lightly. The City Council had reacted with fury when, late in 1879, they had first learned the extent of the Board's proposed changes to their Building Act: the Board 'wanted to arrogate to themselves powers that the law never gave them', and schemed so that 'the officers of the Corporation ... [might] be at their control'. This resentment intensified and extended to the city bureaucracy as well when the Board began hearing appeals against the Council's condemnation orders in 1880, awarding legal costs against the Corporation and overturning the professional judgements of Council officials in proceedings that were labelled 'quite a burlesque' by one angry alderman.[43]

Collaboration between the two authorities broke down almost totally. Hearings before the Board became punctuated by heated exchanges between Sapsford and Board members, especially after the Building Surveyor was instructed by Council to cease carrying out the Board's orders. The Board sought half-heartedly to overcome this impasse by making occasional overtures to the Mayor and proposing joint amendment of the Improvement Act. By 1892, however, it was widely noted in the press that the Town Hall was totally ignoring the Board and was relying exclusively upon the Corporation Act to condemn buildings.

The Improvement Board, hamstrung without the co-operation of the Building Surveyor, launched a systematic press campaign designed simultaneously to encourage the illusion of its relevance in the framing of city improvement policy, and — by vilifying the City Council — to mobilize editorial opinion in support of its calls to Parliament for enhanced powers. The Board's decisions on building appeals were worded carefully to serve as press releases: the publicity was designed both to generate further appeal cases and to pin-point desired legislative amendments for public discussion. Sapsford complained to the Mayor in 1880 that one such newspaper report had been compiled by the Board's secretary, and 'is so constructed as to endeavour to place your officers in as uncomfortable position as possible.'[44]

Letters to the press by the Board's secretary and pseudonymous newspaper commentaries challenged the legality of the mayoral tours, thus helping to expose the illusion of the Council's authority to order the demolition of insanitary buildings. Comprehensive slum clearance was being frustrated, it was alleged, because of the incompetence of the City Council, and because of its pettiness and obstructionism towards the Board. In 1891 the Board worked closely with the *Builder and Contractors News* to prepare a series of articles for the newspaper reviewing the inadequacies of the Improvement Act and urging the Board's transformation into a metropolitan board of works. The Board paid for the articles to be reprinted as pamphlets and distributed to politicians and the press. In the following year the Board placed notices in all the metropolitan newspapers, complaining of the City Council's inaction in referring dilapidated buildings to it, and urging the right of any citizen under the Improvement Act to lodge complaints about such buildings with the Board.

The politics of renewal

The Board's initial impetuosity and lack of diplomacy in asserting sole jurisdiction over building standards in Sydney had been, the *Daily Telegraph* admitted, a 'tactical blunder'. Thereafter the Board and the City Council had 'tried to thwart and circumvent each other.'[45] The arena chosen by both authorities was urban renewal. Prompted by an inexperienced new Building Surveyor, the Improvement Board mistakenly embarked upon an ambitious programme of slum clearance. Mayor Fowler's willingness to embrace the inspection of buildings 'unfit for human habitation' can be interpreted at least in part as a reaction to this initiative. Fowler sought to demonstrate the Council's sole legitimate responsibility for any urban renewal programmes undertaken in Sydney.

By-passed by the Council, and finding that the jurisdiction actually spelt out for them in law did not match the objectives which they had set themselves, members of the Board publicized the issue of slum clearance as they sought legislative changes to give them the powers they wanted. Directly by letters from their secretary to the media, and indirectly by negotiation with editorial staff and by press commentaries under various pseudonyms, the Board contributed enormously to sustaining and enlarging the horizons of community discourse on city improvement. Concentrating on the Council's slum-clearance programme, they questioned both its legality and its sincerity; they targeted municipal performance, firstly alleging tyrannical decision-making in the absence of an effective appeal tribunal, and subsequently suggesting municipal ineptness due to the absence of direction by a strong government board of health and works. Their hidden agenda, always, was that they should become that board.

The Board's strategy depended upon co-operation by the city press. They were not disappointed. Newspaper editorial comment endlessly repeated their arguments: the Board's good work 'in the way of rooting out unhealthy spots' being 'constantly thwarted by municipal jealousy'; the 'utter feebleness of the board' as an appeal body and the resulting 'arbitrary exercise of power' by the mayoral inspection tours; the 'muddled and mismanaged' municipal administration of city improvement, and 'the culpable negligence of the civic authorities in allowing condemned buildings to stand'.[46] In a lucky coincidence for the Board, its squabbling with the City Council suited the purposes of city news editors. The squabblings constituted a ready source of entertaining news. Moreover, the story-line matched a recurring slant in city news reporting. Municipal administration was sensationally and systematically characterized in the press as incomplete, parochial and amateur, and municipal decision-making as unrepresentative, vulgar, and self-serving. Popular journalism contended that city government should devolve to a technocracy, working to a broader ambit, and responsible to a wider electorate. The city press thus espoused for city government what it claimed to recognize in itself: professionalism and accountability.

Two recurring points in particular from the Improvement Board's statements were hammered in newspaper editorials. First, they stated that the Council's urban renewal programme had 'merely skimmed the surface' and that more comprehensive schemes were needed. Second, it was necessary in order to achieve this goal to establish a new body, perhaps akin to 'a Metropolitan Board of Works, acting wholly independently of the City Council'. The urban renewal projects undertaken by the Metropolitan Board of Works in London were watched with great media interest in Sydney: 'Whole quarters of the city were condemned and torn down' in 'stupendous works of reclamation and improvement'.[47]

The city press tilted at many windmills. Only some triggered wide and enduring interest. Their comments about city improvement and its administration exerted influence because they overlapped with broader community discussion of avenues for local-government reform throughout the Sydney metropolitan region.[48] It was noted that as the result 'of municipal reorganisation and civic regeneration' in Birmingham and Glasgow, both cities had been 'practically rebuilt', and the achievements of the new London County Council were frequently cited as another role model: 'It has mown down whole acres of slums, and substituted decent dwellings, wherein are housed thousands of artisans.'[49] The Improvement Board meanwhile bid actively to swing the developing momentum of this debate behind its claims for enlarged powers: metropolitan administration in Sydney was 'an absurd jumble', the Board's registrar wrote to the press in 1891, 'with no central authority ... to secure uniformity of action.' In London, he said, the Metropolitan Board of Works 'failed because it was not strong enough to cope with the other governing bodies, ... and the London County Council Act has been passed to establish a supreme authority such as exists in Glasgow and Birmingham, the two best locally-governed cities in the world.'[50]

Some mechanism for state encouragement of inner-city renewal was inevitable in Sydney by the last quarter of the nineteenth century. The comparisons which were being drawn with apparent models of good city government in the mother country invited local initiatives. News reporting of the changing skylines of big cities in Britain and in the United States simultaneously provided a blueprint in the colonial periphery for the building outcomes which marked a successful modern city. Moreover, piecemeal commercial redevelopment of Sydney's central core was already well in train, and the market-place considerations which sustained this process exerted a preponderant influence upon municipal decision-making as well.

However, the manner in which city improvement strategies came to develop in Sydney, and the forms which they took, lay in 'a realm of contingent detail'.[51] The widespread misinterpretation of the Improvement Act's intent was an accidental result of colonial interest in British city improvement initiatives. Notwithstanding confusion in Sydney between its new Building Act on the one hand, and local application by British cities like Birmingham of the Cross Act on the other, the Sydney City Council's urban renewal programme would still never have evolved as it did were it not also for the persistent debate on city improvement and municipal performance which was sustained by the Improvement Board. The mayoral inspection tours were performances prompted by the schism with the Board. They were designed in part to counter the criticisms and satisfy the expectations generated by the Board's successful manipulation of public opinion: the hard work of municipal inspectors thereby received rare public recognition, and the Mayor's grandstanding won the City Council much-needed newspaper credit.

The City Council was drawn on by community comment and the Board's lobbying of Parliament to prepare legislative amendments of its own to facilitate urban renewal in Sydney. The Building Surveyor drafted a Bill in 1881 which proposed to give the Council full authority to demolish buildings 'unfit for human habitation', to abolish the Improvement Board, and to set up in its stead a new Council committee to hear appeals. The Bill was endorsed by Council and forwarded to the Government, but it was never introduced to Parliament. The Council foreshadowed a fresh Bill to amend the Improvement Act in the late 1880s, and in 1890 framed a Metropolitan Street Improvement Bill designed to grant the Council wide-ranging powers to appropriate and redevelop city properties.[52] Drafting proceeded simultaneously upon a new Corporation Act, which would consolidate existing health laws and the Improvement Act into one statute, and establish a new improvement board made up of aldermen and private citizens. Aldermen expressed enthusiasm during the 1890s for local government reforms that would establish a county council of Sydney along the lines of the London County Council.[53]

It was through this web of contingent happenings that the makers and interpreters of municipal policy sorted out goals and strategies. They struggled to make common-sense choices amid the indeterminacies of multiple-policy options and glimpsed-at outcomes. These confusingly diverse viewpoints and agendas were peddled competitively and often acrimoniously by vying interest groups and partisan individuals. The principles they espoused were appropriated from and in turn served to sustain an international discourse on bourgeois city reform. Yet the motivations lying behind their espousal of grand principle were grounded in local and often pedestrian considerations, parochial in substance and self-serving in their intent.

Notes

[1] *Daily Telegraph*, 15 January 1884, p. 6, Inspection and condemnation of rookeries.

2 ibid., 28 November 1885, p. 5; and 24 November 1888, p. 4, The civic elections. Mayne, 1981.

3 SCC, LR, 1857, vol. 2, no. 424 (Dr Isaac Aaron, September 1857).

4 Mayne, 1982, p. 168. SCC, LR, 1874, vol. 6, no. 814 (Seymour, 9 December 1874).

5 Sydney Building Act of 1837, 8 Wm. IV, no.6 (clause 63); 1850 City Corporation Act, 14 Vic., no.41 (clause 94). The Colonial Secretary is quoted in the *Herald*, 4 October 1878, p. 3, New South Wales Parliament.

6 42 Vic., no.25 (clauses 21, 29).

7 *Herald*, 6 Febuary 1879, p. 7, Legislative Council and new Building Act.

8 R.H. Broderick to the Town Clerk, 26 February 1901, in City of Sydney, 1902, p. 527.

9 See Mayne, 1991a.

10 *Evening News*, 25 June 1885, City Improvement Board, in Improvement Board newspaper cuttings, AONSW, 1/2124. City Auditor's report, pp. 3–5, in City of Sydney, 1889.

11 City Building Surveyor's annual report, in City of Sydney, 1902, p. 527; City of Sydney, 1901, p. 188; City of Sydney, 1902, p. 474.

12 *Daily Telegraph*, 19 March 1880, p. 3, Sydney Municipal Council. Mayne, 1988, pp. 219–41.

13 *Herald*, 13 November 1883, p. 7.

14 ibid., 1 July 1882, p. 5, editorial. Gordon, Gotch, 1888, p. 229.

15 *V&P(NSW LA)*, 1875–6, p. 548. *Herald*, 19 August 1876, p. 4.

16 ibid., 7 February 1879, p. 3, New South Wales parliament. *Daily Telegraph*, 28 May 1880.

17 SCC, LR, 26/168/1539 (Sapsford, 24 August 1880).

18 ibid., 26/171/2241 (30 November 1880) and 26/189/123 (12 January 1883); Annual reports in City of Sydney, 1890, p. 9; City of Sydney, 1901.

19 *Evening News*, 27 May 1880, p. 2, Through the city styes and stews.

20 *Daily Telegraph*, 29 November 1884, p. 4, The City Council elections; 21 November 1891, p. 6, Municipal Elections.

21 ibid., 28 November 1895, p. 2, Municipal elections. Brisbane ward was the municipal district from George Street west to Darling Harbour, and extending from the northern junctions of Sussex and Clarence Streets to King Street in the south.

22 ibid., 30 November 1880, p. 3, The municipal elections; 25 November 1886, p. 6, City elections.

23 ibid., 5 June 1883, p. 3, More crusading amongst the cow-yards; 22 November 1881, p. 3, The municipal elections; 29 November 1888, p. 6, The city elections.

24 ibid., 19 June 1884, p. 4, Demolition of city buildings: advertisement by Hardie and Gorman Ltd., 9 February 1882, p. 3.

25 ibid., 1 December 1885, p. 6, City municipal elections.

26 *Herald*, 16 March 1887, p. 11, City buildings unfit for habitation; 26 November 1887, p. 13, editorial.

27 *Evening News*, 9 December 1887, p. 7, Rookeries reformation: Mayor Riley prepares a scheme.

28 ibid., 11 December 1880, p. 4, Notes on current events; 18 January 1881, p. 2, City council. *Daily Telegraph*, 7 January 1881, p. 3, The rookeries of the city.

29 ibid., 14 April 1886, p. 6, Inspection of rookeries.

30 ibid., 12 May 1886, p. 3; 7 May 1886, p. 7; 20 May 1886, p. 3, The condemnation of buildings. *Evening News*, 19 May 1886, The condemned houses; *Globe*, 19 May 1886, The Building Act: deputation to the mayor, both in Improvement Board newspaper cuttings, AONSW, 1/2124.

[31] *Evening News*, 10 November 1883, The city inspection. *Daily Telegraph*, 21 August 1886, p. 3, City Improvement Board. Sapsford to the Mayor, in SCC, LR, vol. 7, no. 1539 (24 August 1880). City Improvement Board, minutes of evidence relating to appeals, 18 February 1881, AONSW, 4/6897.

[32] *Evening News*, 12 September 1882, p. 3, The City Improvement Act. City Improvement Board, minutes of evidence relating to appeals, AONSW, 4/6897. *Daily Telegraph*, 7 January 1881, p. 3, The rookeries of the city.

[33] *Herald*, 13 November 1883, p. 7, editorial.

[34] City Improvement Board, minutes of evidence relating to appeals, 3 September 1880, AONSW, 4/6897.

[35] *Daily Telegraph*, 28 May 1880, p. 3, The City Improvement Act. *Herald*, 19 March 1880, p. 5; Building Surveyor, Health Officer and Inspector of Nuisances to the Mayor, 16 March 1880, in SCC, LR, 26/164/477.

[36] *Evening News*, 27 August 1880, p. 3, Destruction of fever beds. Sapsford to the Mayor, 24 August 1880, in SCC, LR, 26/168/1539. *Herald*, 18 September 1880, p. 3, City of Sydney Improvement Act.

[37] ibid., 6 June 1882, p. 5. R.H. Broderick, 28 March 1899, in SCC, LR, 26/306/776. *Daily Telegraph*, 19 August 1880, p. 2. City of Sydney, 1902, p. 474.

[38] City of Sydney, 1901, p. 185. *Daily Telegraph*, 19 June 1884, p. 4, The City Surveyor; the city marionettes.

[39] ibid., 26 February 1890, p. 6, City Council.

[40] Thomas Garrett, first chairman of the Board, in the *Herald*, 1 December 1879, p. 7, The City Improvement Act.

[41] Sir Henry Parkes, quoted in the *Herald*, 2 October 1880, p. 6, Deputations. ibid., 6 October 1880, in Improvement Board Newspaper Cuttings, AONSW, 1/2124. Henry Colyer to C.H. Barlee, Secretary of the Board, 9 September 1880, in AONSW, 4/6888.

[42] Improvement Board minutes, 9 October 1888, in AONSW, 1/2129.

[43] *Daily Telegraph*, 26 November 1879, p. 4, Sydney Municipal Council. *Herald*, 22 January 1879, p. 2, City of Sydney Improvement Board. Improvement Board, minutes of evidence relating to appeals, 28 October 1881, AONSW, 4/6897.

[44] CBS to the Mayor, 24 August 1880, SCC, LR, 26/168/1539.

[45] *Daily Telegraph*, 7 November 1884, p. 4, The City Improvement Board.

[46] ibid., 17 March 1891, p. 4, Municipal possibilities; 15 January 1884, p. 4, Improvement of Sydney. *Evening News*, 13 November 1888, p. 4, leader; *Echo*, 12 February 1881, in Improvement Board Newspaper Cuttings, AONSW, 1/2124. *Evening News*, 13 April 1888, p. 4, editorial; *Sunday Times*, 12 January 1890, in Improvement Board Newspaper Cuttings, AONSW, 1/2125.

[47] *Evening News*, 30 August 1886, p. 4 and 15 October 1889, p. 4, leaders. *Daily Telegraph*, 17 March 1891, p. 4, Municipal possibilities.

[48] The Greater Sydney Movement and the Royal Commission for the Improvement of the City of Sydney and its Suburbs were both products of this enlarging community debate. See Robert Gibbons, 'Improving Sydney 1908–1909', in Roe, 1980, pp. 120–33.

[49] *Daily Telegraph*, 28 November 1895, p. 4, editorial; John D. Fitzgerald in ibid., 29 November 1895, p. 3, Municipal reform.

[50] *Echo*, 15 October 1891, The governing bodies of Sydney, in Improvement Board Newspaper Cuttings, AONSW, 1/2125.

[51] Gould, 1989, p. 278.

[52] The bill was considerably watered down in Parliament; see Mayne, 1982, chapter 14.

[53] See Larcombe, 1976.

Part 2

Slums

6

Showcase

In 1901 a Birmingham City Councillor, as he thanked the *Daily Gazette* for publishing *Scenes in Slum-Land*, observed that Walters had revealed 'that instead of living in a municipal Arcadia we are living in a city honeycombed with a terrestrial inferno.' By the turn of the century slumland imagery such as Walters' had become inseparably intertwined with representations of modern cities. The pessimistic discourse which this sensationalism generated periodically punctured the prevailing celebratory talk of city improvement and social progress. Slums were everywhere denounced as constituting a health menace, a moral reproach, and a social danger to society. They were characterized as an aesthetic affront and a functional liability to modern cities. Eliminating slums was therefore advocated as a key responsibility of modern city governments. In Birmingham — touted across the world for the civic benefits supposedly set in train by the improvement policies of progressive city administrators — Corporation Street was applauded for having broken up slums in which 'squalor and crowding had been fearful, and the death-rate outrageous; vice, crime, poverty, and drunkenness flourished there, and the saloon-keepers were the only persons who led endurable lives.'[1]

When Birmingham's improvement scheme was launched in 1875, the term *slum* was becoming well established in everyday usage throughout the English-speaking world. In Sydney during the same year, concerned debate about ill health focused upon the inner city's 'over-crowded dwellings and backslums'. San Francisco's Chinatown, which was singled out by the City Health Officer in 1875 on account of living conditions that he described as being 'totally unfit for the lower animals to live in', was explicitly damned as a 'slum' by the Board of Supervisors and the press a decade later. New World usage implied that the social conditions being described were unwelcome imports. In 1873, for example, the State Board of Health in Massachusetts argued that Boston's appalling tenement-house conditions were perpetuated 'by recruits from the slums and huts of the Old World.'[2] The word had indeed originated in Britain early in the century. *Slum* was a slang expression derived from 'slumber'. Its use in London as a noun, meaning an unsavoury back room or a sleepy and unknown back alley, has been traced to J.H. Vaux's *Flash Dictionary* of 1812. The word's meaning subsequently broadened, and during the second quarter of the century the phrase *back slum* was used to characterize whole London districts. By mid-century this phrase — often bracketed with inverted commas in acknowledgement of its slang origins — was being applied sporadically not only in London but in other British cities, in North America, and in the capital cities of the Australian colonies. In 1857 parts of Melbourne — then scarcely 20 years old — were already being called 'back slums' and likened to London's notorious St Giles.[3]

Expanding usage was a product of linguistic innovation. It was not an accurate measure of urban social change. The phrase '*back slum*' was a racy and evocative synonym for the existing tags, *rookery* and *den*. The new term none the less only gradually replaced these older expressions. Early commentary about the Birmingham improvement scheme frequently referred to 'the terrible rookeries in which the poor now live'. *Slum* and *rookery* were still being used together in Britain during the 1890s, and it remained axiomatic that fever dens were among the chief features of slums. In Birmingham, the words *slum*, *rookery*, and *den* continued to be used interchangeably after the turn of the century. In the United States, too, Jacob Riis's 1892 depiction of New York slum life, *The Children of the Poor*, used the words *slum* and *rookery*. San Francisco's Chinatown was still being called a rookery during the early 1900s.[4]

The phrase *back slum* had begun to be simplified to *slum* in Britain since the middle of the nineteenth century. The shorter expression was popularized by Cardinal Wiseman in 1850, when he denounced the 'labyrinths of lanes and courts, and alleys and slums, nests of ignorance, vice, depravity and crime' that surrounded Westminster Abbey. *Back slum*, however, retained a wide currency. Birmingham's improvement scheme was commended during the 1870s as a device 'for breaking up the dense mass of our back slums'. In Melbourne and Sydney, too, the phrase remained current throughout the 1870s and 1880s. John Freeman used both expressions in his 1888 book, *Lights and Shadows of Melbourne Life*.[5] Although the use of inverted commas had begun to become anachronistic in London during the 1840s, they remained in use 20 years later. A Parliamentary report on housing in 1866 said of Birmingham that there was 'hardly a "slum" in the whole borough'. The city's improvement area was still being labelled a 'wretched "slum area"' at the end of the century. The American, Robert Hunter, wrote of 'our so-called "slums"' in his influential book, *Poverty*, in 1904.[6]

By the 1880s *slum* was also becoming widely used as a verb. 'Slumming' connoted both charitable visits among the urban poor by reformers, and the 'idle curiosity' of bourgeois journalists and tourists. San Francisco's pre-fire Chinatown was described as having been 'undoubtedly the *showplace* of the town'. The writer recalled that it was the slum's 'sinister aspects, its delinquent phases which allured. Worthy citizens ... made tours of lascivious inspection, over and over again.'[7]

It was precisely as a 'showplace' or showcase — an artifice of display — that *slum* became a vogue expression during the last quarter of the century.

It was a construct of bourgeois imagination. Like the phrase *modern city*, with which it was so often juxtaposed, the word enjoyed currency as a universalizing concept. It selectively condensed complex spatial forms and social conditions into readily comprehensible images of deprivation and social pathology. The word did not carry with it a precise description of the material conditions of crowded inner-city living, although its use did powerfully shape community attitudes towards particular city neighbourhoods. The slum was a product of speech, text, and illustration, not of the building and labour markets.

This showcase quality of slumland representation was consolidated in urban popular culture during the 1880s and 1890s as the result of the massive publicity accorded two sensational stories about slum life in the metropolitan cores. The first, an anonymous penny pamphlet called *The Bitter Cry of Outcast London*, was published in October 1883. It had been written by the Reverend Andrew Mearns, secretary of the London Congregational Union, in an effort to mobilize evangelical zeal to proselytize the city poor. The second, by New York police reporter Jacob Riis, initially appeared in *Scribner's Magazine* in December 1889. Expanded into a book, it was published by Scribner's in 1890 as *How the Other Half Lives*. In it, Riis set out to describe tenement life among 'New York's slums'.[8]

These accounts of New York's Lower East Side and London's East End inspired a flood of slumland exposés whose reference points quickly encompassed the entire urban network. When the British Royal Commission on the Housing of the Working Classes released its first report in 1885, the *Birmingham Daily Post* noted that slumland revelations had become familiar to the public 'from long and repeated exposure'. By the time of Cuming Walter's sensational series at the turn of the century, the 'slum question' had entrenched itself as a central issue of public policy debate.[9] The debate crossed classes. In Birmingham the labour movement joined bourgeois reformers in publicizing the 'slum problem'. The debate crossed geographical barriers as well. Mearns considerably influenced American commentary, as did Riis British opinion. This sideways-looking genre of slumland depiction extended as far afield as Australia. *The Bitter Cry* was headline news in Australian cities, and the subsequent reform discourse was reprinted or summarized in the colonial press. Newspapers also kept readers abreast of New York's slum 'scandals'. News reporting from the metropolitan cores generated local slumland sensationalism in imitation. In San Francisco, the local press equated Chinatown with New York's most notorious slumland showcase, 'that sore spot, Five Points, a haunt and breeding place of filth, disease and vice'.[10]

The pessimism of slum representation is now its most apparent feature. The second volume of Charles Booth's massive social survey, *Life and Labour of the People in London*, was called 'the grimmest book of our generation' by the London *Times* when it was published in 1891. This pessimism is evident in two senses. It is recognizable, first, in the widening conviction that slums were not confined to London and New York but were evident in varying degrees of intensity throughout the urban network. This bleak mood was summed up by John Nettlefold in 1908 when he conceded that there 'are slums in every great city'. The pessimism is evident, too, in the characterizations of slums as invasive, cancerous growths within those cities. The *San Francisco Chronicle*'s characterization of Five Points as a spreading sore spot was symptomatic of this prevailing mood. Thirty years earlier observers in Sydney had remarked that slumland poverty was likewise 'mastering' London. Slums were described by one Birmingham newspaper as 'ulcers in our social system', which — as they grew and festered — were 'fostering disease, crime, and poverty'. Walters wrote of the city's slums:

> They stretch out, with infinite ramifications, from the most crowded centre of Birmingham to the uttermost boundaries. You may walk for a day, and not come to the end of the main thoroughfare which, like a polluted river, is fed by a thousand infected tributaries; and you may walk for a week and not have traced the in-and-out convolutions of streets, by-ways, alleys, and courts, which in the mass form the black and festering cancer, ever slowly widening, and sapping the life and strength of the city.[11]

During the 1870s, as usage switched increasingly from back slum to slum, the earlier sense of slums as scattered and containable pockets was replaced by more alarming pictures of slums as vast teeming wildernesses, which were perpetually spilling over and extending their boundaries. In London slumland representation shifted from St Giles to encompass the whole East End. In New York the focus broadened from Five Points to take in the entire Lower East Side. This changing imagery was replicated in the provinces. In Sydney, the measured concern that had been expressed by parliamentary investigators in 1859 about slum pockets like Queen's Place and Durand's Alley was replaced in the mid-1870s by the Sewage and Health Board's perturbing image of Sussex Street, and the whole western portion of the inner city which the street traversed. Commentators on San Francisco's Chinatown, describing 'its byways, its slums, and its purlieus', variously estimated the district as spreading over 9, 12, 14, 20, or more blocks. In 1899 the head of the Birmingham Trades Council declared that hundreds of thousands of Birmingham working people were living 'in dirty and unhealthy slums'.[12]

'The eternal slum question'[13]

The increasing frequency and intensified pessimism of slumland sensationalism during the last quarter of the century was prompted by bourgeois humanitarian disquiet at the extent of urban poverty, by shock at the social ill effects of city improvement policies, and by fear. We shall examine each in turn. Sympathy for slum-dwellers was nevertheless tempered by continuing judgemental assessments that, as the *Sydney Morning Herald* put it in 1878, 'vice and folly create more destitution and suffering than misfortune ever can do.' Charles Booth and Robert Hunter — two of the most influential social investigators at the turn of the century — both perpetuated the distinction between deserving and undeserving mendicants which had dominated bourgeois reform discourse throughout the century. In 1897 Francis Walker, then head of the United States Census, reaffirmed that 'pauperism is largely voluntary ... Those who are paupers are so far more from character than from condition.'[14]

Slurs against the urban poor were increasingly qualified by the caveat that, as Hunter himself noted in 1904, poverty resulted in part from 'deeply seated and fundamental economic disorders' that were perhaps 'essential to our modern system of production'. The argument had been publicized throughout the urban network by a former San Francisco newspaper editor, Henry George. His denunciations of the unequal distribution of wealth generated by industrial society — first publicized in his 1879 book *Progress and Poverty*, and repeated in 1883 in *Social Problems* — were serialized and reprinted throughout the English-speaking world. George spoke to packed halls during his English lecture tour in 1882, and repeated that success during an Australian tour in 1890. His *Progress and Poverty* was described by the Sydney press in 1883 as being 'as popular a book almost as any story by the late Charles Dickens'. By the early twentieth century even moderates like Nettlefold conceded that the 'advance of civilisation, which has brought greater comfort and well-being to the richer classes, has actually increased the sufferings of the poorer town-dwellers.'[15]

That admission was supported by the accumulated findings of 30 years' intense outreach work by charities and city missionaries, and the survey work of statistical societies and government health inspectors. In 1892 state investigators styled Boston's tenement-dwellers as 'slaves of circumstances'. Investigators in cities throughout the urban network confronted — and newspapers publicized — the tenuous lifestyles of the secondary labour force, confronted as they were by the erratic demands for labour at the docks and warehouses, the insecurity of long-term employment in manufacturing and the building industry, and the exploitation of women piece-workers. In the supposedly Australian 'Working Man's Paradise', it was being widely conceded by the daily press even before the onset of the Great Depression of the 1890s that 'there is in all cities a class who through no fault of their own are unable to get sufficient employment to insure even a poor livelihood.' In Birmingham, the *Daily Gazette* likewise publicized the plight of labouring people 'whose poverty compels them to live in foul dens close to the centre of the city.' Witness after witness who appeared before the City Council's 1903 investigation of working-class housing conditions confirmed that working people caught in the secondary labour market were tied to the inner city by low-paying and irregular jobs, by long hours if they had the luck to find work, and by the cost of commuter travel. The general secretary of New York's influential Charity Organization Society, Edward Devine, argued simultaneously that poverty was an economic and social category rather than a moral and personal blemish of character.[16]

A new consensus was emerging among social investigators and reform leaders that urban poverty was perpetuated by inadequate wages and exploitative housing markets rather than by individual pathologies. Benjamin Seebohm Rowntree's 1901 study of York, *Poverty: A Study of Town Life*, confirmed Booth's findings in *Life and Labour of the People in London* that at least one-quarter of Britons lived in poverty. Influenced by Booth and Rowntree, Hunter embarked upon a poverty survey of Americans, and generated shock waves of his own when in 1904 he published *Poverty*, in which he argued that almost the same proportion of Americans lived in poverty in the populous northern industrial states.[17] Booth, Rowntree, and Hunter all focused on the dismal equation between employment, earnings, and needs. They argued, in common with many other commentators, that slums were the horrifying consequence of that disequilibrium. The British sanitary pioneer Sir John Simon insisted upon the 'inseparability' of slum housing from that equation. His blunt message was that 'scanty earnings can buy but scantily of the necessaries and comforts of life.' This message was massively underlined in the United States by the meticulous documentation of the Pittsburgh Survey, which was published in six volumes between 1909 and 1914. The Survey concluded that two-thirds of industrial Pittsburgh worked long hours for inadequate pay and lived in substandard housing. Pittsburgh's 'social neglect', it seemed, was representative of the new urban order.[18]

The contrasting faces of urban wealth and poverty dismayed influential segments of the bourgeois intelligentsia. It seemed that everywhere the 'greatest wealth exists in our modern cities, side by side with the greatest poverty.' Cities actively seemed to exacerbate the miseries of the poor: in 'every part of the world where population is closely concentrated extreme misery and suffering have been found to prevail among a large number of the people, even in times of comparative prosperity.' Residents of Sydney were cautioned against complacency that the conditions described in *The Bitter Cry of Outcast London* 'are altogether confined to the cities of the old world. More or less, we have them in the midst of us in this very city.' In 1881 the *Sydney Daily Telegraph* worried that behind the city's main streets and their 'thin veneer of respectability lurk all the horrors of civilised degradation, and, if the term can be used, of modern barbarism.'[19]

Slumland mocked the apparent progress of the age. The *Sydney Morning Herald* worried that readers would judge from *The Bitter Cry* 'that our civilisation is a failure, and that we are going from bad to worse'. Joseph Chamberlain had conceded during the mid-1870s that in Birmingham, notwithstanding the improvement schemes of private reformers and politicians,

they were continually brought face to face with the disheartening fact that they seemed only to be scraping the surface, and that all around them there was a mass of misery, poverty, and crime which they seemed powerless to deal with and unable to touch. In the course of the last thirty years Birmingham had made marvellous progress in every respect. The population had more than doubled, its wealth had greatly increased, its public buildings had multiplied, its institutions enlarged and extended in all directions.

Yet, he said, 'We find bad air, polluted water, crowded and filthy homes, and ill-ventilated courts everywhere prevailing in the midst of our boasted wealth, luxury, and civilisation'. Fifteen years of apparent improvement later, a Liberal Unionist politician conceded that the slums remained a 'great blot on modern civilisation'. In 1904 the American reformer, Josiah Strong, addressing the first International Garden City Conference in London, declared that the rise of cities challenged all of Western civilization.[20]

To many social commentators, the gulf between city wealth and slumland poverty visualized the unravelling ethical bonds and responsibilities of modern society. Strong styled 'The Modern City a Menace', contending that 'the moral development of the city has by no means kept pace with material growth.' His friend, Jacob Riis, argued that New York's slums resulted from 'Greed and reckless selfishness'. In *How the Other Half Lives, The Children of the Poor*, and his later works, *The Battle with the Slum* (1902) and *The Peril and the Preservation of the Home* (1903), Riis represented the metropolis as typifying society's retreat from Christian fraternity.[21] Strong and Riis were tapping a well-established stream of big-city criticism. A member of New York's 1884 slum investigation committee had concluded that the city needed 'a revival of civic pride in her citizens to stimulate them ... to public duties. Our people are too absorbed in their private affairs and content to delegate responsibilities to ill-paid and harassed officials.' Theodore Roosevelt declared in the following year that 'people of means in all great cities have ... shamefully neglected their ... duties.' In Chicago, too, it was contended during the 1890s that the 'chief cause of the slums is the abandonment of the poor by the well-to-do.' Chicago's business leadership was accused by William Stead of displaying 'cynical neglect of civic duty and indifference to the responsibilities and obligations of citizenship.' Social survey workers in the Massachusetts manufacturing city of Lawrence concluded similarly in 1911 that because the mill owners lived outside the city, they felt no 'direct sense of shame and personal responsibility' about the city's appalling housing conditions and eschewed the responsibilities of city government.[22]

In England, Birmingham churchmen — radicalized by Walters — preached that slum reform required an awakened 'sense of civic duty'. Birmingham was accused of having succumbed to 'the contagion of ... commercialism ... People rush in from the outside in the eager hunt for money. They simply strive to "make their pile" and haste away again. Among such a population it is difficult to spread altruistic ideas: it is a wild endeavour all round after business each for himself, and but few pause to consider what are their duties to society.'[23]

In Australia, also, commentators cautioned that the 'civilised heathenism of our great cities' extended through all classes, because the impersonal urban settings which made it inevitable 'that one half the world does not know how the other half lives' broke down the moral integrity of community and encouraged mutual exploitation. Australian clergymen — protesting against this urban 'delusion that ... everyone is at liberty to do what he likes with his own' — questioned the moral underpinnings of market-place progress.[24]

Humanitarian quibbles at the contrasts between wealth and poverty were intensified by mounting evidence of the ill effects which flowed from the so-called city improvement works undertaken by commercial developers. A swelling chorus of accusations were heard during the last quarter of the century that cities had single-mindedly pursued improvement strategies geared only to maximize 'Wharves and shipping, warehouses and commerce, money-making and keen competition'. It was claimed that the deleterious effects of such decision-making upon the poor questioned 'the much-vaunted progress of the age'. In 1873 the Massachusetts Board of Health expressed alarm that mass evictions caused by railway making in Boston had intensified the 'already surfeited' crowding of the city's poor. Sydney's *Echo* newspaper noted a decade later that as 'the poorer class of tenements are giving way to the insatiable demands of business ... the poor ... must huddle closer together. If each family cannot obtain a house for itself, several must collect under one roof — a necessity that has fallen upon thousands of the humbler classes of older cities, to their degradation and ruin.' A writer to the *Herald* was concerned in 1887 that the commercial building boom gave a misleading 'impression of the improvement and advancement of the city':

To the wharf labourer and the like, whose occupations must be entered upon and carried on through all hours of the day and night as occasions require, this wholesale destruction of tenements, unless followed by the erection of other and better ones, has a debasing influence by causing such to crowd together in the available houses of the same district; and city missionaries and others who constantly visit from house to house can testify to the fact that where two families occupied a house previously, now another, and in cases two families more, are sharing the same house.[25]

Critics blamed government improvement strategies for exacerbating the harmful effects of commercial redevelopment. In London, disquiet had been expressed since the 1840s that street-improvement-enabling laws had intensified slumland overcrowding. The New Oxford Street improvement scheme, which had been launched with fanfare in the late 1830s, was being blamed by mid-century for having aggravated overcrowding in St Giles. During the third quarter of the century the London press gave increasing publicity to the social ill effects of evictions caused by Parliament-endorsed railway and street improvement schemes.[26] *The Bitter Cry* carried that message to the provinces. In Birmingham, the *Daily Gazette* noted in 1883 that 'Vast public improvements — new streets, public buildings, factories, business establishments, and railways — have swept away whole colonies of artisans' dwellings in all large towns', but cautioned that their effect had been to worsen overcrowding. It was already being said of Birmingham's own improvement scheme that many 'poor people instead of having better houses had been driven to crowd together in those that were left.' In 1891 the *Daily Mail* concluded that the scheme had indeed aggravated the miseries of 'that unlucky residue of the population who must live in the town yet whose pockets will not afford more than the barest of rents.'[27]

Bourgeois preoccupation with the slum question was also sustained by fear. Worries about slumland were inseparably tied to concerns about city ill health. The Sydney *Herald*, warning of points of unimagined contact between city wealth and poverty, cautioned in 1875 that city dwellers 'are miserably at each other's mercy. The germs of disease that are generated in back slums travel to front thoroughfares ... , and thus the unhealth of the few becomes that of the million.' The newspaper noted perceptively during a smallpox epidemic in 1881 that it required a disease 'panic ... to show half the world how the other half live.'[28] The first comprehensive surveys of working-class living conditions in British, North American, and Australian cities during the 1840s and 1850s had been partially prompted by anxiety about epidemic cholera and other diseases.

Slumland worriers had in mind more than the sickness and death caused by poverty-bred infections. They also voiced concerns about the economic burden of disease. In America fear of pestilence was augmented by the worry — intensifying as immigration accelerated late in the century — that immigrant slums imposed an intolerable drain upon private and state charity. In Birmingham, Chamberlain calculated in pounds, shillings, and pence the productivity loss caused by insanitary housing. Moreover, slums were blamed not only for filling the hospitals and asylums, but also the gaols. Supporters of Birmingham's improvement scheme contended that the targeted '"slums" ... are the haunts of thieves and the receivers of stolen goods.' This sort of slumland pessimism blended with worries about economic slump and anticipations of poverty-generated criminality and insurrection. In Britain, the pioneering sanitary investigations of the 1840s had been influenced not only by disease, but by economic depression and the rise of Chartism. The trail-blazing 1865 sanitary report on slum living by the Citizens' Association of New York had likewise been prompted not only by cholera, but by bourgeois alarm at the 1863 draft riots. Slum-clearance proposals for the city's Mulberry Bend, which Riis carried through in the mid-1890s, dated back to 1829, when the Common Council had first contemplated ridding the city of that 'place of great disorder and crime.'[29]

These concerns intensified during the last quarter of the century. In the United States, the protracted depression of the 1870s, and simmering labour unrest which exploded in the 1877 national railway strike, fuelled a gloomy discourse about poverty-bred criminality and insurgency. The Chicago's Citizen's Association, dominated by millionaire businessmen, gave the city police department rifles, cannons, and a gatling gun.[30] The key phrase from the title of Charles Brace's influential 1880 book, *The Dangerous Classes of New York*, quickly entered bourgeois vocabulary. Their fears — widely broadcast by cable news — intensified with the massive rail strike of 1885 and Chicago's Haymarket riot in 1886. Talk of social crisis reached a climax during the depression of 1893–7.

In Britain, social commentary during the early 1880s was preoccupied with the 'Great Depression' and its attendant slumland turmoils. The *Birmingham Daily Mail* commented of *The Bitter Cry* that these 'outcasts, degraded as they are, are a menace to our social fabric. The slums are the great recruiting grounds of vice and crime ... It is out of such conditions that the madness of revolutions is born.'[31] London's Trafalgar Square riot in 1886 introduced an additional note of hysteria about the metropolitan poor. Early twentieth-century debate about slums took place against a backdrop of chronic unemployment and mass demonstration.

Sensational news coverage of mass protest and bourgeois hand-wringing in the metropolitan cores circulated throughout the urban network. The Melbourne *Argus* warned in 1884 that within the city's 'back slums ... crime conspires, and epidemics breed, and drunkenness flourishes, and vice assumes a character of lawless insolence.' In 1888 Freeman predicted that these conditions were nurturing a revolutionary mob as dangerous as any history had seen in Paris: 'We, too, have a dangerous class in our midst, lurking in holes and corners away from the public gaze, where they mature undisturbed their plans against society.' Alarmists in Sydney warned that Australian society was conceivably 'laying the foundations of those social revolutions that have occurred in the old world.'[32]

The greatest fear, however, was ultimately generated not so much by the possibility of slum-induced riot as by the likelihood of radical politicians hijacking public policy-making with chimerical promises of slum reform to mass electorates. Chamberlain worried that working-class voters would be seduced by 'wild creeds' like those of Henry George, and Australian bourgeois liberals also blamed George for fuelling radical proposals demanded by 'the impatient socialist'. In Britain, the Manchester *Guardian* denounced even Lord Salisbury's proposed housing reforms in response to *The Bitter Cry* as 'State Socialism pure and simple'.[33] Worries in Britain about an emerging socialist threat to *laissez-faire* orthodoxies intensified with the formation of the Social Democratic Federation and the Fabian Society in 1883, and with the extension of the manhood suffrage in 1884. In the opinion of traditionalists, the insidious effect of this electoral reform was highlighted in 1892 by the election of independent Labour representatives to the House of Commons. In local Birmingham politics Neville Chamberlain was still fulminating in 1907 against this new party of extremists and faddists 'who called themselves Socialists'.[34] In the United States concerns that California's Union Labour Party might spread nationally prompted an unlikely coalition of Democrats, Republicans, and Progressives in the protracted witch hunt against municipal corruption in San Francisco during the early twentieth century.

Reformers

The *Birmingham Daily Gazette* remarked late in 1883, as it reviewed the exchanges sparked by *The Bitter Cry*, that 'the sad pictures which have been drawn during the last two months are not new to earnest philanthropists, parish doctors, clergymen, and district visitors'.[35] The pessimistic slumland images that were drawn by bourgeois urban reform movements had powerfully influenced popular opinion since early in the century. Yet the pessimism of the reformers' message is deceiving. The 'sad pictures' were not simple depictions of the uneven material conditions of city living.

Rather, the vignettes were carefully selected and fashioned. Reformist discourse had fashioned the slum as a showcase of the imagination.

The reformers' contrived pessimism was in fact grounded in their underlying confidence that the problem they thus presented lay on the edges of social progress. Reformers maintained that — with a modicum of state encouragement — the slum problem was well within the power of the city building and labour markets to resolve. Nettlefold insisted that slums were not a necessary feature of urbanization, but were a passing phase that had resulted from the inadequacy of government oversight during the initial spurt of urbanization. 'Like Topsy,' he said, 'our cities have "growed" in a haphazard manner without any foresight or general supervision.' That rationalization had especial currency among the frontier cities of the New World. 'The Vagabond', writing in Melbourne during the late 1870s, argued that the city's slum pockets stemmed 'from past irregular and ill considered arrangements, which has [sic] arisen under the influence of a most unprecedented state of things, and which, perhaps, has never before existed in a civilized society, it we except our contemporaries of California.' As it was with the built environment, so it was with employment and wages. In 1863 a little-known Melbourne economist, William Hearn, published a book, *Plutology*, in which he predicted a virtually infinite potential for economic growth in maturing capitalist societies. Hearn's argument was noted by the influential British economist Alfred Marshall, who from the early 1870s predicted the steadily increasing prosperity of all classes of society. In 1914 the Johns Hopkins professor of political economy, Jacob Hollander, argued in his *Abolition of Poverty* that poverty was 'an incident of historical evolution, not an essential of economic structure'. City inequalities were therefore resolvable by wise social policy as city and national economies developed.[36]

The imagined slum was constructed as an agent of mobilization. It was not a symptom of despair and hopelessness. Notwithstanding the contrived anxiety about the invasive spread of slum borders, slumland representation was in fact a symptom of the bourgeoisie's drive to consolidate their own hegemony. The slum 'became an indispensable image of social degradation'[37] with which to define issues and press goals, and thereby harness electoral opinion in support of moderate reform strategies. Against a backdrop of slumland horrors, bourgeois spokespeople asserted their readings of the borders of wise political authority and policy-making. The rise of the Birmingham Liberal Association's civic gospel during the 1860s and 1870s, and of Phelan's reform coalition in San Francisco at the turn of the century, are cases in point. In New York during the 1860s and 1870s the urban bourgeoisie had similarly asserted leadership 'by forging new models of social stewardship'.[38] In Australia the third quarter of the century saw the wresting of class dominance from conservative pastoralists by a city-based liberal alliance of merchants, financiers, and professionals. This loose alliance entrenched a distinctive style of populist politics in which city problem-solving emerged as an arena within which contending political factions sought to establish and maintain electoral credibility.

The discourse on slum reform represented an assertion of paternalistic leadership over the pluralism of big cities. The style was pioneered by the English reformer, Octavia Hill, whose work amongst the homes of the London poor — aimed at 'disciplining our immense poor population ... by individual influence' — was cited by charity leaders and city governments throughout the urban network. Hill advocated 'an ever-present, all-pervading, informal, but most active body of volunteer inspectors', who — 'watchful and kind' — would influence the home and neighbourhood lives of all slum-dwellers. Commending Hill's model of training volunteers to provide 'personal service and sympathy' to the poor, a Birmingham church mission worker warned in 1903 that 'Where the relations of tenant and owner are reduced to a cash nexus, the absence of human sympathy, of personal knowledge and friendship hardens life.' That model was widely applied. At the annual general meeting of the Sydney Ragged Schools in 1883, a clergyman had remarked that 'by fostering generous sympathies on the one hand, and respect on the other, the bonds of society would be mutually strengthened and its progress be permanently assured.'[39]

Paternalistic oversight was consolidated by the proliferating Charity Organization Societies, the first of which had been established — with Hill a key participant — in London during 1869. The movement spread to the Australian colonies in the late 1870s and to the United States early in the next decade. This bourgeois paternalism was capped by the settlement-house movement, which was begun in England by the Anglican clergyman the Reverend Samuel Barnett, in reaction to *The Bitter Cry*. Barnett spoke at Oxford in November 1883, and in answer to the 'revelations of recent pamphlets' proposed the founding of a university settlement in London's East End in order to build upon the Charity Organization Society's friendly visitor work with which he was closely associated. Toynbee Hall was subsequently established in Whitechapel in 1884. Barnett advocated, like Hill, 'the power of friendship to harmonize conflicting interests.' It was anticipated that settlement residents would act as 'wise counsellors' and as 'trusted advisers of the poor', teaching them friendship as a basis upon which to demonstrate the broader 'duties and obligations of social life'. The settlements would thus function as 'bridges over ... the gulf between the classes which modern civilization has created.' In the United States likewise, the settlement houses — beginning with the establishment of Hull House in Chicago in 1889 and proliferating in the years before the First World War — represented an effort to 'establish neighborly friendship' with slum dwellers in order thereby 'to reconstruct the human family'.[40]

The popular genre of slumland representation late in the nineteenth century was nurtured by the publicizing activities of these bourgeois reformers. A trickle of slumland tracts was generated in Britain during the 1830s in pursuit of legislative controls to curb urban ill health. This campaign found fuller expression in Edwin Chadwick's *Report on the Sanitary Condition of the Labouring Population* (1842) and the Royal Commission on the Sanitary State of Large Towns in 1844. As reformist interest shifted from sewage to housing conditions, a broader audience was reached through the works of writers such as Hector Gavin, who in 1848 described Bethnal Green in his *Sanitary Ramblings,* and Henry Mayhew, whose *London Labour and the London Poor* was first published in serial form in the *Morning Chronicle* in 1849–50, published as a book in 1851, and reissued in 1861. Such efforts bore early but bitter fruit in the short-lived General Board of Health between 1848 and 1858. Meanwhile in the United States, sanitarians such as William Channing in Boston and John Griscom in New York were also spurred by Chadwick to publicize inner-city living conditions in order to mobilize support for health reforms. Griscom's 1845 tract, *The Sanitary Condition of the Laboring Population of New York with Suggestions for its Improvement,* influenced a generation of later reform writers.

The lobbying effort continued in both countries throughout the 1850s and 1860s, by means of public lectures, pamphlets, journals, and commissioned reports. The New York Citizens' Association sanitary report during the mid-1860s, for example, was a powerful stimulus behind the establishment of the Metropolitan Board of Health in 1866 and the 1867 tenement code: the first comprehensive health legislation in any American city. In Britain, the sanitary exposés of the 1840s were reinforced by works such as Thomas Beames's *The Rookeries of London* in 1852, George Godwin's *London Shadows* in 1854, and John Hollinghead's *Ragged London* in 1861. Moreover, as the denunciations of Birmingham slumlands at the 1868 conference of the Social Science Association demonstrated, the message was also being carried to the provinces. However, in both countries the sanitarians gained only a relatively small and specialist readership, and sparked only sporadic interest among the daily press.

A similar picture is evident in the Australian colonies. In Sydney sanitarians generated an advanced but specialist reform literature in imitation of British precedents. W.S. Jevons' sophisticated but unpublished social survey of the city, undertaken during the mid-1850s, was publicized in a series of newspaper articles late in 1859. In the same year a Parliamentary Select Committee on the Condition of the Working Classes of the Metropolis publicized the slumland viewpoints of health officials, the clergy, and the police. The city's Health Officer, first appointed in 1857, used his quarterly and annual reports —modelled on those of Simon in London and reprinted in the local press — to lobby for enlarged public health legislation.[41]

Not until the 1870s and 1880s did the reformers' slumland representations reach a mass audience. This was due in part, as in San Francisco, to the establishment of boards of health and to the professional organization of the medical officers and municipal engineers who serviced them. It was due, also, to the increasing scale and organization of the public health movement. In Britain, the Charity Organization Society established a standing committee on working-class housing, which publicized health and housing issues before parliament and the general public. The American Public Health Association, founded in 1872, likewise targeted the tenement-house conditions as they lobbied lawmakers for health reform. Publicity generated by New York reformers during the late 1870s and early 1880s paved the way for state investigations and reform initiatives. Most of all, however, the reformers' slumland diatribes galvanized attention as discourse on working-class housing transcended the sanitary preoccupations of the early reformers to address the broader and interconnected social issues of urban poverty.

One symptom of this changing mood was the widespread publicity belatedly given during the 1870s to Octavia Hill's experiments, begun the decade before, in the rehabilitation and controlled rental of working-class housing in London. The more grandiose schemes of philanthropic housing companies also finally caught the popular imagination. The earliest of these model dwelling companies had been formed in London during the 1840s, and were copied in the United States during the 1850s by the New York Association for Improving the Condition of the Poor. It was not, however, until the 1860s that the movement fully established itself, with the establishment in London — funded by the American banker George Peabody — of the Peabody Trust in 1862, Sir Sydney Waterlow's Improved Industrial Dwellings Company in 1863, and the Artisans', Labourers' and General Dwelling Company in 1867. Thereafter philanthropic housing schemes occupied a central place in nineteenth- and early twentieth-century discussions of the slum problem. These initiatives sparked overseas imitators. In 1872, for example, the Boston Co-operative Building Company renovated and operated a model tenement, and in 1877, 1879, and 1890 the philanthropist, Alfred Threadway White, translated Waterlow designs to Brooklyn. City and Suburban Homes Company, formed in 1896, built model tenements in Manhattan and cottages in the suburbs. Attempts to apply Octavia Hill's housing rehabilitation schemes in New York also received publicity during the 1880s and 1890s. In Sydney, a Model Lodging House Company was launched in 1878 and abortive efforts were made in 1885 and 1888 to establish a Workingmen's Improved Dwellings Company. An Improved Dwellings and Lodging House Company opened model accommodation in Melbourne for working men in 1884.

Another symptom of the changing mood was the bracketing — axiomatic by the mid-1880s — of the concepts *housing* and *poverty*. The changing paradigm was highlighted by the impact of *The Bitter Cry*. Newspaper commentary in Birmingham drew attention to the 'excitement' and 'agitation' which Mearns's tract had produced, and Joseph Chamberlain exclaimed that 'Social reform is in the air.' A flood of books, pamphlets, periodical articles, and daily newspaper depictions of slums thereafter directed community attention to the interconnectivity of poor housing, wages, and employment. Reform debate was fuelled by Charles Booth's massive survey of *Life and Labour of the People in London*. Preliminary results, presented to the Royal Statistical Society in 1887 and 1888, suggested that one-third of London was 'sinking into want'.[42] In the following year Booth released the first volume of *Life and Labour*, which quickly sold out and generated a mass of reviews in periodicals and press. Slummer discourse was further fuelled and popularized by General William

Booth, founder of the Salvation Army, who published *In Darkest England and the Way Out* in 1890.

In the United States, a spate of inner-city social surveys likewise followed in the wake of Riis. The journal *Arena* began a series of slumland features in 1890, and continued them throughout the decade. The economist Marcus Reynolds released *The Housing of the Poor in American Cities* during 1893, and in the following year the United States Department of Labor published *The Slums of Baltimore, Chicago, New York and Philadelphia*. Elgin Gould, president of the City and Suburban Homes Company, produced a massive report — *The Housing of the Working People* — for the Commissioner of Labor during 1895. Much of the momentum of slumland investigation was sustained by settlement-house activists. In Chicago, residents at Hull House collaborated with the Department of Labor's slum survey and then released their own report, *Hull House Maps and Papers*, in 1895. During the next year the head of Boston's South End House, Robert A. Woods, edited *The Poor in Great Cities*, a massive publicizing tract by a dozen reform leaders, the chapters of which had originally been published by *Scribner's Magazine* during the early 1890s. In 1898 Woods also edited South End House's own Boston survey, *The City Wilderness: A Settlement Study*. Robert Hunter was a member of Hull House, and — before writing *Poverty* — had in 1901 produced *Tenement Conditions in Chicago*, a stinging indictment of Chicago's 'wilderness of bad housing and sanitary neglect', which prompted the city belatedly to overhaul its primitive building regulations.[43]

The use of slumland sensationalism as a catalyst for legislative reform was highlighted by the New York Charity Organization Society. In 1900 the Society staged an exhibition of photographs, maps, statistical tables, and models in order to dramatize its arguments for housing reform, and then engineered a massive state investigation of tenement conditions which resulted in a total overhaul of the city's building codes. The Society's example was imitated by reformers and city governments around the nation. Meanwhile, the New York Charity Organization Society and the settlement house movement, whose respective journals had merged in 1905 to establish *Charities and the Commons* (renamed *The Survey* in 1909), embarked upon the massive Pittsburgh Survey. In thus attempting to survey an entire industrial city, reformers explicitly widened the parameters of concern from the slum problem to a galaxy of overlapping social issues within which ill health, housing, and poverty were embedded.

These widening preoccupations were also evident in Britain, sustained by concerns about bolstering national efficiency in the face of stiffening German competition and the embarrassing reverses of the Boer War. In 1901 Charles Masterman's book, *The Heart of the Empire*, represented the slums of imperial London as sapping the vitality of the British race. The high rejection rate for soldier enlistments during the conflict in South Africa appeared to authenticate that claim, and in so doing blended discussions of slums with the newer vogue themes of city and national planning. The release in 1904 of a major government report on physical deterioration cemented this new synthesis, prompting an intensified reformist debate about housing, planning, and social engineering which unfolded amid lurid newspaper accounts of excursions into London's slums. Here was the genesis of the Liberal reform programme after 1905, and the construction of the welfare state.

In both Britain and America, urban planning — as a policy agenda for reformers, a new professional affiliation, a programme for lawmakers and administrators — was an outcome of these synthesizing developments. In the newly federated nation of Australia, as well, slum reform shaded into the planning of better cities as a means of engineering national fitness. This trend was highlighted by Melbourne's Select Committee on the Housing of the People in the Metropolis, 1913–14, the 1917 Royal Commission on the Housing of the People of the Metropolis, and — in Sydney — by the 1909 Royal Commission for the Improvement of the City of Sydney and its Suburbs. By the early twentieth century, reform innovators in all three nations were thus moving beyond concern with slums to define the city as a whole as the pre-eminent field of interest.[44]

Entertainers

We confront an apparent paradox. The last quarter of the nineteenth century and the pre-war years of the twentieth century shared a preoccupation with slums. These years were characterized by intensive organizational and lobbying effort to address the so-called slum question. Yet, as the chapter on the Birmingham Improvement Scheme has already suggested, the reform results were paltry. The slumland exposés and long drawn-out reformist discourse were not matched by sustained popular interest in the reformers' agendas.

In Britain, the Cross Act was already by the late 1870s being judged a failure. The Housing of the Working Classes Acts of 1885, 1890, 1900, and 1903 — prompted by reform agitation in the wake of *The Bitter Cry* — were also disappointing in their results. The reform movement in the United States likewise struggled in the face of indifference on the part of lawmakers and the general public. In 1921 the settlement-house leader Mary McDowell conceded that for all the reform efforts there 'has been very little real improvement in housing.'[45] The focus of city improvement policies remained firmly fixed upon commercial renewal, not housing reform. No real housing reforms were achieved in London until the 1930s. There were no more large-scale clearances of working-class housing in Birmingham until after the Second World War, although municipal house building got under way in the suburbs during the inter-war years.[46] In Sydney, notwithstanding extensive land clearances by the Sydney Harbour Trust early in the century, and sporadic Labor Party experiments in public housing — the State Government's Daceyville model village scheme in 1912, and projects by the City Council during the mid-1920s — housing reform lost momentum during the 1920s. Renewed reform agitation during the 1930s led to the establishment of a State Housing Commission in 1942, but clearance and public housing programmes did not get under way until the 1950s. In Melbourne too, despite intensive newspaper campaigns and the appointment of a Housing Investigation and Slum Abolition Board in the 1930s, no significant programme of inner-city clearances and public housing emerged until the 1950s.[47] In the United States public housing was stillborn, and the federal government's provisions for slum clearance programmes in the 1930s were applied to central-city 'blight' in the interests of business redevelopment.[48]

The undoubted popularity of slumland sensationalism was not grounded in the objectives of bourgeois reformers. It lay partially instead in quirky boosterism of the modern city's two faces. In provincial centres especially, where it had been repeatedly relayed that all great cities contained slums, the possession of contrasting lights and shadows was regarded by many as a defining feature of metropolitan style. In 1886, for example, the exotic allure of San Francisco's Chinatown 'pest hole' was presented as confirming San Francisco's status as a 'cosmopolitan city'. More importantly, the bizarrely alien quality of slumland depictions enjoyed mass appeal because they were 'curiosities': entertaining diversions from the humdrum routines of big-city life. Bourgeois slummers represented the congested living areas of inner cities as picturesque showcases of low life. The appeal of this 'spectacle' lay in its manifest difference from everyday living.[49]

Charles Dickens had championed this theatrical style in *Household Words* during the 1850s. His collaborator, the writer and journalist George Augustus Sala, was captivated by far-flung cities. He admired Melbourne's glitter and styled the city 'Marvellous'. He was enchanted, too, by city badlands. Sala emerged from a night-time tour through the 'fetid precincts' of San Francisco's Chinatown in 1885 exclaiming excitedly that the 'sights he observed he never before had believed could exist.'[50] Walter Besant had similarly exploited the romance of London's East End in his 1882 novel, *All Sorts and Conditions of Men*. The American H.O. Bunner, editor of *Puck* from 1878 to 1896, called himself 'an ardent collector of slums', and thought Riis's favourite slumland specimen, Mulberry Bend, 'the most picturesque and interesting' of them all. In 1913 another connoisseur of New York low life, the British literary critic Stephen Graham, called the Lower East Side 'slums at their intensest'. A Melbourne journalist and bohemian, John Arthur Andrews, who wrote a series on 'Australia's Slums' for the *Tocsin* in 1901, recalled that he had begun to investigate Melbourne's slums during the 1880s, attracted by their 'picturesqueness'.[51]

Immigrant neighbourhoods seemed especially exotic to these writers. San Francisco's 'Latin quarter' was a case in point. Slum romancer Will Irwin wrote that on 'the slopes of Telegraph Hill dwelt the Mexicans and Spanish, in low houses, which they had transformed by balconies into a semblance of Spain. Above, and streaming over the hill, were the Italians ... The effect was picturesque, and this hill was the delight of painters. It was all more like Italy than anything in the Italian quarter of New York and Chicago.' It was generally agreed by these slumland *aficionados* that San Francisco's Chinatown was especially 'diverting and outlandish'. The imaginative reconstruction of Chinatown as it had been before the fire into 'a thing of beauty' was championed by Irwin and photographer Arnold Genthe, who together published a book of photographs and text in 1909. Irwin rhapsodized that in Chinatown even 'the crime was ... picturesque'. He teased his readers 'What tragedies ... what comedies, what horror stories, what melodramas!'[52]

The writings of these publicists stimulated a vast entertainment industry. It found partial expression in tourism. Slumming became a popular 'hobby'. In 1888 a family visiting Melbourne made a special excursion to that city's Chinatown, and exclaimed that it was 'a real treat to see the different grades of Chinkeys.' Visitors' guides in San Francisco extolled the showcase features of their Chinatown: 'No other city in the United States contains an exhibit of Oriental life and customs so large and complete in all details as San Francisco.'[53] The place was 'picturesque in the extreme.' Indeed, the picturesqueness lay in its extremes. Chinatown was advertised as *fantastic, odd, strange, bizarre,* and *weird.* These were the qualities which made it so impressive. The tourists' high point lay in the midnight frenzy which marked the beginning of the Chinese New Year: 'Streets crowded with jostling Chinese, sidewalks and alleys covered with peddlers' stands, bright-colored costumes and the deafening popping of countless firecrackers.'[54]

These slumland 'spectacles' enticed a stream of tourists to Chinatown 'to inhale its myriad of smells, to penetrate its dens.' Chinatown was called 'the best show in the city.' Irwin and Genthe recalled that the district 'was the first thing which the tourist asked to see, the first thing which the guides offered to show.' When a party of fashionable sightseers were arrested as they viewed a Chinatown brothel in 1900, the *Examiner* snorted that such sightseeing had 'become a part of the trade of the noisome quarter.' Tourists loved to tell stories 'of the hairbreadth' scapes from the ... deadly highbinder [gangs]; of the fearsome debaucheries of opium dens leagues under ground; of wild essays at fan tan, or the whispered awfulness of things too horrible for human speech.'[55]

More significant than tourism, however, were the showcase dramas by the theatre, illustration, literature, and the daily press, all of which catered to the general public's imaginative yearning for slumland discovery tours. A genre of cheap and sensational low-life tales had become well established in London, New York, Boston, and Philadelphia during the 1840s and 1850s. Moreover, the genre quickly became well known to readers in provincial cities, too, a familiarity which in turn made it possible for local imitators to experiment upon so familiar a theme. The chief vehicle for this transfer was Dickens. He translated poor Mr Micawber from London penury to a new start in Australia in *Hard Times.* His 1842 depiction of New York's Five Points district in *American Notes* startled Americans, and generated a host of imitators over the next half century. Five Points became entrenched in American popular culture as a spectacular showcase of seedy haunts and degraded social types. A sensational genre of 'mysteries and miseries' novels boomed after publication in 1844 of *Mysteries of Boston* and

Dragon – Chinese procession, San Francisco (from Park, 1906)

Miseries of New York. San Francisco produced its own *Mysteries and Miseries* in 1853. The mysteries style was still a potent force in popular imagination when the Sydney *Evening News* alluded to it in the early 1880s.[56]

It was indeed in the daily press that slumland story-telling reached its widest audience. The entertaining sensationalism of journalists, far more than the 'sad pictures' of earnest reformers, constructed the slum in popular imagination. Moreover, the influence of reform discourse upon public opinion and lawmakers was greatest when it overlapped with and was appropriated by the entertainments of city journalism. Hollinghead's *Ragged London* in 1861, for example, had its genesis in a series of articles for the *Morning Post*. Mearns's *Bitter Cry* was anticipated in 1883 by George Sims' graphically illustrated 'How the Poor Live' series in the *Pictorial World* and his series on 'Horrible London' in the *Daily News*. Sims's work was reprinted in city newspapers throughout the urban network: he was as well known to newspaper readers in Sydney and Birmingham as he was in London. Charles Booth's massive social survey work in London first received public recognition when the press seized upon his preliminary report in 1887 and cabled news of 'London's Suffering Millions' in headlines around the world.[57] Much of William Booth's best seller, *In Darkest England and the Way Out*, was in fact written by William Stead, editor of the *Pall Mall Gazette*. James Cuming Walters, the writer of *Scenes in Slum-Land*, was not only a prominent churchman but was assistant editor of the *Birmingham Daily Gazette*.

In Australia, bourgeois interest in slum life was stirred by Marcus Clarke's stories of city low life for the Melbourne *Argus* during the late 1860s, and by John Stanley James' tales in the *Argus* and *Sydney Morning Herald* during the 1870s. New York dailies such as the *Tribune* and *Daily Graphic* and periodicals such as *Frank Leslie's Illustrated Newspaper* and *Harper's Weekly* devoted considerable space to slumland articles. In 1872 *Frank Leslie's* began a major series of stories on 'Our Homeless Poor; Or, How the Other Half of the World Lives'. New York's Tenement House Commission of 1894 and redrafted tenement-house laws which followed it were sparked off by a series of articles in the *Press*.[58]

This showcase literature of slumland exoticism was reinforced by the frequent reissuing of newspaper tales such as Hollinghead's as books. Stanley James's articles were published as *The Vagabond Papers* in 1877. Sims's London tales were likewise amalgamated and published, as were Walters' *Scenes*. Journalists also turned directly to book writing, with an eye to mass audiences. In 1893 B.O. Flower wrote about Boston low life in *Civilization's Inferno; or Studies in the Social Cellar*. Stephen Crane's New York novel *Maggie: A Girl of the Streets* was published in the same year. Abraham Cahan's *Yekl: A Tale of the New York Ghetto* appeared in 1896, and Frank Norris' novel *McTeague: A Story of San Francisco* was published in 1899.

The stamp of newspaper sensationalism was responsible for the runaway impact of both *The Bitter Cry* and *How the Other Half Lives*. Many of Riis's chapters were simply expanded versions of earlier newspaper articles he had written. Mearns's social survey work was primitive, but few could surpass him in sensational grandstanding upon slum living. One who could, the journalist William Stead, chose instead to publicize Mearns's story in the *Pall Mall Gazette*. Stead, who had become editor of the *Gazette* in 1883, selected *The Bitter Cry* as his first 'crusade' in the 'new journalism' of entertaining city newsmaking.[59]

Notes

[1] *Daily Gazette*, 15 April 1901, p. 6, Correspondence. Ralph, 1890, pp. 107–8.

[2] *Herald*, 20 August 1875, p. 4, editorial. San Francisco Board of Supervisors, 1875, p. 31. *Chronicle*, 17 February 1885, p. 8, Chinatown slums; San Francisco Board of Supervisors, 1885, p. 5. Massachusetts State Board of Health, 1873, p. 429.

[3] Davison, G. and Dunstan, D., This moral pandemonium: images of low life, in Davison, Dunstan, McConville, 1985, p. 30. On the English derivation of 'slum', see Dyos, 1967, pp. 7–8; and Dyos, H.J., Reeder, D.A., Slums and suburbs, in Dyos, Wolff, 1973, pp. 362–3. See also Partridge, 1966. The word's application in the United States long predates the references to it in 1870 and 1884 that are noted by Warner, S.B. Jr., The management of multiple urban images, in Fraser, Sutcliffe, 1983, p. 386.

[4] Joseph Chamberlain, in Borough of Birmingham, 1875a, p. 81; see *Daily Mail*, 9 February 1875, p. 2, leader; *Daily Post*, 23 October 1901, p. 9, The municipal elections. Riis, 1892, p. 10. *Chronicle*, 3 July 1900, p. 12 , Chinatown problem should be solved, say the merchants. Photograph entitled Court of Chinese rookery, Chinatown, San Francisco, in Rieder, 1904, n.p.

[5] Cardinal Wiseman, quoted in Wohl, 1977, p. 5. *Daily Post*, 12 October 1875, p. 5, editorial; and see *Daily Gazette*, 5 October 1875, p. 4, leader, and Borough of Birmingham,1875b, p. 10. Freeman, 1888, pp. 16, 18.

[6] Dr Henry Julian Hunter, Report on the housing of the poorer parts of the populations in towns, in *BPP*, 1866, p. 102. Dolman, 1895, p. 10. Hunter, 1904, p. 265.

[7] *Daily Telegraph*, 25 February 1884, p. 5, The housing of the poor. Dobie, 1936, p. 233 (my italics).

[8] Riis, 1971, p. 13. See Mearns, 1970.

[9] *Daily Post*, 9 May 1885, p. 4, leader. *Daily Gazette*, 6 March 1901, p. 4, leader.

[10] *Daily Post*, 29 October 1903, p. 11, Municipal elections. *Herald*, 19 November 1883, p. 4, Our American letter. *Chronicle*, 1 July 1900, p. 11, Widen streets of Chinatown and purge place of its evils.

[11] Simey, 1960, p. 116. Nettlefold, 1908a, p. 13. *Herald*, 2 March 1869, p. 4, editorial. *Daily Mail*, 16 August 1875, p. 2, leader. Walters, 1901a, p. 18.

[12] San Francisco Board of Supervisors, 1885, p. 5. *Daily Post*, 9 October 1899, p. 8, The housing of the working classes: conference in Birmingham.

[13] *Daily Post*, 17 October 1906, p. 4, The municipal elections.

[14] *Herald*, 20 April 1878, p. 4, editorial. Walker is quoted in Paterson, 1981, p. 21.

[15] Hunter, 1904, p. 331. *Daily Telegraph*, 3 March 1884, p. 5, Our London letter. Nettlefold, 1908a, p. 15.

[16] Ward, 1989, p. 83. *Daily Telegraph*, 2 August 1890, p. 4, leader; and see the satirization of the 'Working Man's Paradise' in Lane, 1980. *Daily Gazette*, 6 February 1901, p. 4, editorial. Appendix, in City of Birmingham, 1903b. Devine is quoted in Paterson, 1981, p. 22.

[17] See ibid., pp. 8–9; also Gilbert, 1966. Bremner, 1956, chapters 2 and 8.

[18] Simon, 1897, pp. 435, 445. Devine, Edward T., Pittsburgh the year of the survey, in Kellogg, 1974, p. 4.

[19] Nettlefold, 1908a, p. 15. *Daily Telegraph*, 2 August 1890, p. 4, leader. *Weekly Advocate*, 19 January 1884, p. 340. *Daily Telegraph*, 10 May 1881, p. 3, editorial.

[20] *Herald*, 14 January 1884, p. 6, editorial. Joseph Chamberlain, press cuttings of speeches, 12 October 1874 and 13 January 1875, in Joseph Chamberlain Papers, JC 4/1, UBA. *Daily Post*, 8 October 1890, p. 8, The municipal elections (Councillor Arthur Dixon). Buder, 1990, pp. 157–8.

[21] Strong, 1907, p. 50. Riis, 1971, p. 1. Fried, 1990, p. 11.

[22] Charles F Wingate, quoted in Plunz, 1990, p. 36. Roosevelt is quoted in Schiesl, 1977, p. 10. The Reverend W.E. McLennan, quoted in Philpott, 1978, p. 61. Stead, 1964, p. 95. Todd and Sanborn, 1912, p. 111.

[23] *Daily Gazette*, 1 July 1901, p. 4, leader. *Lancet*, 31 July 1897, p. 284, Hospital abuse.

[24] *Weekly Advocate*, 15 December 1883, p. 300, A dark picture. *Australian Churchman*, 29 November 1883, p. 241, leader.

[25] ibid., 13 January 1881, p. 170, leader. Massachusetts State Board of Health, 1873, p. 399. The *Echo*, quoted in Mayne, 1982, p. 195. *Herald*, 22 November 1887, p. 4, Improved artisan dwellings.

[26] See Yelling, 1986, pp. 14–15; Jones, 1984, pp. 161–83; Wohl, 1977, chapter 2; and Wohl's introduction to Mearns, 1970, pp. 9–37; Olsen, 1979, pp. 301–2.

[27] *Daily Gazette*, 26 October 1883, p. 4, leader; 18 October 1882, p. 5 and 25 October 1882, p. 5, The municipal elections. *Daily Mail*, 25 February 1891, p. 2, Notes and news.

[28] *Herald*, 4 March 1875, p. 4 and 27 June 1881, p. 4, leader.

[29] *Daily Gazette*, 5 October 1875, p. 4, leader. Plunz, 1990, p. 51.

[30] Philpott, 1978, pp. 44–5.

[31] *Daily Mail*, 15 November 1883, p. 2, leader.

[32] *Argus*, 23 July 1884, p. 4, editorial. Freeman, 1888, p. 14. *Daily Telegraph*, 27 February 1886, p. 6, Poverty in Sydney.

[33] Chamberlain, 1883, p. 762. Mayne, 1982, pp. 131–2. Wohl, 1977, p. 229.

[34] *Daily Post*, 30 October 1907, p. 5, The municipal elections.

[35] *Daily Gazette*, 12 December 1883, p. 4, editorial.

[36] Nettlefold, 1908a, p. 15. James, 1983, p. 96. Mayne, 1982, p. 127. Paterson, 1981, p. 23.

[37] Ward, 1989, p. 43.

[38] Scobey, 1989, p. 275.

[39] Hill, 1869, p. 219; 1891, pp. 163–4. The Reverend T. Pipe, in appendices to City of Birmingham, 1903b, p. 15. The Reverend Mr Bryant, in *Herald*, 1 October 1883, p. 11, Sydney Ragged Schools.

[40] Barnett, A.S., Settlements of university men in great towns, in Pimlott, 1935, p. 266. Sir John Gorst, 'Settlements' in England and America, in Knapp, 1895, pp. 10, 17, 21. Barnett in ibid., p. 66. Stead, 1964, pp. 400–1.

[41] Kelly, 1978, pp. 66–80; Mayne, 1982. Jevons' Remarks upon the social map of Sydney, 1858, is held in the Mitchell Library, Sydney.

[42] *Daily Gazette*, 12 December 1883, p. 4, editorial. Chamberlain, 1883, p. 761. Simey, 1960, p. 95.

[43] Quoted in Philpott, 1978, p. 29.

[44] Buder, 1990, p. 72. The emerging urban planning movement in Sydney is discussed in Roberts, 1979; and Gibbons, R., Improving Sydney 1908–1909, in Roe, 1980, pp. 120–33.

45 Philpott, 1978, p. 90.
46 See Briggs, 1952, chapter 8; also Rex, Moore, 1967; Lambert, 1970; Newton, 1976; Dunleavy, 1981, pp. 255–302.
47 See Jones, 1972; Kendig, 1979. Spearritt, 1974, pp. 65–81. Spearritt, 1978, pp. 11–15. For Melbourne see Howe, 1988, chapters 1–2.
48 Greer, 1965, p. 32; and see Scott, 1969, chapters 4–6; Wright, 1981, chapter 12; Abrams, 1965.
49 Raymond, 1886, p. 3. Walters, 1901a, pp. 24, 25.
50 *Examiner*, 16 February 1885, p. 2, The Chinese New Year.
51 Bremner, 1956, p. 99. Still, 1956, p. 267. Davison, Dunstan, McConville, 1985, p. 54.
52 Irwin, 1906, pp. 45–6. Dobie, 1936, pp. 234, 235. Genthe, Irwin, 1909, p. 48.
53 *Daily Telegraph*, 25 February 1884, p. 5, The housing of the poor. Davison, Dunstan, McConville, 1985, p. 1. Robertson, 1895, p. 40.
54 Bancroft Company, 1893, p. 5. Lloyd, 1876, p. 223; *Chronicle*, 23 January 1903, p. 9, Chinese observe ancient custom; Banks, Read, 1906, p. 161. San Francisco Passenger Department, 1901, p. 93. *Examiner*, 16 February 1901, p. 5, Flowers and noise tell of the New Year.
55 Banks, Read, 1906, p. 162. Steele, 1909, p. 96. Genthe, Irwin, 1909, p. 1. *Examiner*, 22 March 1900, p. 7, To stop vulgar shows in Chinatown.
56 Stout, 1976, pp. 37–45. *Evening News*, 17 May 1881, p. 2, Another sanitary crusade. See Himmelfarb, 1984, pp. 435–52.
57 Simey, 1960, p.92.
58 Hergenhan, 1972, pp.100–73; James, 1983; Davison, Dunstan, McConville, 1985, pp.37–41. Bremner, 1956, p.68; Duffy, 1974, p.227. Lubove, 1962, p.89.
59 Gilbert, 1966, pp. 29–30.

7

Threshold

'You cannot imagine the conditions. I cannot write them. It would take Charles Dickens to do it.' So wrote the harassed federal official in charge of plague eradication measures in San Francisco's Chinatown during 1901. In New York, too, Riis's slumland depictions echoed Dickens. Slums were, after all, fictions. They were fashioned as showcases of the imagination. In 1882 the *Birmingham Daily Mail*, striving to encapsulate in text the character of the city's improvement area, characterized it as comprising the 'vilest rookeries" which the imagination can well conceive.'[1]

Slumland representations were cultural performances which explored and sought to resolve bourgeois concerns about the indeterminacies of urban scale and the resulting contentiousness of urban policy-making. Newspaper slumland serials such as Birmingham's *Scenes in Slum-Land*, San Francisco's exposés of gang warfare, illegal gambling, and prostitution in Chinatown, and Sydney's press coverage of the municipal crackdown on houses unfit for human habitation, all clearly sought to influence the direction of local government policy-making and administration. However the popularity of such story-telling lay more in the entertaining zestfulness of slumland sensationalism. The slumland showcase amused and titillated, and in so doing it educated. Chinatown's 'squalid picturesqueness and moral filth' were described in 1901 as making the district 'a source of much amusement *and instruction*'.[2]

The apparently encroaching borders of slumland were uniformly represented as a moral threshold between decency and degeneracy. The prevailing mood was well expressed by a Liberal politician in Birmingham's municipal elections of 1908: 'Slums ... were a disgrace, and were physically, mentally, and morally degrading to many of those who lived in them.' By construing an imagined schism — what *Scenes in Slum-Land* labelled an 'abyss of unknown depth which baffles human sight and imagination' — between slum and modern city, between slum denizen and citizen, these sensational newspaper performances served to condense and display a core of agreeable principles about the ethics and priorities appropriate to decent everyday city living and responsible decision-making.[3]

The schism drawn between city heartlands and bad-lands consolidated bourgeois common-sense opinion. To contemplate anything else would be to capitulate to slumland's insidious advance, with the inevitable corollary 'that the moral will become immoral, the pure-minded vicious, and the worthy citizen a genuine slumite.' Because this scenario was as credible to audiences in the fantasy of theatrical performance as it was unthinkable to them in their own lives, the slumland genre affirmed the strengths of the modern city and of the belief systems which underpinned it. In 1889 Cassell's *Picturesque Australasia* concluded its depiction of Melbourne's Chinatown by emphasizing that the district was indeed 'a world apart from the City of Melbourne'.[4]

By charting the moral borders of the imagined slum, representations of the abominations supposedly given free reign beyond the slumland threshold framed and extended the broad moral commonwealth of bourgeois community. As the *Birmingham Daily Gazette* remarked in 1883, the 'harrowing pictures of penury and disease, immorality and crime, which are so frequently placed before society, are used ... to "point a moral".' That moral message had been to the fore in the conclusions drawn by Sydney's first comprehensive official investigation of working-class living conditions, over 30 years earlier. The parliamentary committee, after having sensationally depicted the depth of slumland depravity, concluded that 'there is another side to the picture; the region of depravity and moral death is limited ... These dark features do not belong to the character of the laboring masses of society ... , [who have] a high character for honesty, intelligence, and sobriety.' A similar moral purpose is evident in the United States, where Riis's popularity lay not so much in originality of observation as in the moral intensity and sensational delivery of his presentation. Riis's characterizations of New York's slums 'took on the dimensions of a universal morality play', in which complicated social and economic questions were recast as essentially ethical ones to which answers could readily be given from a pool of core values. He constructed slums 'as the symbols and gauge of society', set against which common-sense agreement could readily be made concerning 'those virtues that made for unity (thrift, temperance, language, theology), and those that subverted the city by breaching all these values.' [5]

All slumland usage — the supposedly objective social surveys and serious reform discourse as well as the genre of popular entertainment — operated within this 'unshakeable moral framework'. It is evident in part in the moral environmentalism of urban reformers, whose policy agendas presupposed 'the close alliance which exists between physical want and misery and moral degradation.' Charity, improvement projects, and housing schemes were therefore advertised by them as the best means of integrating slum denizens as 'cleanly, provident, and industrious' participants in the shared moral order of a united society. The *Sydney Morning Herald* argued in 1876 that housing improvement 'will do more to make a people orderly and well-behaved than the largest corps of the best disciplined police.' In 1884, responding to the reform agitation that had been generated by *The Bitter Cry*, the newspaper predicted that 'Vice and misery, like vermin, haunt all places of squalor, filth, and decay. They cannot breathe the air of respectability and health. Improve the conditions, and you must improve the people.'[6]

This moral purpose also characterized the photographers who first turned their cameras on the urban working classes. Their images were carefully composed so as to complement the genre of slumland exposé and substantiate the reformers' message of moral environmentalism. This purpose is evident in the pioneering Sydney photographs and social surveying undertaken in the late 1850s by William Stanley Jevons, then an assayist at the Sydney mint. It is evident, too, in Thomas Annan's stark photographs of Glasgow tenements during the 1860s and 1870s, which were widely circulated as 'depicting, with absolute faithfulness, the gloom and squalor of the slums.' By the early twentieth century, Labour politicians in Birmingham regularly used photographs in public lectures as they hammered home their moralistic interpretation of the city's 'slum problem'. Slum photography in the United States was pioneered by Riis. In 1888 he presented a lecture entitled '"The Other Half" — How It Lives and Dies in New York', which he illustrated with 100 slides. The city press called the images 'object lessons in squalor, vice and unclean and degraded humanity'. Although Riis abandoned photography early in the twentieth century, another reformer, Lewis W. Hine, began developing a potent new style of 'photographic social work' with which to complement the reform agendas of the influential philanthropic magazine, *Charities and the Commons*, the National Child Labor Committee, and the Pittsburgh Survey.[7]

Bourgeois moralism is also evident in the indignation that was expressed by a small band of social novelists. The English writer George Gissing characterized slums as the sick centre of the modern city in his novels *Workers in the Dawn* (1880), *The Unclassed* (1884), *The Nether World* (1889), and *New Grub Street* (1891).[8] A similar moral passion characterized Israel Zangwill's *Children of the Ghetto* (1892), and Arthur Morrison's *Tales of Mean Streets* (1894), and *A Child of the Jago* (1896). A comparable moralism is also evident in the United States in Stephen Crane's 1893 novel *Maggie*, Theodore Dreiser's *Sister Carrie* (1901), and Upton Sinclair's *The Jungle* (1906). It also permeated the late nineteenth-century American genre of utopian novels, the best known of which — Edward Bellamy's *Looking Backward* — influenced popular imagination throughout the English-speaking world.

Sensational depictions of the moral threshold between slums and cities were most evident in the interplay between illustration, theatre, and fiction which characterized urban popular culture. In Britain the eighteenth-century painter and engraver, William Hogarth, mightily influenced nineteenth-century opinion with his serials *A Harlot's Progress*, *A Rake's Progress*, *Industry and Idleness*, *Gin Lane*, and *Beer Street*. Hogarth's moral messages were reinforced by the nineteenth-century artist, caricaturist, and engraver, George Cruikshank, in productions such as *Life in London*, *The Bottle* and *The Drunkard's Children*. British melodrama was by the late 1860s translating Hogarth's and Cruikshank's images of London low life on to the stage with spectacular effect. During the early 1880s

George Sims, too, successfully represented London's East End to mass markets through the multiple planes of melodrama, illustration, and serialized fiction. Cruikshank's influence, like Sims's, was also felt in fiction as well as illustration and drama. He illustrated Dickens' *Oliver Twist* and other popular works of fiction. In 1872 Gustave Doré's illustrations of city low life in Blanchard Gerrold's *London: A Pilgrimage* became a catalyst for slumland illustrators on both sides of the Atlantic. Doré's bleak imagery also considerably influenced textual representation. Innovations in text in turn influenced illustration. Publication of *The Bitter Cry* prompted *Punch* and the *Illustrated London News* to take up the slumland theme with cartoons such as 'Mammon's Rents' and 'A Sigh from the Slums', which then circulated throughout the urban network.[9]

In the United States, engravers had selected Five Points as the threshold symbol of city bad-lands since the 1820s. During the second half of the century, *Harper's Weekly* popularized slum illustration, and in so doing included many illustrations of Chinese scenes and opium dens. The comic strip 'Hogan's Alley', begun in 1894, further capitalized upon popular interest in New York slum life. American theatre, too, influenced by British precedents, had presented melodramas on the seamy side of city life since the 1820s. During the late 1870s and 1880s Edward Harrigan produced a long series of popular New York slum comedies. Harrigan in turn influenced American popular fiction, just as the melodramatic plots of successful slumland novels had long been adapted to the stage. Popular low-life novels, many of them overlaid with temperance messages, had multiplied from the mid-nineteenth century. Imitating illustration and the theatre, they fashioned urban forms into a moral topography of city heartlands and bad-lands with which to teach bourgeois moral codes for big-city living. The 1853 thriller, *The Mysteries and Miseries of San Francisco*, especially captivated readers because of the 'absence of moral restraints' which seemed to characterize frontier towns.[10]

Borderlands

Representation of the slumland threshold found its widest application in the city press. Daily newspapers in Birmingham, San Francisco, and Sydney — all vying with competitors for circulation — consistently exploited slumland sensationalism in their local news columns, telegraphic news, editorials, special features, and weekend magazine supplements. By the 1890s and early 1900s, illustration and photography emerged — in San Francisco especially — as major devices for slumland sensationalism. The newspaper styles of these three cities typified news reporting throughout the urban network. Newspapers copied, interpreted, and improvised from the entire field of slumland representation. Moreover, crucially, they communicated the slumland performance to mass audiences in informal settings which no other medium of cultural performance could fully match.

The relationship of newspaper reporting to the wider genre of slumland performance is explicit. Newspapers strove to imitate the spontaneity and intimacy between artist and audience which characterized popular theatre and vaudeville. Their presentations are billed as providing 'entertainment', 'spectacle', and 'thrilling' scenes.[11] They were designed to engage and hold an audience among casual readers who were attuned to easy amusement, and who might turn the page on sober commentary. The entertainment appeal anchored the newspaper performances within their readers' everyday frameworks of comprehension and relevance. Significantly, the melodramatic story-lines, sentimental and comic interludes, and contrasts of rectitude and debasement also fashioned threshold sensationalism into a make-believe medium which could translate precise social description into all-embracing moral diatribes without unduly straining readers' credulity.

This performance was sustained in part by incorporating easily recognizable fragments drawn from popular drama, narrative, and illustration. Shakespeare was universally raided for familiar phrases. In Birmingham, *Scenes in Slum-Land* was described as 'graphic pen-pictures' by one reviewer, and in Sydney, newspaper representation of slum exploration was bracketed with references to the 'pencil of Gustave Doré' and the 'repulsive characters ... depicted by Hogarth or Cruikshank.'[12] The San Francisco *Examiner* and *Chronicle* vied with one another in applying photography and illustration to sensationalize stories of violence and vice in Chinatown. Popular fiction was also a ready source with which to prompt the imagination of abominations lying beyond the threshold of civilized living. Dickens was a model everywhere. Walters, for example, was described as 'an ardent Dickensian'. The 'horrors' of San Francisco's Chinatown were claimed by the *Examiner* in 1901 to be 'infinitely worse than those described by Harriet Beecher Stowe in the thrilling pages of "Uncle Tom's Cabin".' The *Chronicle* quoted from the novelist Frank Norris in 1903 as it conjured Chinatown's 'human vermin that even the guides do not see.' In 1906 the *Chicago Tribune* asserted that the district's inhabitants revelled in 'bacchanalian orgies like the infamous intimates of Javert in "Les Miserables".'[13]

References to French low-life sensationalism peppered English-language slumland representation. The recurring expression 'how the other half lives' — as current in Britain and the Australian colonies as in the United States — was borrowed from François Rabelais. One Sydney journalist in 1881 equated his own slumland story-telling to that of the French novelist Eugène Sue, translations of whose *Les Mystères de Paris* (1842–3) were still immensely popular. In San Francisco, too, it was said of Chinatown's underground labyrinth that 'Eugene Sue, himself, never conceived anything more loathsome.' More influential still were the late-nineteenth century novels of Émile Zola. The *Pall Mall Gazette* derided the newspaper sensationalism which followed *The Bitter Cry* as being the outcome of 'scores of would-be Zolas'. Walters' *Scenes in Slum-Land* asserted that the 'pen of Zola could scarcely do justice to the filthy horrors of this slum.'[14]

Newspaper performances were sustained to an even more important degree by revolving the drama of their unfolding story-lines around the threshold between everyday experience and its surmised slumland antithesis. Newspaper sensationalism thereby became a vehicle for their readers' imaginations with which to visualize slumland boundaries and thereby penetrate to the liminal zone beyond. The texts abound with contrived scenes which set up pairs of starkly contrasting metaphors: one immediately familiar to readers for its equation with their own everyday city lives, the other a negation of the first. Like a psychic magic lantern, the texts throw up polarized images of normalcy and otherness with which to visualize the threshold to the slum.

Architectural contrasts are among the most obvious. The slumland threshold is constructed by juxtaposing familiar and prized landmarks with their hitherto unimagined and horrible opposites. In San Francisco, for example, the *Examiner* in 1900 dramatized the incongruity of finding the city's new Hall of Justice located 'almost within the borders of Chinatown'. The device was familiar to provincial readers from its long use in the metropolitan cores. In New York writers had regularly contrasted Five Points with the glitter of Broadway. In San Francisco, juxtaposition of the Chinese slum at the foot of Nob Hill and 'the residence section of San Francisco's millionaires and leading financiers and business men' at its top was a well-established representational convention. It had been peddled successfully in 1876 by Benjamin Lloyd, in *Lights and Shades in San Francisco*. The implied contrast — of morals as well as of wealth — had been stated bluntly by the Workingmen's Party of California in 1880. In their tract, *Chinatown Declared A Nuisance!*, the party announced sensationally that even behind the city's cathedral there lurked a slumland abyss of 'terrible filth, stink and slime'. Sydney newspapers exploited the same technique to the full in their coverage of municipal inspection tours during the 1880s: the hidden slum just behind a prestigious social club, another close to the town residence of the Lieutenant-Governor, a seedy alleyway at the rear of ornamental banks and insurance offices. In 1880 a reporter for the *Evening News*, describing how one inspection party had suddenly found itself overlooking Darling Harbour as it condemned insanitary houses in the Kent Street district, exclaimed that the 'view of the steamships and sailing vessels at anchor, and of the numerous small craft plying about was splendid, but a terrific contrast was presented by the sight immediately around.'[15]

The effect of such threshold dramas was to give undercurrents of ambiguity even to familiar places. Reality dissolves in proportion as the threshold is visualized. As the *Sydney Daily Telegraph* remarked in 1889, 'it would surprise many to see some of the rookeries which are to be found in many of our leading and most fashionable thoroughfares side by side with mansions and large places of business.' In Birmingham, Walters assured his readers that they 'would be amazed to learn that almost within a stone's throw' of 'the centre of the city, with its spacious streets and imposing buildings', there existed back slums — 'secret and hidden' — in which 'signs of wretchedness, poverty, and despondency are visible everywhere.'[16] These rhetorical flourishes had a long currency. The Birmingham improvement scheme had been introduced to the Council in 1875 with the comment that the slumland abyss could be 'scarcely ... believed'. A reporter for the

Daily Mail thereupon traced the proposed route of Corporation Street and confirmed that it 'lay among scenes which I had never dreamed Birmingham contained.'[17]

Newspaper writers also conjured the slumland threshold by ironic twists of language. These serve to invert common-sense usage when applying labels which contradict what is being described. The device was popular among Sydney journalists: 'a lady' for a slumland slut, 'the parlour' within a cramped hovel, 'the "bed"' for a stretcher in a common lodging house, a 'delightful neighbourhood' for rookery, 'fashionable thoroughfare' for mean-street, and 'desirable city properties', 'palatial residences', 'private family villa residences', and 'so-called houses' for broken-down tenements.[18] In Birmingham, Walters exploited the topsy-turvy effect of this technique to its furthest limits. 'Names,' he said, 'seem to go by contraries in Slum-Land.' He interrupts one passage to exclaim that 'squalid children ... are "playing" — a term to make the cynic sneer — in the well-filled gutters.' On another occasion he halts a description of slumland living quarters to query, 'Houses? — well, they are occupied by human beings, and we suppose that name must be retained. Perhaps "warrens" would be a better word.' The ultimate contradiction, Walters asserted, was the presence of slums at all in 'what some king of humorists has called "the best-governed city in the world"'. The recurring implication of this turning of common-sense meaning upon its head was that slumland idiom amounted to a foreign language. Its 'euphemistic terms', said Walters, had constantly to be 'translated into plain English.' The use by Sydney journalists of slang terms for the neighbourhoods they describe — spots 'known as the "Puzzle"', for example, and 'Harrington-lane, better known to the habitues as the Suez Canal' — likewise implies foreign territories and idioms.[19]

Suggestions of foreign idioms powerfully consolidated the slumland threshold as though it stood as a physical border between two discrete and polarized lands. This connection was assisted in part by drawing upon easily recognizable references to Heaven and Hell. Sydney journalists often incorporated phrases from the Bible in their descriptions of slum investigations. San Francisco's Chinatown is styled 'the precincts of Satan', and Walters calls Birmingham's slums 'an inferno'. His disclosures revealed that 'we have hells of infamy and misery and disease in our midst', announced the *Birmingham Daily Gazette*. Passing the threshold to the slum thus transported visitors from 'the surface' to a 'submerged' underworld of unknown, unimaginable, unguessed-at depths.[20] Writers even more frequently represented city and slum as radically different and antagonistic nation states. It was commonly suggested that to pass beyond the borders of the city heartland was to enter a separate 'slum-*region*'. Birmingham's improvement scheme was commended by the *Daily Post* in 1882 for eliminating '*regions* which were the habitual seats of ... the dangerous classes.'[21] The suggestion of territorial difference was heightened by frequent reference to slums as *purlieus*: borderlands or outlying regions. Walters even implied, with his terms 'Slum-Land' and 'Slumdom', that to cross the slum's threshold was actually to enter a separate kingdom.[22]

The characterization of slums as separate lands had a long currency in slum representation. In 1845 Benjamin Disraeli in his novel *Sybil* had popularized the idea of 'Two nations; between whom there is no intercourse and no sympathy; who are as ignorant of each other's habits, thoughts, and feelings, as if they were dwellers in different zones, or inhabitants of different planets.' In the United States the prominent Unitarian missionary William Ellery Channing had simultaneously applied the same metaphor in Boston. These characterizations echoed the language of European exploration and imperialism. In 1842 James Grant asserted in *Lights and Shadows of London Life* that Londoners 'are as ignorant of the destitution and distress which prevail in large districts of London ... as if the wretched creatures were living in the very centre of Africa.' Bethnal Green was described two years later as being as little known as the 'wilds of Australia or the islands of the South Seas'. Henry Mayhew further popularized the concept in *London Labour and the London Poor*. Mayhew argued that less was known about the city's poor than about 'the most distant tribes of the earth'. In 1894 William Stead asserted that the slums of Chicago were almost as unknown to the well-to-do 'as the territory of Timbuctoo'.[23]

The topsy-turvy effect of these analogies was strengthened because popular culture had long likened slums not just to distant, but to primitive and debased, lands. In 1900 the *San Francisco Chronicle* referred to Chinatown's highbinder gangs as 'head hunters'. British illustration and fiction had conventionally represented the urban poor as repulsive savages since the early nineteenth century. Mayhew depicted the London poor as tribes from 'savage nations'.[24] Joseph Chamberlain knew he would trigger a responsive chord when he suggested in 1874 that 'we have in our midst a vast population more ignorant than the barbarians whom we affect to despise, more brutal than the savages whom we profess to convert, more miserable than the most wretched in other countries to whom we attempt from time to time to carry succour and relief.' Liberal Unionist and Conservative voters were told in 1901 that thousands of slum-dwellers were living a stone's throw from the Council Chamber in conditions that would 'disgrace the Hottentots of South Africa'. The *Birmingham Magnet* announced that 'we would very much rather make our abode with a Solomon Islander, a Hottentot, or any other heathen than dwell in any of the slums of Birmingham.' It was axiomatic that slumland savages were wilfully defiant of common-sense norms. Stead called them 'the stunted squalid savages of civilization', and General Booth questioned whether, just as 'there is a darkest Africa, is there not also a darkest England? Civilisation, which can breed its own barbarians, does it not also breed its own pygmies?'[25]

The most alarming feature of such pictures was that the geographical as well as the moral distance which separated European civilization from 'savagery' was not replicated in the threshold between slumland and modern city. Here, decent people and brutes practically rubbed shoulders. Theatrical preoccupation with close-set borders is especially evident in San Francisco, where Chinatown was conventionally represented as 'an Oriental city within an American city', in which 'the Chinese live much as they do in China'. Its 'bizarre effects' were said to mock 'every tenet of decency, order and Christianity'.[26] The City Board of Health declared in 1880 that the San Francisco Chinese, 'with laws, customs, courts and institutions of their own, [were] utterly at variance with and dangerous to the health, morals and prosperity of our city.' The Chinese were repeatedly styled 'a law unto themselves', contemptuous of American sanitary and criminal codes, and resorting instead to secret tribunals which levied taxes, imposed punishments, and even enforced death sentences 'in utter defiance of the laws of the State.'[27] Tourist guidebooks and newspaper stories promised that to enter the borders of Chinatown was to enter 'another world' and be 'enveloped in a sort of mystery': surrounded by slumland denizens 'jabbering their unintelligible dialects', seeing shops full of 'strange jewellery' that had been fashioned by 'queer tools', produce markets displaying preserved foods in 'fantastic forms', and peculiar restaurants 'decorated with gaudy ornaments'. The frontages of once-European buildings, refurbished, now presented 'a riot of color'. The joss houses, especially, were renowned for their 'garish and inharmonious mingling of color', and inside, amid 'bizarre surroundings', visitors could see where 'grotesquely hideous heathen gods are worshipped'. Topsy-turvy reversals are intensified in the Chinese theatres 'where the female roles are taken by men, and where the gongs and cymbals, horns, tom-toms and squeaky fiddles keep up a wild revel of sound.'[28]

Slumland thresholds were commonly dramatized by metaphors drawn from descriptions of frontier expansion and border conflict. The 1885 Chinatown investigation committee of the San Francisco Board of Supervisors was preoccupied with the necessity of policing the 'boundaries' of Chinatown, and applauded the nightly stationing of police 'at each end of the alleys leading slumward in Chinatown' to frisk passers-by for weapons. Chinatown's outermost boundaries were characterized by a succession of writers as having been 'captured' by the 'Mongolian advance guard', and the buildings 'occupied' by the Chinese as they battled 'to get a foothold' in the surrounding areas. In 1900 the *Examiner* noted that the moment the plague quarantine cordon around Chinatown was removed, the Chinese 'began to swarm in and out'.[29] This sense of foreign intrusion was strengthened by styling Chinatown a 'colony'. The term was widely used in American cities to characterize poor immigrant districts. In 1904 Robert Hunter argued that the slum problem was perpetuated by the 'millions of foreigners [who] have established colonies in the very hearts of our urban and industrial communities.' Sydney's Chinatown had also long been characterized a 'Mongolian colony'. Moreover, in Sydney the term 'colony' was applied not only to Chinese neighbourhoods but to slum neighbourhoods in general. In 1877 Birmingham's slums, too, were referred to as 'these colonies of disorder and sin'.[30]

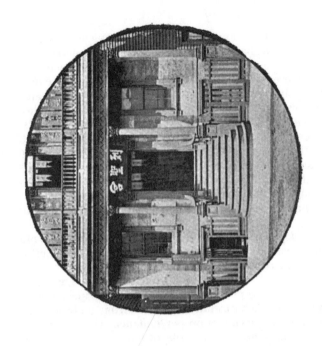

Joss House in Chinatown, San Francisco (from Park, 1906)

Alley in Chinatown, San Francisco (from Park, 1906)

The Crossing

The common effect of threshold representations was to suggest that slums were so grotesque and alien that their existence had been tolerated only because their presence was hidden and their borders shunned. As a corollary, although the threshold between city and slum was always close to hand, it was not easy to find and still less so to penetrate. The performances insist that special resolve and courage are needed to cross the threshold. The story-lines are contrived to include readers as imaginary participants in the crossing. This act of crossing was structured into a universal set of rites of passage between the readers' everyday and fantasy worlds. Challenges and obstacles are thrown in the path of the readers' imaginary progress. They function to heighten anticipation of the moral affronts surely to come, and to signal a change in gears from forms of reasoning grounded in verifiable facts to that constrained by nothing more than imaginative possibility.

Scenes in Slum-Land hesitates before venturing to 'look into the depths' and — poised on the threshold — cautions that at 'this point we respectfully but earnestly ask our lady-readers to read no further unless they are quite prepared for pain and shock.' Even with the requisite courage, special guidance is needed in order to proceed. In Sydney, newspaper narrators emphasize that slumland 'is often carefully concealed from public gaze, and is only unearthed by special visits under proper guidance.' Their stories cast the municipal sanitary inspectors in the role of guides who act as key-keepers to slumland thresholds. In San Francisco, Chinatown tourists normally hired guides because it had long been emphasized that 'none but the Chinese themselves, and a few of the police officers can thread their way with certainty' through the borders of the slum. Sometimes Chinatown tours were advertised in terms of navigation through dangerous shoals: in 1895 the guides were advertised as serving 'to pilot strangers'.[31]

The most powerful metaphor, however, by which newspaper story-tellers — and other slummer writers — accomplished the imaginative leap necessary for readers to visualize the slum and cross its threshold was borrowed from the language of travel and exploration. Mayhew had pioneered the style, characterizing himself a 'traveller in the undiscovered country of the poor'. *Scenes in Slum-Land* is presented as a series of gruelling hikes through rough country: 'We have tramped over the whole area of Slumdom,' declares Walters. The *San Francisco Chronicle* in 1869 equated walks through Chinatown's back alleys to the explorations by 'the compilers of the early maps of California'. Walter Raymond's 1886 fantasy story about San Francisco's Chinatown, *Horrors of the Mongolian Settle-ment*, was presented as a discovery tour through 'devious ways', replete with compass and chart, by a police detective, a retired municipal officer, an artist, and a journalist.[32] Representation of slumland as a hidden world and of visitors as bands of explorers among foreign tribes in unmapped territories, watched over by a narrator who imaginatively guides readers in the explorers' steps, and whose common-sense judgements renders slum-land comprehensible to them, had become a universal form by the last quarter of the century. In Sydney slumland is 'discovered' by 'municipal expeditions' which set forth to 'explore' the 'wilds'. *Scenes in Slum-Land* likewise revolves around the key word, 'discovery'. A quarter of a century earlier, Chamberlain had similarly characterized his first inspection of Birmingham's improvement area as 'a veritable tour of discovery amid the "slums" of Birmingham'.[33]

This sense of discovery is strengthened by analogies of foreign evangelization and conquest. Walters spoke to Birmingham church-goers about the need for missionaries to dwell amongst the 'den dwellers in St Marys and St Bartholomews [wards] as much as in mid Africa'. In Sydney and San Francisco, the depictions draw from folk lore of frontier law enforcement. Sydney's municipal inspection parties are called *patrols*. In San Francisco Sala's 1885 tour of Chinatown was described by the *Examiner* as having been led by a police sergeant of 'the Chinatown posse'. The police stationed in Chinatown were routinely labelled 'the Chinatown squad' by the city press, which applauded their 'unrelenting war against the gambling and opium dens and other abodes of vice', and described how their incursions into Chinatown sought to dodge, Custer-like, the 'lookouts' and 'spotters' whom the gambling racketeers had put on their heels.[34]

Rites of passage into the slum are played out in terms of overcoming challenges and obstacles to the explorers' free movement. The people of the slum close in threateningly: in Sydney, 'forbidding-looking men and women with folded arms, too often nursing their wrath to keep it warm, or giving full vent to it, stand at open doors.' *Scenes in Slum-Land* unfold against a background sense of borrowed time: at each street corner stands a menacing group of 'peakies', and on one occasion 'Three hard-headed youths in peaky binder costume eventually decide to take matters seriously in hand. "Who might you be a-wantin'?" is the query, and it is time to make excuses and walk away.' Walters' encounters with peakies in Birmingham are paralleled in Sydney by reference to larrikins, and to hoodlums and Chinese highbinder gangs in San Francisco. The potential for violence is routinely exploited in *Scenes in Slum-Land*. Here, the police 'are almost always to be found in couples. Where a constable is regarded as a natural enemy, and his mere presence an affront to the mob, too much care cannot be taken. Ere now a lonely policeman has been half-murdered or maimed for life in this quarter of Birmingham.' Small surprise to readers, then, that 'more than once, in the course of our journey, we were surrounded by a threatening crowd, shrieked at by women, menaced by men. In one case, we confess, the situation was such as to compel a hasty and undignified retreat.'[35]

This undercurrent of violence is recast as open warfare by the San Francisco press. In June 1900 — simultaneously as it carried headline news of Boxer 'Mobs Rioting in Peking Clamoring for the Blood of the White Men' — the *Examiner* carried sensational stories of Chinese rioting in San Francisco against the plague eradication measures. Mobs were represented as rampaging through Chinatown, surrounding a Board of Health doctor and lunging at him with knives, yelling 'Kill him!' Police wielding clubs intervene, their brave sergeant yelling 'Go at 'em with your clubs, boys', and after much 'hard fighting' the mob is scattered. In 1901 the *Chronicle* described how crowds of 'howling Celestials' attempted to block Federal officers in their 'raids on the slave dens' of Chinese brothel owners, until city police sent them scattering.[36]

These raids were frequently likened to siege operations against enemy fortresses. In 1885 the Board of Supervisors' special Chinese investigation committee had railed against the '"iron-clad," barricaded gambling dens ... which are veritable citadels and strongholds built to defy assault and to baffle police interference.' Their report listed 150 such places, 'the approach to which is through a series of plank and iron doors, in every instance with grated windows, cunningly devised trap-doors for escapes, and in many instances iron-clad walls or partitions.' Before the earthquake and fire the city press regularly carried sensational stories and illustrations of federal marshals and city police battering down 'fortified' doors with axes. In 1903 the *Chronicle* described graphically with photographs and text how 'Shortly before 11 o'clock yesterday morning, after a night of careful siege, the police charged the secret lair of the murderous fighting men of the Hop Sing tong, at 709 Dupont Street, and by means of axes, with which they chopped their way past bolted doors and through a wall, gained entrance to the den which served to shelter the most vicious gang of yellow thugs that has ever terrorized the Chinese quarter.'[37]

The most consistently applied rites of passage to the slum are conjured not so much by the resistance of slum-dwellers as by the physical contrasts and difficulties of passing through the threshold itself. One popular device was the sudden introduction of jarring twists and turns in the route being followed by the explorers: 'turning sharply to the right', for example, or the 'party turned suddenly off the main line of traffic'. *Scenes in Slum-Land* is typical of the style: 'on reaching the top of the narrow Court, you are amazed to find that at right angles to it is a mere gullet leading to another row of houses, practically hidden from sight.' Hazardous stairways, collapsing floorboards and low doorways symbolically test the resolve of the would-be intruders. In Sydney, narrow and boggy alleyways intimidate, and simultaneously beckon the explorers on: 'we pass through the passage, and find ourselves ... '[38]

Walters exploits the metaphor of the maze: the 'labyrinth'. The tales focus on the difficulties of probing a 'tortuous course' through long, narrow 'subterranean' passages into hidden courts of back-to-backs. Readers imaginatively follow the narrator's steps, encouraged by the second- and first-person plural delivery of the text: crouching with him to get through low passageways, and venturing further, 'swallowed up in the darkness' of the threshold. Climbing a narrow and winding staircase, 'You stumble along as best you can, your feet upon the broken and rotting wood, your hands against the black and crumbling wall, your head in danger of striking against ... projecting woodwork'.[39]

The metaphor of the labyrinth also recurs extensively in San Francisco, where it became a cliché to characterize Chinatown in terms of its 'labyrinths of maze-like passages'. The *Examiner* described in 1900 how the 'highbinder tongs have turned almost the whole of Chinatown into a gigantic Chinese puzzle of trap doors, mysterious electric wires, trick stairs that fall to pieces when certain steps are pressed upon, and floors that are made of paper, painted to look like boards, with nothing underneath but a twenty-foot drop.' With every passing year, 'the puzzle grows, and its labyrinths twist and become more complex.' Predictably, the most popular rite of passage into the Chinese slum consists of descriptions of traversing 'the underworld' of Chinatown's reputed maze of hidden trap doors, sliding panels, and underground passages, all leading to 'a buried city'. This, literally, was a 'descent into ... unknown depths'. Will Irwin echoed the drama of Dante's Inferno to characterize these underground routes as 'passageways of the Third Circle'.[40]

By participating in these threshold performances, readers clambered Alice-like through the keyhole and into the topsy-turvy world of the slum. They find themselves arrived in a strange and repugnant liminal zone, 'a sort of moral antipodes' in which bourgeois normalcy has been turned upside down: 'Here we are in the very depths. Poverty unredeemed is found everywhere. Humanity is in its lowest and most corrupt and degraded state. Filth abounds. Morality is at its worst. A hundred streams of pollution seem to pour their poison into that pit of crime and slime.'[41] The topsy-turvy underworld beyond the slumland threshold is performed on two interacting planes: slum-*land* and slum-*people*. In the next chapter we will explore the representation of urban forms into stylized slumland sets. In the following chapter we will examine the recurring character sketches of generic slumland types, whose exchanges serve to highlight the represented strengths of bourgeois morality and of its creation, the market-place city.

Notes

1 White to Wyman, 18 April 1901, Public Health Service, box 550, NA. *Daily Mail*, 24 May 1882, p. 2, leader.

2 San Francisco Passenger Department, 1901, p. 95 (my italics).

3 *Daily Post*, 14 October 1908, p. 11, Birmingham municipal elections. Walters, 1901b, p. 24.

4 ibid., p. 10. Davison, Dunstan, and McConville,1985, p. 1.

5 *Daily Gazette*, 22 November 1883, p. 4, leader. *V&P(NSW LA)*, 1859–60, p. 1272. Lane, 1974, p. 32. Fried, 1990, pp. 50–1.

6 Davis, G., Beyond the Georgian façade: the Avon street district of Bath, in Gaskell, 1990, p. 144; and see Himmelfarb, 1984, p. 526. Massachusetts State Board of Health, 1873, p. 428; and see Schultz, 1989. *Herald*, 29 July 1876, p. 4, editorial; and 13 February 1884, p. 4, Rehousing the poor.

7 William Young, Introduction, n.p., in Annan, 1900. *Daily Post*, 29 October 1903, p. 11, Municipal elections. Fried, 1990, p.10. Trachtenberg, 1989, p. 166; and see Bremner, 1956, pp. 196–7.

8 See Poole, 1975.

9 Meisel, 1983. Sutherland, G., Cruikshank and London; and Nadel, I.B., Gustave Doré: English Art and London life, both in Nadel, Schwarzbach, 1980. Dyos, 1967,

pp. 20–1. See the references to 'A sigh from the slums' in *Daily Telegraph*, 25 February 1884, p. 5, The housing of the poor.

10 Siegel, 1981, pp. 108–9. See Bremner, 1956, chapters 6 and 7; Dunlap, 1965; Blayney, G.H., City life in American drama, 1825–1860, in Wallace, Ross, 1958, pp. 99–128.

11 *Daily Telegraph*, 29 May 1883, p. 3, Crusading amongst the cow-yards; 29 April 1884, p. 5, The rookeries on the rocks. Walters, 1901a, preface.

12 Walters, 1901b, p. ii. *Herald*, 8 February 1878, p. 5, The common lodging-houses of Sydney. *Evening News*, 21 February 1881, p. 2, Mayoral inspection of dilapidation.

13 *Manchester City News*, Mr. J. Cuming Walters: a journalist's long and varied career, n.d., newspaper cuttings, BCL. *Examiner*, 27 April 1901, p. 1, Grand jury recommends the removal of police chief and rebukes Mayor Phelan. *Chronicle*, 16 August 1903, Sunday Supplement, p. 5, Chinese boy is running an undertaking establishment to keep himself in school. Banks, Read, 1906, p. 103.

14 *Evening News*, 17 May 1881, p. 2, Another sanitary crusade. Dobie, 1936, p. 246. Wohl, 1977, p. 201. Walters, 1901a, p. 15.

15 *Examiner*, 4 October 1900, p. 7, Chinatown gamblers open many new games and boldly defy the law. Banks, Read, 1906, p. 155; see Lloyd, 1876. Workingmen's Party of California, 1880, p. 14. *Evening News*, 28 May 1880, p. 3, The homes of the larrikins.

16 *Daily Telegraph*, 9 February 1889, p. 6, Some city rookeries. Walters, 1901a, p. 31. Walters, 1901b, p. 5. Walters, The housing problem, in *Daily Gazette*, 21 June 1901, p. 4.

17 Borough of Birmingham, 1875b, p. 12. *Daily Mail*, 4 October 1875, p. 2, The proposed new street: a sketch of the doomed rookeries.

18 *Daily Telegraph*, 15 January 1884, p. 6, Inspection and condemnation of rookeries; 25 February 1885, p. 6, Among the rookeries; 17 September 1881, p. 6, Sydney rookeries; *Evening News*, 31 October 1883, p. 6, City inspection; *Daily Telegraph*, 30 October 1883, p. 3, More city properties condemned; *Evening News*, 7 November 1883, p. 3, More rotten buildings condemned; 25 January 1883, p. 2, City rookeries; *Daily Telegraph*, 23 September 1881, p. 3, Sydney rookeries. Numerous variations upon these expressions are found throughout the Sydney newspaper stories.

19 Walters, 1901a, pp. 3, 8, 11, 20. Walters, 1901b, p. 5. *Daily Telegraph*, 25 November 1887, p. 3, More buildings condemned; and 16 September 1884, p. 6, Dilapidated properties.

20 Bancroft, 1907, p. 57. Walters, 1901a, pp. 9, 15; Walters, 1901b, p. 8. *Daily Gazette*, 6 March 1901, p. 4, leader. See Mayne, 1991a, part 2.

21 Walters, 1901a, p. 18; *Evening News*, 26 June 1882, p. 2, Cheap lodging houses; Robertson, 1895, p. 40 (my italics). *Daily Post*, 24 May 1882, p. 4, leader (my italics).

22 *Daily Telegraph*, 25 February 1885, p. 6, Among the rookeries. Banks, Read, 1906, pp. 103, 157. Walters, 1901a, pp. 4, 11, 27.

23 Disraeli is quoted in Himmelfarb, 1984, p. 493. Grant is quoted in Dyos, 1967, pp. 14–15. Wohl, 1977, p. 5. Mayhew is quoted in Himmelfarb, 1984, p. 332. Stead, 1964, p. 401. See Keating, 1976, pp. 11–32.

24 *Chronicle*, 21 March 1900, p. 5, Highbinders arrested. Smith, S.M. 'Savages and martyrs': images of the urban poor in Victorian literature and art, in Nadel, Schwarzbach, 1980, pp. 14–29. Wohl, 1991, p. 88.

25 Chamberlain, 1874, p. 414. *Daily Gazette*, 6 February 1901, p. 8, The city council. *Birmingham Magnet*, 10 August 1901, p. 9, Mr. J. Cuming Walters. Lees, 1985, pp. 109, 111.

26 Linthicum, 1906, pp. 4, 246. *Chronicle*, 4 April 1903, p. 16, Ask removal of Chinatown. San Francisco Passenger Department, 1901, p. 93.

27 Workingmen's Party of California, 1880, p. 3. *Examiner*, 10 July 1900, p. 4, The danger from Chinatown. San Francisco Board of Supervisors, 1885, p. 28. Raymond, 1886, pp. 72–3.

28 *Chronicle*, 7 August 1904, p. 5, How white women doctors are called in by the wealthy to cure ills of Chinatown. San Francisco Passenger Department, 1901, pp. 94–5, 96. Disturnell, 1883, p. 107. Linthicum, 1906, p. 247. The Bancroft Company, 1893, p. 4. See Hittell, 1888, p. 49.

29 San Francisco Board of Supervisors, 1885, pp. 3, 43, 63. San Francisco Passenger Department, 1901, p. 93. *Chronicle*, 20 February 1903, p. 9, Want to keep back Chinese. *Examiner*, 11 March 1900, p. 14, Quarantine of Chinatown raised, all fears groundless.

30 Hunter, 1904, p. 265. *Evening News*, 17 May 1881, Another sanitary crusade. *Daily Post*, 16 October 1877, p. 8, The municipal elections. See also the 1900 report of the city bacteriologist in San Francisco Department of Public Health, 1901a, p. 144; also *Chronicle*, 29 May 1900, p. 7, Bubonic fake is dying hard.

31 Walters, 1901a, pp. 19, 15. *Daily Telegraph*, 10 May 1881, p. 3, The rookeries of Sydney. The Bancroft Company, 1893, p. 2. Robertson, 1895, p. 40.

32 Himmelfarb, 1984, p. 332. Walters, 1901a, p. 30. *Chronicle*, quoted in Dobie, 1936, p. 189. Raymond, 1886, p. 12.

33 *Evening News*, 17 May 1881, p. 2, Another sanitary crusade. *Daily Gazette*, 20 October 1875, p. 5, The proposed new street; and see Walters, 1901a, pp. 27, 31.

34 *Daily Gazette*, 3 June 1901, p. 5, Scenes in slum-land. *Daily Telegraph*, 10 May 1881, p. 3, The rookeries of Sydney. *Examiner*, 16 February 1885, p. 2, The Chinese New Year. *Chronicle*, 9 September 1903, p. 7, Fan tan game raided; 3 March 1900, p. 6, Suppression of Chinese lawlessness. *Examiner*, 4 August 1900, p. 3, Chinese move gambling games that were unmolested for weeks to elude the new police squad.

35 *Evening News*, 16 March 1887, p. 3, The condemned 'sell'. Walters, 1901a, pp. 4, 5, 10. See Lloyd, 1876, p. 298.

36 *Examiner*, 12 June 1900, pp. 2, 8, Chinese wreck Mongol morgue; and 10 June 1900, p. 34, Officers are attacked by the Chinese. See Dr Williamson to Mayor Phelan, 30 June 1900, in San Francisco Department of Public Health, 1901a, p. 16. *Chronicle*, 21 April 1901, p. 12, Government lays strong hand on Chinese slave trade.

37 San Francisco Board of Supervisors, 1885, pp. 35–6. *Chronicle*, 11 December 1903, p. 16, Hop sing highbinders kill rival tong man; 16 December 1903, p. 9, Raid highbinder den; capture hatchet men.

38 Raymond, 1886, p. 4. *Evening News*, 17 May 1881, p. 2, Another sanitary crusade. Walters, 1901a, p. 25. *Daily Telegraph*, 17 September 1881, p. 6, Sydney rookeries.

39 Walters, 1901a, pp. 6–7.

40 *Chronicle*, 20 January 1903, p. 9, Chinese will reward murder. *Sunday Examiner Magazine*, 18 March 1900, Why Chinese murderers escape; showing Chinatown's loopholes for highbinders. Dobie, 1936, p. 245. Raymond, 1886, pp. 7, 11. Genthe, Irwin 1909, pp. 52, 44.

41 Scobey, 1989, p. 425. Walters, 1901a, p. 31.

8

Slumland

Crossing imaginatively through the slum's threshold, participants in the newspaper performances find their illusions of slumland sojourns sustained by threads of narrative which flow between their common-sense certainties — based on personal experience and local knowledge — and increasingly more abstract concepts that are based upon pooled and mediated knowledge. Audience comprehension is sustained — and the contentiousness and indeterminacies which so often cloud public knowledge are overridden — by endless repetition of key words and phrases. These trigger easy recognition because of their reflexive relationship to personal experience, and then relocate common-sense certainties at ever higher levels of abstraction. Three of the spiralling narrative sequences through which these trigger devices operate revolve around concepts of time, smell, and territory. Notwithstanding subtle regional and temporal variations of emphasis, each of these sequences recurred in newspaper representations and general city discourse across the urban network throughout the late nineteenth and early twentieth centuries. They served to delineate and, in so doing, to contain the imaginary borders of the slum. They did so by juxtaposing the abhorrent conditions which supposedly typified slumland with common-sense bench-marks of taste, propriety, utility, and comfort in the modern city. Each sequence thereby became an avenue for imposing bourgeois logic upon the indeterminacies of urban society.

Time

The first dramatic sequence to address the readers' attention is that of time. The device is introduced simply by juxtaposition of daytime and night-time. The *Birmingham Daily Gazette*'s trampings through slumland are, with one jarring exception, set in daylight. Newspaper sensationalism about San Francisco's Chinatown was also conventionally presented through the press reporters' daytime eyes, although the stories they pursued frequently related back to the previous night's happenings. Referencing to time was still more explicit in the slumland stories carried by the Sydney press. These articles invariably begin by locating the journeys of slumland discovery within the shared time clock of the urban bourgeoisie. They begin and end at familiar times adjusted to the work rhythms of Town Hall and the press: from 'shortly after 10 o'clock ... until dinner time' at 'a little after 12 o'clock'.[1]

An immediate and basic conflict is thereby introduced between conventional city work time — which became increasingly regulated by standardized clock times in the last decades of the nineteenth century — and its slumland antithesis. Visitors to the slums are represented as purposeful and energetic. Sydney's hard-working expeditioners are characterized as being 'pressed for time', and their tours are said to proceed according to overall plan and timetable. By contrast, time in the city's slums is disregarded. Life seems directionless and lethargic: 'one or two men are smoking from apparent want of something to do.' The *Birmingham Daily Gazette* likewise contrasts the earnest purposefulness of its tours with the aimlessness of the slum's inhabitants: 'trollops ... idle around', and at 'the street corners cluster groups of men, out o' work or unwilling to work, hanging about listlessly.' The San Francisco Board of Health's efforts during 1900 to eradicate plague from Chinatown was contrasted by the city press with the obstructionist indolence attributed to the Chinese, who are pictured as simultaneously 'sleeping snugly packed in vile, unventilated underground holes, the very nest and breeding place of disease.'[2] The storylines describe the imposition of city time upon the slums. Sydney's explorers find the slum's inhabitants lying in bed, and urge them that it is 'time to get up'. Walters exults that as the result of the embarrassment his tours had given to municipal officials and landlords, 'in the stagnant Birmingham slums there are the signs of bustle and stir'.[3]

Trigger words adjust readers' easy comprehension of distinctions between energy and slothfulness to more sophisticated levels of discourse. On one plane the performances explore the theme of sleep in order to consolidate the contrasts being drawn between the city's daytime bustle of legitimate social activities and the slum's indolence by day and excesses by night. On a still higher plane of abstraction the performances pursue juxtaposed images of slum time and city time in order better to authenticate notions of market-place progress.

On the first of these planes, newspapers present slums as places of daytime slumber. In so doing, their performances assist audience comprehension by linking the implied associations between sleepiness, concealment, and subterfuge with the origins of the word *slum* in popular usage. When, in 1903, San Francisco police closed in upon the Chinatown hide-away of a notorious highbinder gang, the *Chronicle* described how the gang's members — thwarted in their efforts to escape — pretend to be 'deep in slumber' as the police crashed down their door. Walters stumbles upon slumland denizens 'in ... heavy slumber', the women 'dozing', and their husbands 'snoring in ... drunken sleep'.[4] His readers, imaginatively joining the discovery tours, find everywhere 'a drowsy air'. The slum by day is a 'dull' place, all activity paralysed by 'general dreariness'. Sydney's rookeries are similarly characterized as places of 'ennui'. In 1903 the *San Francisco Examiner* likewise styled daytime Chinatown a place of 'monotony'. The characterization was a familiar one. In 1876 Lloyd's *Lights and Shades in San Francisco* alleged that the city's bustling main streets stood in contrast to Chinatown, where 'vigorous life' was suspended by day, and the streets given over to 'listless idlers lolling upon the curb or against the walls'. In 1888 John Hittell's *Guide-Book To San Francisco* referred to 'a kind of sluggish activity in Chinatown' during the day.[5]

Implications of suspended and illicit slumland activity are strengthened by reference to imprisoned time. Walters remarks upon the frequent and 'perfectly nonchalant manner in which women speak of the imprisonment of their husbands ... [who] ... were away "doing time".' His wanderings through slumland are punctuated with references to 'cell-like rooms' and 'prison-like houses'. Living space in San Francisco's Chinatown is likewise described as 'little cells' by a writer for the *Chicago Chronicle* in 1906. Journalists and slummer publicists delighted to recount stories of Chinese women enticed to the city and imprisoned as 'slaves' in underground 'dungeons' for purposes of prostitution.[6]

Recurring references to slumber and sleep also prompt recognition of familiar biblical conceptual frames: the sleep of the soul — with its associations of supineness, indolence, and stupidity — and more ominously, the sleep of death. Walters calls Birmingham's slums 'deadly dull'. As the stories unfold it becomes clear that throughout slumland 'there is little life; no healthy stir, no cheery activity.' In Sydney, patrons of slumland opium dens are found lying in 'death-like sleep'. These word associations become a means in turn of encapsulating slums in funereal, mournful hues. *Scenes in Slum-Land* repeatedly presented Birmingham's slums as 'dismal' and 'forlorn' places, in which even the buildings were 'dejected-looking' and 'bowed down with despondency'.[7]

Word associations between slumber and death are particularly evident in newspaper representations of Chinatown in San Francisco. The stories are invariably intertwined with images of opium dens in which addicts lay 'wrapped in the dream smoke of opium'. To touch Chinese people was to be struck by their 'uncanny clamminess'. The *Examiner* explicitly labelled Chinatown's reputed maze of underground rooms and passages a burial place, calling it 'a strange labyrinth of burrows ... like the Roman catacombs'.[8] The catacombs metaphor was also popular in books. It was particularly frequent after the outbreak of plague in 1900, when journalists repeated the City Board of Health's complaints that Chinatown was 'honeycombed by passages and blind alleys' in which the sick were hidden and the dead buried.[9] Such sensationalism built upon a long tradition of associations between opium sleep and death. The Workingmen's Party of California, publicizing its 1880 inspection of Chinatown, had declared that their investigators peered through the opium smoke in one packed lodging house to find that the 'inmates have a ghastly look, and are covered with a clammy perspiration.' In 1885 the Board of Supervisors' special Chinatown investigation committee reported that day and night, visitors to opium dens were confronted by 'the spectacle of pallid men in a condition of death-stupor ... such as would seem to furnish fit subjects for the Coroner and the morgue.' In the following year Walter Raymond, in *Horrors of the Mongolian Settlement*, wrote that inside the opium dens, smokers 'lie in a grotesque attitude, ... having the look of plague-stricken corpses.'[10]

Representations of slum time in terms of difference and repulsion are cemented by juxtaposition of day with night. The message is straightforward: whereas the busy world of legitimate and useful city industry was suspended at dusk and respectable people went to sleep, the hitherto drowsy denizens of the slum burst into life. Theirs, however, was a parody of decent codes for living. *Scenes in Slum-Land* dramatized the contrast: 'At night comes a change. In the darkness these slum-dwellers can shout and riot and indulge in their coarse play, and quarrel over their drink, and brawl over women, and so pass away the time much to their taste.' They had bided their time during the day, preferring 'stealth and darkness because their deeds are evil.' Night-times, consequently, 'are a drunken saturnalia. Saturday night is an inferno.' The climactic centre-piece in the second series of Walters' stories is entitled 'The City of Dreadful Night'.[11]

In Sydney slumland representation, too, neighbourhoods visited without incident by day are represented as being 'the nightly resort of questionable characters and a great trouble to the police.' Dwellings found empty in the light of day 'bore evidence of being nightly occupied ... by homeless outcasts, if not for even more reprehensible purposes'. In the slum neighbourhood known as Little Canton, 'tables were found fitted up for Mongolian games of chance, which are here nightly played amidst a chatter of tongues that would prove perfectly bewildering to a European.' An *Evening News* depiction of slumland exploration in 1880 asserted that none of the places visited along Clarence and Kent Streets, in the bustling dockside district alongside Darling Harbour, 'are resided in by any of the merchants and wharfingers who keep the place tolerably lively all day. At night they depart, leaving the locality to the young and old larrikins and their families to disport themselves at their own sweet will, as any police-officer can testify.' In San Francisco, it was axiomatic in newspaper depictions of Chinatown vice that it was only when 'darkness came [that] the highbinders left their retreats.'[12]

Dramatic effect is strengthened by repetition of words such as *gloom, dark, shadow,* and *black.* They function in part as synonyms for night: thus a reporter for the *Sydney Daily Telegraph* notes that 'under the light of noonday, [the locality] did not riot in the saturnalia of debauchery which belongs to it after dark.' The words also switch comprehension from contrasts of day and night to contrasting patterns of social behaviour: 'vice ... in its darkest light' is juxtaposed with legitimate social behaviour. In so doing, the slumland narratives become allegories with which to visualize the margins of 'the darkest side of life'.[13] The alien and reprehensible character of Sydney's Little Canton is therefore signalled by labelling its buildings 'dark, noisome places', and San Francisco's Chinatown is called a 'dark and repulsive quarter ... ' Slumland rooms in Birmingham are characterized as 'dark and grim'. As Walters' stories unfold the 'pictures [become] blacker and blacker', and climax with the telling of 'the horrors that come in the darkest hours'.[14] The words cement representations of slums as abhorrent places which were tolerated by decent people only so long as they remained hidden and unknown. Walters styled the Midland slums 'black and unknown Birmingham'. San Francisco's Chinatown vice was said to flourish only because decent people were 'in the dark', and law-enforcement officers are represented as pegging back the darkness by striving 'to bring the facts to light'.[15] The joint effect of these linked word associations between general discourse and newspaper representation is twofold. First, slum-dweller and slum behaviour are sublimated to slum-land. The place and the people become undifferentiated; hence the precept that 'Immorality and infamy in their darker forms have always been associated with squalid and wretched homes.'[16] Second, the social effects of slum clearance programmes are henceforth to be grasped through sim-plified image substitution of light for dark.

Readers' comprehension was easily sustained as the words' associations switched between contrasts of time and behaviour because concepts of light and dark echoed their equations of familiarity with propriety as they navigated the streets at dusk. Whereas familiar places were judged respectable because they were illuminated by municipal street lamps, the back streets and alleys suggested criminality and deviancy because they were shrouded in gloom. Lloyd's *Lights and Shades in San Francisco* drew attention the the 'striking contrast' between the 'brilliantly lighted' shop fronts of Kearny Street, where 'every surrounding is indicative of refine-ment, comfort, happiness and prosperity', and the shadowy 'Chinatown, only a few blocks away, [where] the streets and narrow lanes are mantled in dismal gloom'. Hittell's 1888 *Guide-Book to San Francisco* likewise advised tourists that an evening's 'walk of a few blocks from the most brilliantly lighted portion of Kearny Street will take the visitor to the dingiest portion of the Chinese quarter, where the streets are narrowest and most gloomy.' In Sydney, critics of inadequate municipal street lighting regularly claimed that the 'city after dark teems with vice', and urged the erection of lamps in all the lanes and side streets as an antidote: the city must 'not [be] left in darkness!' Austin Chamberlain likewise emphasized the need to illuminate Birmingham's back courts when he campaigned in the municipal elections of 1889: 'the lighting of courts was a thing necessary for the peace and the good order of the town.'[17]

Streetwise references to light and dark were replicated in general city discourse, in which the contrasts functioned as common-sense bench-marks of the borders between good and bad. Slums were universally characterized as 'dark spots' and 'blots'[18] in newspaper editorials, police and criminal court reports, and in comments by public health officials, charity workers, and politicians. Accounts by proselytizing city clergymen of lighting up dark corners had regularly appeared in print since the 1860s. More importantly, juxtaposition of light and shadow was a familiar device in the titles and plots of city novels during the last quarter of the century, which in turn echoed the earlier fiction style of 'mysteries and miseries'.[19] The genre had traditionally served to introduce topsy-turvy reversals. Dickens had asserted in *Household Words* in 1850 that, just 'as the brightest lights cast the deepest shadows, so are the splendours and luxuries of the West End found in juxtaposition with the most deplorable manifestations of human wretchedness and depravity.' The lights and shadows style, long popular in the metropolitan cores, was also well established in provincial cities. A London journalist, Frank Fowler, had applied the style to the Australian colonies in 1859 when he depicted Melbourne in *Southern Lights and Shadows*. Benjamin Lloyd published his dramatic *Lights and Shades in San Francisco* in 1876. [20]

Metaphors of darkness act as bridges to conceptualizations of time on a second and more abstract plane than that of day and night. They introduce conceptualizations of historical change. Walters visualizes slum settings for his readers by reference to 'time-blackened old-fashioned dwellings'. He demands municipal action to ensure that 'this Slum-Land ceases to exist and becomes but a black memory of the sad and wicked past.'[21] This sense of long-term time change is introduced simply in newspaper stories by reference to personal knowledge of human ageing. Slumland buildings are represented as 'rickety' old structures which totter on their 'last legs' and are 'hardly able to hold up their heads from old age'.[22] Mention of the 'hand of Time' also linked readers' experiences of depreciation through time to representations of slumland obsolescence. Everyone understood 'the changes which time bring[s] about'. Slumland, too, is said to be a product of the 'ravages of time', as buildings once 'considered fine ... in days gone by' were reduced by time to 'crumbling ruin'. *Scenes In Slum-Land* characterizes Birmingham's slum houses as 'crumbling away with age'. Representation so framed enabled precise description of inner-city streetscapes to be easily subsumed into generalized images of decay and obsolescence.[23]

Slumland obsolescence is contrasted with city modernity. This comparison is also anchored within the local horizons of personal knowledge. Depictions of the ageing ugliness of slum housing provided readers with bench-marks for making comparisons between slumland living conditions and the new standards for utility and comfort laid down by the style manuals and standardized plans which had shaped their own modern suburban homes. Slumland is again etched as irredeemably alien. Its dwellings appeared flimsy and poky, lacking in the ornamentation, the larger and more easily opened windows, and the modern plumbing found in newer suburban homes. They violated the minimum standards and uniform dimensions set down in later building and sanitary by-laws; they possessed little of the privacy and specialization of domestic space found in suburban houses. Bourgeois domesticity is offended. Yards are said to be 'not so large as an ordinary room', and their *ad hoc* additions are described as presenting scenes of 'chaos' and 'confusion'. The houses' few rooms were 'used indiscriminately' for multiple functions.[24]

Juxtaposition of slumland decrepitude and city modernity is strengthened by remarking upon contrasts in height between modern buildings and slumland hovels. The comparison jelled with every reader's street sense of old and new buildings. Moreover, the comparison echoed familiar themes in newspaper and guidebook publicity of improvement projects by commercial developers and city governments. Birmingham's slums are represented by Walters as the 'low quarters of the city'. Supporters of Corporation Street argued that as a result of its construction, 'nests and rookeries of dwellings of the lowest and vilest description were swept away from the city's centre, and upon their sites rose the blocks of handsome and aspiring buildings, which go so far to render our city so fair in the eyes of the stranger.' Sydney news reporters commented in 1882 that as a result of commercial redevelopment, 'stately structures, three, four, and five stories in height', many of them 'noble warehouses and other business places[,] now stand upon what were before then the sites of some of the lowest and most unhealthy of city dens.'[25] In San Francisco, the *Chronicle* hoped that Chinatown would be obliterated as investors 'put up good modern structures' in its place. The newspaper championed the erection of 'tall and costly building[s] which will conform with the demands of the times ... [and] be an ornament to the city.' In the aftermath of the city's earthquake and fire in 1906, confidence was expressed that the disaster had presented an opportunity for the erection of 'lofty and solid steel and concrete buildings and of the sweeping away of the slums.'[26]

One effect of the contrasts being drawn between slumland dilapidation and city modernity was to emphasize the impressive evolution of cities since 'olden times'. Time is used as a measuring stick with which to visualize past and present, and thereby celebrate social progress. Sydney journalists noted the incongruity of seeing old buildings on the slum's fringes standing alongside newer commercial buildings: the *Herald* noted in one such instance that the former had 'done duty for upwards of 40 years, and since the handsome warehouses ... in the neighbourhood have been erected, the antiquated appearance of [these] ... buildings has been rendered more noticeable.' During 1900 the *San Francisco Chronicle* likewise drew attention to the tearing down of an unlikely 'landmark' to the city's past: a 'little, black, shaky building' in Sacramento Street. 'Although few remember it,' the newspaper noted, 'this was the commercial center of the city in the early 50's', and had once been occupied by the now-giant Pacific Mail Steamship Company. The newspaper echoed a recurrent theme in celebrations of the vigorous pace of commercial redevelopment. In 1888 a city guidebook had crowed that 'year by year the wooden buildings that form the landmarks of earlier days are being crowded out by substantial brick and iron edifices.'[27]

Another effect of the slum writers' harnessing of time was to support the logic of familiar bourgeois arguments about the necessity for ongoing spatial and functional renewal in order to sustain the modernization process. The case is introduced in simple, matter-of-fact terms: the ageing ugliness of slumland is an 'architectural eye-sore' which disfigures 'the appearance of the city'.[28] The implications of this argument are rapidly extended to include criteria other than architectural aesthetics. These eyesores from the past are judged to constitute a disgrace not only to the appearance but also to the achievements of modern cities. During the 1880s Sydney's 'back slums' were labelled an 'eternal disgrace' to a society that 'claim[ed] ... boastfully ... to be building up a great nation under these southern skies', and in San Francisco the condition of Chinatown was simultaneously being described as 'a disgrace to the civilization of the age'.[29] In Birmingham, the improvement scheme had been proposed in 1875 with the comment that the city's slums were 'a disgrace and a scandal to our civilization'. That characterization was repeated into the next century, and was echoed by Walters: slumland '[is] a disgrace to our humanity and civilisation.'[30] Time had become a device for simultaneously visualizing the ageing obsolescence of slumland and the bustling modernity of city business cores. Sydney newspaper stories characterized slums as 'unwhole-some relics of "ancient" Sydney', which had necessarily become 'quite unequal to modern requirements', and had thus 'outlived ... [their] useful-ness'. Conversely, the municipal inspectors' work in condemning these 'relics' was represented as 'useful ... beyond denial'.[31]

By couching story-lines in terms of utility and progress, the substitution of slums by modern commercial buildings becomes a logical and unconten-tious proposition. It overlapped with familiar arguments in support of city improvement strategies. Thus, in Birmingham, the building of Corporation Street was justified in terms of the 'new and stately buildings' which were erected along its length, and which were judged 'a credit to the town'. Newspaper commentaries in Sydney argued that it was 'vain to hope for the creation of a city fit to be compared with other modern capitals' so long as the unsightly slums remained. The Mayor's actions in 'sweeping away the rookeries which disgrace different parts of the city' therefore entitled him 'to the thanks of the citizens and stamps him as a friend of progress. It is high time that the owners of those unsightly decaying tenements should be ordered to ... keep pace with the times.' Municipal slum clearance was hailed by the Sydney press for having 'produced order out of chaos, established uniformity out of confusion, pleased the eye, [and] cultivated the taste ... of the community':

When the Legislature passed the 'City of Sydney Improvement Act', an important step forward in the social progress of the country was made. If the present appearance of the city ... be contrasted with the state of things that existed ... say ten years ago, the change will be found a striking one indeed. Buildings palatial in their magnificence have sprung up on sites previously occupied by hovels. Splendor has appeared where squalor lurked or hideousness was painfully to the front. As if by the touch of a magician's wand, ugliness has vanished, and beauty and grace have taken its place.[32]

The elimination of hovels thus becomes synonymous in the newspaper performance with logical appreciation of progress and modernity. Progress and city improvement have been recast as impersonal and inexorable processes; social costs and alternative agendas have faded from common-sense recognition; the inhabitants of the inner city have been lost with the

Corner of Henn and Balloon Streets, Birmingham, c.1882–84

remodelling of the landscape of slumland. Slum-dwellers can vanish unproblematically as 'respectable warehouses or shops' displace 'the disgraceful rookeries'.[33]

Smell

The second sequence of interactions which is quickly introduced between local experience and newspaper performance centres upon smell. Slum representation through the allegory of smell made possible the most dramatic performances of all because the textual images meshed so closely with basic personal knowledge. Contrasts of smell were built into the discourse of everyday contact, and the bourgeois suburban preference for 'pure air' and 'greater salubrity ... compared with the city'[34] decisively shaped every city's evolving socio-spatial form. Smell functions in the newspaper stories to sustain the illusion of slums as an alien world. It is also used to remind readers of the seemingly intimate associations between dirt and disease. In so connecting, the theme of smells enables the newspaper performances to restate community concerns about ill health, crime, and immorality, and to hold slumland responsible for these social ills. Once again, the effect of the stories is the justification of slum clearance as a logical policy choice for progressive city governments.

Contrasts of smell add potency to representations of slums as foreign lands. Walters writes of slumland that 'throughout their whole wide region in Birmingham, pure fresh air is almost unknown.' Common reference is made in newspaper stories in all three cities to the slummers' noses, which are continually assailed and offended by vile *stinks*, stifling *odours*, and noxious *vapours*. In so doing, the writers build upon a tradition of local and imported representation. In San Francisco, for example, the City Health Officer had repeatedly publicized the 'stifling and disgusting' air in Chinatown during the last quarter of the nineteenth century. The Board of Supervisors' special report on Chinatown in 1885 asserted that the slum's amalgam of smells 'make up a perfume which can neither be imagined nor described.'[35]

Imaginatively tramping through the slum in the newspaper stories, readers find the stench 'almost unendurable'. The stories unfold recurring scenes in which the explorers 'beat a hasty retreat' from alien surroundings where their senses reel, 'overcome by foul and nauseating smells', to re-emerge on the familiar main streets 'panting for fresh air'.[36] The stories exploit the personal horror of vomiting. A news reporter for the Sydney *Herald* exclaims that 'the bad smell given out in some of the houses ... was strong and unpleasant enough to produce nausea', and journalists who visited San Francisco's Chinatown recall that the 'odour was nauseating'. It was commonplace in San Francisco to read that the air inside Chinatown's underground rooms was 'so foul that I defy any white man to live in it over night.' *Scenes in Slum-Land* tells of a visit to Love Lane. The name, says Walters, suggests grassy glades and ... the odour of early violets and primroses ... [the reality is] a gloomy horror ... with grim old-built houses of darkened bricks ... And the perfume! The new-comer, not warned in advance, will feel as if he had been smitten on the head or thumped in the stomach, or otherwise deadened and sickened by some sudden shock ... As you breathe in the pungent odours you cough or spit, perhaps retch, for the acid vapours assail the lungs like poison and set up nausea.[37]

Smell was intimately associated with filth in popular consciousness. Smell and filth in turn defined the slum in popular imagination. Sydney's Kent and Sussex Streets districts, located behind Darling Harbour, were conventionally represented as 'dirty back slums'. The San Francisco *Examiner* sought to encapsulate the essence of Chinatown in 1885 with metaphors of 'reeking ... filth'. References to slumland dirtiness reinforced the journalists' recurring play upon images of black spots and time-accumulating eyesores. The sleazy threshold to San Francisco's Chinatown is introduced in terms of 'pick[ing] your way by the aid of the policeman's candle along ... dark and narrow passageway[s], black and grimy with a quarter of a century's accumulation of filth.'[38]

Nineteenth-century cities faced immense difficulties maintaining minimum building standards, devising efficient schemes for waste removal, and making, repairing, and cleaning streets, gutters, and footpaths. Words with personal immediacy such as *rubbish, filth, drains, dirt, damp, grime, slime,* and *mud* repeatedly underlined these problems. Chinatown was called 'the unclean abode of a thousand smells'. When plague was discovered there in 1900 newspapers sensationalized the disgust expressed by city and federal health officials at the 'vast amount of garbage and filth' which the cleansing teams collected, and which 'blended [together] every imaginable foul odour and stench'. With characteristic bluntness the federal health officer, Joseph Kinyoun, called Chinatown a place 'of filth and refuse'. The press demanded that the slum be obliterated, clamouring that not even the slums of New York were such a dirty spot. It was a well-worn characterization. In 1885 the Board of Supervisors had styled Chinatown 'the filthiest spot inhabited by men, women and children on the American continent.'[39]

This fixation with the dirt of slum living was encouraged by dread of infectious disease. Slumland stench was not just unpleasant, it 'was something fearful'. Slums were places of 'sickening filth'. Pressmen habitually gave prominence to sanitary reformers' urgings that 'the "dominion of dirt" means the dominion of disease', and styled slumland scourges such as cholera 'filth diseases'.[40] Understanding of germ theory was still influenced by earlier assumptions that diseases were spread by dangerous gases or miasmic poisons in the air which had been generated by the smells of decaying filth. References to filth in the newspaper stories are consequently invariably bracketed with the adjectives *decaying, rotting, putrescent, festering, decomposing,* or *reeking,* all of them intimately connected with personal experience. Slumland neighbourhoods are identified as seedbeds of 'reeking rottenness' and as 'certain disease breeders'. The most popular metaphor was the characterization of slums as *hotbeds of dirt and disease.* The phrase was in general and frequent use in the press and in general city discourse. Smells are likened to *miasma* and *poison* which are 'enough to breed disease'. Slum dwellings are represented as being 'crowded with men, women, and children who dwelt in a stench that the inspectors, though used to foul smells, said was enough to poison them.'[41] Deathbed scenes of pathos visualize the consequences of such conditions. Walters makes the moral explicit: 'the stench is unbearable ... Is it to be wondered at that some of the residents complain of sores, and bad eyes, and are constantly "feeling bad"?' The *Evening News* had likewise noted of the tours of 'Sydney's Slums and Rookeries' that 'we should cease to wonder when children with swollen faces and bandaged throats open the door to the appeal of "The Mayor of Sydney wishes to inspect the dwelling", and in answer to the medical officer's inquiry reply that they are nearly always "not well", or that baby died a week or so ago.'[42]

Personal experience of the widespread incidence of infant morbidity and mortality readily confirmed these slumland scenes. Moreover, everyone knew that cities were alarmingly infectious places for people of all ages. Traditionally, their worries had focused on the smelliest and dirtiest places: the inner-city slums. San Francisco newspapers warned that Chinatown 'furnishes a starting point from which ... disease may spread to other localities.' Chinatown had long been likened to 'a slumbering pest, likely at any time to generate and spread disease.' In Birmingham, the press characterized the 'foul slums' within the improvement area as 'breeding-centres' and 'hotbeds of infectious disease' which 'threw out ... deadly radii in all directions' to endanger 'more salubrious neighbourhoods'.[43] Trigger words consolidated readers' comprehension by reference to personal ill health. *Scenes in Slum-Land* depicts the city's slums as 'a festering sore', and warns that its 'mass of festering horrors and iniquities ... has eaten at the heart of the city like a malignant cancer.' The analogy of heart disease was especially popular in San Francisco, where newspaper stories — drawing upon many decades of similar commentary by the city health department and by exposé tracts — railed against 'the menace of a filthy Asiatic quarter in the heart of the city'.[44]

Repetition of the word *epidemic* further emphasizes the theme of slumland menace. The explosive quality of slumland diseases is constantly reiterated. Sydney newspaper stories caution that if the diseases generated by the smells of decaying slumland filth ever 'got a hold', they 'would spread with lightning-like rapidity'. Walters interrupts his commentaries to exclaim that 'you can veritably taste the pestilential air.' The stories echoed the frequent warnings issued by sanitarians and city health authorities. Sydney's parliamentary investigation into overcrowding in 1876 had concluded that the city's slums invited 'the outbreak of some deadly epidemic', a message that journalists sensationalized during smallpox outbreaks in 1881 and 1884. In San Francisco, the negative publicity given to Chinatown during the 1870s and 1880s by the city health authorities was prompted by local outbreaks of smallpox and by a global pandemic of cholera. City health officials characterized the Chinese slum as a 'plague spot' long before the outbreak of plague in 1900.[45]

References to pestilence were so readily comprehensible that they often functioned as well to translate attention from infectious disease to the contagious qualities of moral disease: violence, robbery, and vice. News coverage of highbinder rivalry in San Francisco asserted that 'an epidemic of murder ... is raging in Chinatown.' Chinese gambling, opium smoking, and prostitution were blamed for having 'inoculated our youth ... with the virus of immorality.'[46] *Scenes in Slum-Land* contends that 'disease and crime are epidemic' in Birmingham's slums, and that a 'pestilence of immorality sweeps through ... [its] streets and courts.' The *Birmingham Daily Gazette*, as it drew attention to the end of Walters' first series in 1901, editorialized that slums were 'centres of moral and physical disease'.[47] The characterization had been in general circulation a quarter of a century earlier, when it formed the dramatic centrepiece of memorials presented to Parliament by the Charity Organization Society and the Royal College of Physicians in 1874 as they pressured the Tories for housing reform. In 1876 the London *Times* noted that Birmingham slum life entailed

something like a permanent plague in respect to sickness and death; but it also means a moral plague, infinitely worse than any mere loss of physical life. It means the impossibility of decency, and of the moral sensitiveness which is impossible without decency; it means an utter depression of those higher functions of the brain upon which the exercise of will, intelligence, and self-command is dependent; it means a constant craving for excitement, and an unquenchable thirst for strong stimulants.

In San Francisco, too, City Health Officers throughout the 1870s and 1880s called 'Chinatown ... a moral and social plague spot, productive of continual annoyance and much disease.'[48]

The implied correlation between physical and moral disease is clarified in newspaper performances by repetition of words and phrases that are normally used to describe the generation and spread of infections. In 1901 headlines in the *San Francisco Examiner* proclaimed Chinatown a 'Hot Bed of Vice and Corruption', while in Birmingham Walters described the city's slums as 'centres of depravity and corruption'.[49] The word *corruption* capitalizes upon associations between decay, smell, and disease generation, and echoes characterizations of slums in terms of death. The *Birmingham Daily Gazette* characterized the city's slums in 1901 as 'foul dens where vice and disease are fostered. They are points of moral and physical *contagion.*' References to miasmic hypotheses of disease generation are also common. In 1875 the *Daily Mail* had described the improvement area as 'noisesome nests and layers of pollution which ... are little else but hot-beds of *festering* vice, crime, and disease.' The *Daily Gazette* announced in 1888 that 'the rookeries ... reek with violence and heathenism.' The currency of such metaphors was constantly renewed by metropolitan usage. In the wake of *The Bitter Cry*, Birmingham reporters repeated the representations of London's East End as 'hotbeds of vice, immorality, and crime'.[50] Colonial usage was characteristically similar. During Sydney's smallpox epidemic of 1881 the long-notorious and now-infected Sussex

Street district was depicted as having been for years 'hot-beds of crime, degradation and disease, ... festering, and frothing up the greater number of cases that come before our police courts.'[51]

The associations being thus drawn between physical and moral disease were also assisted by the stories' appeal to readers' personal experiences of smell and filth. Characterizations of Sydney slum life in terms of drug abuse and organized crime are introduced by reference to sickly smells. The stench in Sydney's Chinese 'opium and gambling dens', 'reeking with the fumes of opium, stale beer and other abominable smells', was 'sufficient to turn the strongest stomach'. The stories abound with contrasts between cleanliness and dirt. The juxtaposition serves to visualize the boundaries between degradation and respectability: in one such slumland script, two wooden cottages are found, 'the one kept clean and neat with flowers and shrubs in front, the other a filthy hovel, in which a man half stupid lay on a mattress reeking with dirt, from which a horrible stench came.' Such comparisons were regularly reinforced by city news commentaries: in 1883 an editorial leader in the *Birmingham Daily Gazette* reminded readers that 'In the same court in every large town houses are to be met with, clean, tidy, and healthy, opposite to or alongside of filthy, untidy, and unhealthy houses. The difference is not in the houses, but in the tenants.'[52]

Decent people had been taught to abominate smells and filth. It was therefore common sense that people who seemingly revelled in them were savages. During the 1880s San Francisco's Health Officer railed against Chinatown's 'filthy habits and *customs*'. The slum's smell and dirt thus become symptomatic of a deeper moral malaise: slumland 'presented a scene of dirt *and disorder*.' It 'offended the nostrils *and all sense of taste or decency*.'[53] Smells and filth become moral offences, and blame was sheeted home to blemishes of character amongst those who most dwelt amongst them. Such performances highlighted familiar reformist arguments about 'the dirty slums' that invariably fused images of dirty people and dirty places. It was axiomatic in such discourse that 'the lowest haunts of large centres of population are made what they are by the people who live in them.' In Birmingham, Joseph Chamberlain and his political allies were already by 1878 complaining that their efforts to ameliorate housing conditions within the improvement area were being undermined by 'the apparently incorrigibly dirty and slovenly mode of life among many of the inhabitants', who seemed to be 'completely without any fundamental notions of decency and cleanliness.'[54] The *San Francisco Chronicle* asserted in 1900 that Chinatown's residents were 'addicted to dirty habits'. Smell thus becomes an index of behaviour, and both in turn serve to consolidate understanding of social progress and its antithesis. In 1885 the Board of Supervisors had concluded that 'Thus, with its filth, its odors, its vices and the general repulsive character of its people, Chinatown stands to-day a barrier against the advancement of the city.'[55]

With audience comprehension thus assured, the newspaper narratives present the bourgeois case for sanitary reform by slum clearance. In Sydney municipal inspection tours were applauded as 'a crusade ... against the

Kingdom of Dirt'. Word associations with smell and filth enabled the case to be made in common-sense terms of domestic cleanliness. One writer characterized the destruction of San Francisco's old Chinatown in 1906 as 'house cleaning day'. The analogy used was generally that of wielding the broom: the slum, says Walters, must be 'swept away'. The phrase peppered newspaper slumland tales and general news reporting throughout the urban network. It was often coupled with the analogy of the mop: the slums were to be 'wiped off from the face of the town'.[56] The performances thus appeal to consensus grounded incontestably in domestic hygiene. In Birmingham, the Independent Labour Party joined Liberals, Conservatives, and Unionists in demanding that the City Council 'sweep away the slums'. Moreover, this sweeping away of the slums is invariably bracketed with their substitution by 'splendid buildings'. In San Francisco, the *Chronicle*'s John Young expressed satisfaction that the otherwise calamitous fire of 1906 'had swept away all the rookeries ..., and in the place of the destroyed buildings substantial brick structures were erected.'[57]

Territory

The final interplay between newspaper representation of slumland and the personal experiences of the newspapers' readers revolves around concepts of territoriality. The newspaper performances build upon the rites of passage associated with discovery and exploration of the slumland threshold in order to engage each reader's instinctive mapping out of space into my place, our place, and stranger's place. These mental borders between personal space, local community, and city thereby become reference points against which to visualize the territory of the slum. Walters declares sensationally that 'Birmingham's Slum-Land is no small and easily-dealt-with area, but is a wide hinterland, beginning just outside the city's centre, and extending far on all sides.'[58] Communities of strangers stand juxtaposed to the familiar neighbourhood networks and associations of readers' everyday lives.

Among the most potent examples of territorial referencing is newspaper story-telling in San Francisco about 'the mysterious nooks and corners of *underground Chinatown*, where few white men ever penetrate.' These netherworld stories were credible to readers because allegations of the 'honeycombed condition of Chinatown' had regularly been aired during the last quarter of the nineteenth century by politicians, health officials, and publicists of the city's tourist attractions.[59] Dramatic representations of this mythical Chinatown underground territory synthesized the other representational sequences in the newspaper performances. In the aftermath of the district's destruction in 1906, sensational accounts circulated the nation of how the Chinese had

burrowed like rats, and countless tunnels, foul-smelling and repellant, were thronged with opium-smoking hordes of celestials. Crimes of every character were committed in these underground retreats, almost without fear of punishment.

Honeycombing the quarter with a system of tunnels, frequently reaching a depth of fifty feet, it is estimated that nearly one-half of the people of the quarter lived therein, removed from the light of the sun.

It was underground Chinatown which 'gave visitors the most terrifying ... thrill ... Actually an ingenious labyrinth contrived out of connecting basements and narrow passageways one level below the street, it grew in legend until practically every stranger as well as most of the natives of San Fransisco repeated marvellous tales of how it burrowed down five, six, seven, eight stories underground.'[60]

Identification of slumland as an alien and debased territory was powerfully assisted in both the newspaper stories and the broader genre of slumland representation by recurring metaphors of territoriality in the natural world. Darwinists and Creationists agreed that the arrangement of species in the natural world was strictly hierarchical. The San Francisco Board of Supervisors' special report on Chinatown in 1885 had declared that 'Here it may truly be said that human beings exist under conditions ... scarcely one degree above those under which the rats of our water-front and other vermin live, breath and have their being. And this order of things seems inseparable from the very nature of the race.'[61]

The commonest synonym for slum was *rookery*, whose primary meaning related to colonies of nesting birds. Inner-city neighbourhoods were also commonly represented in Birmingham, San Francisco, and Sydney — and, indeed, throughout the urban network — as *dens, hides, nests, burrows, rat holes, lairs, bee hives*, and *rabbit warrens*. Associated metaphors suggest imprisonment: *hutches* and *pigsties*. *Scenes in Slum-Land* likens slum dwellers to 'stabled and kenneled beasts'. The Chinese in San Francisco are commonly represented as being 'packed in like sardines in a tin box'.[62] Animal metaphors echoed long-established usage in the metropolitan cores. They completed the representation of slum dwellers into abstractions, a mutated genus that was inseparable from the grotesque props with which they were cast. Slum-dwellers *infest* and *swarm*. They 'herd together like swine.' The San Francisco Chinese are said to live 'like so many prairie dogs', and are represented as 'chattering' like monkeys. Sometimes their status is reduced further, to that of invertebrate parasites: the *San Francisco Chronicle* likened the Chinese to 'human scum'.[63] Similar words and expressions recurred widely in political and reformist discourse, and in other genres of popular slumland representation. Slum-dwellers thereby become the wretched fauna distinctive to an alien environment. The newspaper explorers who penetrated the territory of the 'so-called rookeries ... found human beings huddled together in noisome dens.' Reformist commentary on both sides of the Atlantic likewise described slumland families as 'herding like swine' and 'herd[ing] together like sheep'.[64]

This blending of the images of territoriality to encompass both landscape and native is reinforced as the newspaper stories distance audience from natives by exclamations grounded in the horizons of the readers' daily lives. Sydney journalists remark that the 'question frequently arose how it was possible for *human beings* to exist in such stys [sic]', and marvel that since the 'majority of these places are fever-hutches ... it is a matter of wonderment how *people* can live or exist in them.' Such dramatic exclamations echoed the rhetoric of sanitarians and reform politicians: stump orators in Birmingham told electors that the so-called houses in the city's back courts were not fit for animals. Chamberlain announced that 'Houses which were not not fit for pigs to live in sheltered ... whole families who herded together in utter defiance of all sanitary laws, and with a total disregard of every consideration of decency.'[65] San Francisco's Health Officer expressed concern during the 1870s at the 'many shanties totally unfit for the lower animals to live in, but which are tenanted by human beings. This is notoriously the case concerning the Chinese, but is not confined wholly to them.' Walters' *Scenes in Slum-Land* remarks of tenants living in 'pen'-like dwellings that an 'animal-like attachment seems to tie them to the places, however bad.' Occupants of the back-to-backs 'are filthy in their habits, and behave with less decency than animals.'[66] Performance thus gave new meaning to the expression 'unfit for *human* habitation', as slum-dwellers are transformed into animals or — at best — weird tribespeople distinct from normal city people.

The suggestions and connections made possible by territorial character-izations of inner-city working people as 'primitive dwellers in the wilds' rendered plausible the newspapers' generalizations that any slum 'tene-ments visited were ... occupied by the usual class of tenant found in such places.' The play upon territoriality thus reinforced the other strands of slumland performance, and extended the theme of inexorable moral contamination within the slums' borders. Throughout the nineteenth century, reformers and entertainers contended that the slumland environ-ment 'gradually destroys the moral feelings of the people, [and] renders them brutal, reckless, and drunken.' Boston investigators in 1849 had asserted that the territorial conditioning of slums made it inevitable that their inhabitants should behave 'like brutes'. In Birmingham, it was predicted that as the slum-dwellers' humanity was thus unravelled, so 'gratification of their animal passions will be their chief object.'[67]

Theatrical representations of slums as foreign territories and primitive communities dramatically visualized and thereby confirmed the imaginary slum line between healthy and blighted city districts which had been pictured by bourgeois improvement discourse throughout the nineteenth century. In so doing they blended pooled opinion regarding the borders of economic, social, and aesthetic good sense with characterizations of slums as havens of brutishness and misery. Territory thereby becomes palpable in inseparably spatial and moral terms.

Audience responsiveness to these synthesizing representations of ter-ritoriality provided a common-sense context for reasserting the inevitability of what the Massachusetts Board of Health called 'the natural encroach-ments of business' upon the seedy slumland fringe areas around city business cores. The city press again simplified and popularized the arguments of bourgeois reformers. Journalists applauded the renewal process whereby 'old places ... [in] the heart of the city' were swept away, to be replaced by 'stores, factories and the palaces of commerce'.[68] In San Francisco journalists, city government, and business organizations all contended that Chinatown — lying 'between the best business and finest residential sections' of the city — was 'too valuable to be used as a slum'.[69] They anticipated its 'remodelling ... as a part of the regular business quarters of San Francisco, whose expansion is now prevented by present conditions.' By thus assaulting the territory of the slum, they would 'remake Chinatown into a modern district'. It was inevitable, they contended, that because Chinatown stood on 'part of the best quarter of the city ... sooner or later these improvements will be made and Chinatown will become a thing of the past.'[70]

Thus was measured modern city progress! In Sydney the *Echo* enthused that 'private enterprise is lining our streets with noble buildings — temples, one might almost call them, of the God of Commerce.' Guidebooks recommended a stroll down the city's main streets so that visitors might chart how 'the old order of things changeth, giving place unto the new.' A slumland narrator in the *Daily Telegraph* described how, on 'the site once occupied by some hovels known in their time as "Canary Row", or the "Twelve Apostles", which were held and frequented by the very dregs of society, and where vice and crime reigned supreme, are now ... handsome warehouses ... This is an instance of the changes that have been effected and the progress still going on in one locality, and others could be given to almost any number.' In Birmingham similarly, it was contended that as the result of forming Corporation Street, 'Slums and rookeries, pestilential morally and physically, have disappeared as if by magic, and have given place to streets and buildings worthy of occupying the centre of a great town.'[71]

The beneficial effects that were widely predicted to flow from such spatial redevelopment is distilled and thus underlined in the newspaper stories by translating the imagery from the broad canvas of the whole city to the immediate horizons of the readers. Often this is achieved by invoking homely references to gardening. It was contended in San Francisco that the only way to abate 'the blight' of Chinatown was to 'root ... out' the 'entire Chinese colony, root and branch'. *Blight* was a widely used slumland metaphor. In Sydney the *Herald* referred to the City Council's slum-clearance programme as a 'weeding-out process'.[72]

Judgement

The combined effect of these newspaper performances was simultaneously to visualize the otherness of slumland, by metaphor linked with common-sense suggestion, and systematically to peg back the slum's borders by stamping bourgeois order and modernity upon the alien settings which had been thus constructed. The essential elements of bourgeois common sense were thereby consolidated. In so doing, the complexity and diversity of evolving inner-city spatial forms were reduced by the performances to a recurring set of stylized stage props, designed to convey simple truths to the audience as they meshed with personal experience and with representations of slums and city progress which were carried in general community discourse.

The story-line for slumland necessarily ends in judgement. The destruction of San Francisco's old Chinatown was represented in quasi-biblical tones as a 'blessing' for the city: 'Fire has reclaimed to civilization and cleanliness the Chinese ghetto, and no Chinatown will be permitted in the borders of the city.' *Scenes in Slum-Land* capitalizes upon the *double entendre* quality of the City Health Department's responsibility to *condemn* slum dwellings. The same device is exploited routinely by the Sydney press, in which ritual performances — sketched with trigger words which echo the language of the city's criminal courts — signal the slum's death-knell: the municipal inspectors' unhesitating 'verdict' is that the territory of the slum be 'condemned ... to undergo ... the "capital sentence"'.[73]

Notes

[1] *Herald*, 16 September 1881, p. 5; *Evening News*, 16 September 1884, p. 2, Among the rookeries.

[2] *Daily Telegraph*, 12 August 1884, p. 5, Condemned buildings; 17 September 1881, p. 6, Sydney rookeries. Walters, 1901a , pp. 4, 3. *Chronicle*, 4 July 1900, p. 8, Wiping out of Chinatown evil must come before long.

[3] *Daily Telegraph*, 29 April 1884. Walters, 1901b, p. 7.

[4] *Chronicle*, 16 December 1903, p. 9, Raid highbinder den; capture hatchet men. Walters, 1901b, pp. 23, 11.

[5] Walters, 1901a, pp. 5, 8. Walters, 1901b, p. 9. *Evening News*, 17 May 1881, p. 2, Another sanitary crusade. *Examiner*, 14 December 1903, p. 5, More life-taking expected in Chinatown. Lloyd, 1876, p. 254. Hittell, 1888, p. 47.

[6] Walters, 1901a, pp. 12, 7, 3. Linthicum, 1906, p. 248. Tyler, 1906, p. 309. Wilson, 1906, p. 175.

[7] See Cruden, n.d., pp. 451–2. Walters, 1901a, p. 5. *Daily Telegraph*, 16 September 1884, p. 6, Dilapidated properties. Walters, 1901b, p. 5.

[8] *Sunday Examiner Magazine*, 18 March 1900, Why Chinese murderers escape; showing Chinatown's loopholes for highbinders. *Chronicle*, 7 August 1904, p. 5, How white women doctors are called in by the wealthy to cure ills of Chinatown. *Examiner*, 18 January 1900, p. 2, Oriental vengeance like a tiger asleep in Chinatown.

[9] ibid., 4 July 1900 p. 9, Health Board has report on plague; see Banks, Read, 1906, p. 158; Wilson, 1906, p. 175.

[10] Workingmen's Party of California, 1880, p. 4. San Francisco Board of Supervisors, 1885, pp. 26–7. Raymond, 1886, p. 13.

[11] Walters, 1901a, p. 15. Walters, 1901b, pp. 22–5.

[12] *Daily Telegraph*, 9 February 1889, p. 6, Some city rookeries; 17 January 1881, p. 3, The rookeries of the city. *Evening News*, 10 July, 1882, p. 2, Inspection of rookeries; 28 May 1880, p. 3, The homes of the larrikins. *Chronicle*, 20 January 1903, p. 9, Chinese will reward murder.

[13] *Daily Telegraph*, 10 May 1881, p. 3; 1 February 1881, p. 3, The rookeries of Sydney. ibid., 28 May 1880, p. 3, The City Improvement Act.

14 ibid.,17 May 1881, p. 3, The rookeries of Sydney. *Examiner*, 17 February 1885, p. 3, The Chinese quarter. Walters, 1901b, pp. 9, 1, 24.

15 Walters, 1901a, p. 31. *Chronicle*, 12 September 1903, p. 16, Chinese bureau again outwitted by the ring; ibid., Six young Mongolians transformed into old men during trip from jail to a steamer; and see 14 September 1903, p. 12, Substituting Chinese a profitable business; also 12 May 1903, p. 5, Chinese conspiracies to murder.

16 *Evening News*, 27 August 1880, p. 2, leader, Destruction of fever dens.

17 Lloyd, 1876, p. 254. Hittell, 1888, p. 47. *Daily Telegraph*, 31 July 1882, p. 3, The city in darkness; 30 November 1893, p. 5, The city elections. *Daily Post*, 31 October 1889, p. 5, The municipal elections.

18 *Evening News*, 9 July 1885, p. 3, The dark spots of Sydney. BCCHC, 6 April 1881. Walters, 1901b, p. 7. Tyler, 1906, p. 308.

19 See Dyos, 1967, p. 17; Taylor, W.R., The launching of a commercial culture: New York city, 1860–1930, in Mollenkopf, 1988, p. 117; See Fried, 1990, p. 31; Siegel, 1981, chapter 3; Gates, 1987, p. 50.

20 Wohl, 1977, p. 5. See Fowler, 1975; Lloyd, 1876.

21 Walters, 1901a, p. 3; Walters, 1901b, p. 27.

22 *Daily Telegraph*, 30 October 1885, p. 5, The mayor on the war-path; 7 January 1881, p. 3, The rookeries of the city; 3 October 1881, p. 4, Sydney rookeries. See also *Chronicle*, 4 July 1900, p. 8, Wiping out of Chinatown evil must come before long; Workingmen's Party of California, 1880, p. 16.

23 *Evening News*, 27 May 1880, p. 2, Through the city styes and stews; 30 July 1884, p. 5, Sydney slums and rookeries. *Daily Telegraph*, 6 June 1882, p. 3, Inspection of rookeries. Walters, 1901b, p. 7.

24 *Evening News*, 23 March 1886, p. 3, Buildings condemned; 8 July 1880, p. 2, Another raid on the hovels and rookeries of the city; 6 January 1881, p. 2, Civic raid on Phillip Street.

25 Walters, 1901a, p. 11. Workmen's Cottages, Lawrence Street, 1893, p. 191. *Herald*, 29 April 1884, p. 5, Condemnation of tenements. *Evening News*, 12 June 1882, p. 2, City inspection.

26 *Chronicle*, 4 July 1900, p. 8, Wiping out of Chinatown evil must come before long; 24 April 1901, p. 6, Height restrictions removed. Linthicum, 1906, p. 256.

27 *Daily Telegraph*, 7 November 1883, p. 3. More rotten buildings condemned. *Herald*, 15 February 1881, p. 6, Old buildings marked for destruction. *Chronicle*, 11 July 1900, p. 12, Another historic building doomed to destruction. Hittell,1888, p. 25.

28 *Daily Telegraph*, 28 May 1880, p. 3, The City Improvement Act. *Herald*, 25 January 1883, p. 9.

29 *Australian Churchman*, 5 June 1884, p. 266, City rookeries; 29 November 1883, p. 241, Homes for the poor. Workingmen's Party of California, 1880, p. 3.

30 Borough of Birmingham,1875b, p. 11. *Daily Post*, 4 May 1892, p. 7, The City Council; 16 October 1903, p. 12, Municipal elections. Walters, 1901a, p. 18.

31 *Daily Telegraph*, 13 June 1882, p. 3, Inspection of rookeries; 21 February 1881, p. 4, The city rookeries. *Evening News*, 15 February 1881, p. 2, More rookeries condemned. *Daily Telegraph*, 7 January 1881, p. 3, The rookeries of the city.

32 *Daily Post*, 24 May 1882, p. 4, leader. *Evening News*, 18 February 1881, p. 4, Demolition of city rookeries; 26 January 1881, p. 4, Notes on current events; 30 August 1886, p. 4, City improvement.

33 *Daily Telegraph*, 10 October 1882, p. 3, City omissions and complaints.

34 *Evening News*, 23 February 1886, p. 3 Sanitation; 3 September 1886, p. 4, The public health.

[35] Walters, 1901a, p. 20. San Francisco Department of Public Health, 1882, p. 9. San Francisco Board of Supervisors, 1885, p. 19.

[36] *Herald*, 13 June 1882, p. 5. *Evening News*, 30 July 1884, p. 5, Sydney slums and rookeries. Walters, 1901b, p. 10. *Daily Telegraph*, 23 January 1883, p. 3, Slum surveying expedition.

[37] *Herald*, 16 March 1887, p. 11, City buildings unfit for habitation. *Chronicle*, 7 August 1904, p. 5, How white women doctors are called in by the wealthy to cure ills of Chinatown; 3 July 1900, p. 12, Chinatown problem should be solved, say the merchants. Walters, 1901a, p. 13.

[38] John Young in the *Herald*, 31 July 1876. *Examiner*, 17 February 1885, p. 3, The Chinese quarter. San Francisco Board of Supervisors, 1885, p. 25.

[39] *Chronicle*, 4 April 1903, p. 16, Ask removal of Chinatown. Examiner, 1 June 1900, p. 3, Board of Health called upon to provide for the quarantined inhabitants of Chinatown; 4 July 1900, p. 9, Health Board has report on plague. Kinyoun to Wyman, 6 December 1900, in Public Health Service box 497, NA. *Examiner*, 10 July 1900, p. 4, The danger from Chinatown. San Francisco Board of Supervisors, 1885, p. 5.

[40] *Daily Telegraph*, 8 July 1880, p. 3, Purifying the city. Workingmen's Party of California, 1880, p. 4. *Daily Telegraph*, 29 June 1882, p. 4, editorial. *Daily Post*, 7 October 1892, p. 3, Society of Medical Officers of Health.

[41] *Daily Telegraph*, 21 February 1881, p. 4, The city rookeries; 11 November 1887, p. 5, Hotbeds of dirt and disease; 9 February 1889, p. 6, Some city rookeries. *Herald*, 29 April 1884, p. 5, Condemnation of tenements.

[42] Walters, 1901a, p. 14. *Evening News*, 11 November 1884, p. 6, Fever dens.

[43] *Examiner*, 4 July 1900, p. 9, Health Board has report on plague. San Francisco Board of Supervisors, 1885, p. 4. Raymond, 1886, p. 12. *Daily Mail*, 24 May 1882, p. 2, leader. *Daily Gazette*, 27 July 1898, p. 4, leader.

[44] Walters, 1901b, pp. 9, 27. *Chronicle*, 1 July 1900, p. 11, Widen streets of Chinatown and purge place of its evils. Workingmen's Party of California, 1880, p. 4.

[45] *Daily Telegraph*, 12 August 1884, p. 5, Condemned buildings. *Evening News*, 27 May 1880, p. 2, Through the city styes and stews. Walters, 1901a, p. 3. *V&P(NSW LA)*, 1875–6, pp. 549, 620. Health Officer's Report, 1 July 1896, p. 7, in San Francisco Department of Public Health, 1896. San Francisco Board of Supervisors, 1885, p. 18.

[46] *Examiner*, 17 January 1900, p. 1, Another murderous attack, victim seriously wounded. San Francisco Board of Supervisors, 1885, p. 39. Workingmen's Party of California, 1880, p. 12.

[47] Walters, 1901a, pp. 19, 15. *Daily Gazette*, 3 April 1901, p. 4, leader.

[48] *The Times*, quoted in *Daily Mail*, 15 April 1876, p. 2, The Birmingham improvement scheme. See the COS and Royal College of Physicians' memorials in *BPP*, 1874, vol. 52, pp. 675–8. Health Officer's Report, p. 5, in San Francisco Department of Public Health, 1879; see also the Health Officer's Report, p. 5, in San Francisco Department of Public Health, 1881.

[49] *Examiner*, 11 February 1901, p. 1, Pulpits ring with denunciation of officials too weak to battle with the wiles of oriental vice. Walters, 1901b, p. 18.

[50] *Daily Gazette*, 1 July 1901, p. 4, leader. *Daily Mail*, 4 October 1875, p. 2, The proposed new street: a sketch of the doomed rookeries. *Daily Gazette*, 17 November 1888, p. 4, leader (my emphases). ibid., 26 October 1883, p. 4, leader.

[51] *Daily Telegraph*, 27 July 1881, p. 4, The plague spots of Sydney.

[52] ibid., 1 February 1881, p. 3, The rookeries of the city; 26 August 1885, p. 5, Among the rookeries; 9 February 1889, p. 6, Some city rookeries. *Daily Gazette*, 27 November 1883, p. 4, leader.

53 Health Officer's report, p. 5, in San Francisco Department of Public Health, 1881; ibid., San Francisco Department of Public Health, 1885, p. 4; *Daily Telegraph*, 3 October 1881, p. 4, Sydney rookeries (my italics).

54 *Evening News*, 26 June 1885, p. 4, Sanitary reform. *Herald*, 28 January 1878, p. 4, leader. BCCHC, 5 March 1878. Chamberlain, quoted in *Daily Post*, 24 November 1878, p. 5, Infant mortality in Birmingham.

55 *Chronicle*, 3 July 1900, p. 6, Rebuilding Chinatown. San Francisco Board of Supervisors, 1885, p. 65.

56 *Echo*, 25 January 1883, Improvement Board Newspaper Cuttings, 1/2124, AONSW. Park, 1906, n.p. Walters, 1901b, p. 5. *Daily Post*, 25 October 1880, p. 8, The municipal elections; see also *Chronicle*, 4 April 1903, p. 16, Ask removal of Chinatown.

57 *Daily Post*, 24 October 1913, p. 11, Municipal elections. *Daily Mail*, 24 May 1882, p. 2, leader. Young, 1912, p. 903.

58 Walters, 1901a, p. 31.

59 *Examiner*, 18 January 1900, p. 2, Oriental vengeance like a tiger asleep in Chinatown. Workingmen's Party of California, 1880, p. 16.

60 Banks, Read, 1906, p. 161. Dobie, 1936, p. 245; and see Wilson, 1906, pp. 173–4.

61 San Francisco Board of Supervisors, 1885, p. 5.

62 Walters, 1901a, p. 7. *Chronicle*, 3 July 1900, p. 12, Chinatown problem should be solved, say the merchants.

63 Walters, 1901a, p. 15. Wilson, 1906, p. 173. *Examiner*, 16 June 1900, p. 5, Court decrees the raising of quarantine. *Chronicle*, 1 July 1900, p. 11, Widen streets of Chinatown and purge place of its evils.

64 *Daily Telegraph*, 25 November 1887, p. 3, More buildings condemned. *Daily Gazette*, 6 February 1901, p. 4, leader. *New York Times*, 15 May 1880, quoted in Lubove, 1962, p. 45.

65 *Evening News*, 21 February 1881, p. 2, Mayoral inspection of dilapidation; 25 November 1887, p. 6, Wretched rookeries (my italics). *Daily Post*, 4 May 1892, p. 7, The city council. *Daily Gazette*, 20 October 1875, p. 5, The proposed New Street. Walters, 1901b, p. 5.

66 San Francisco Board of Supervisors, 1875, p. 31. Walters, 1901b, pp. 12, 20.

67 *Daily Telegraph*, 5 June 1883, p. 3, More crusading amongst the cow-yards. *Herald*, 25 February 1885, p. 9. Robert A. Slaney, Report on the state of Birmingham and other towns, pp. 14, 19, *BPP*, 1845. Schultz, 1989, p. 119.

68 Massachusetts State Board of Health, 1873, p. 397. *Herald*, 1 July 1882, editorial; *Daily Telegraph*, 14 November 1887, p. 3, The rebuilding of Sydney.

69 Tyler, 1906, p. 308. *Chronicle*, 3 July 1900, p. 6, Rebuilding Chinatown; see San Francisco Board of Supervisors, 1885, pp. 42, 63.

70 *Chronicle*, 19 November 1904, p. 4, The Chinatown problem; 4 July 1900, p. 8, Wiping out of Chinatown evil must come before long; 3 July 1900, p. 12, Chinatown problem should be solved, say the merchants. See ibid., 1 July 1900, p. 11, Widen streets of Chinatown and purge place of its evils; Linthicum, 1906, p. 256.

71 *Echo*, 20 October 1883, Street improvement and the City Improvement Board, in Improvement Board Newspaper Cuttings, 1/2124, AONSW. Gibbs, Shallard and Company, 1884, p. 37. *Daily Telegraph*, 13 June 1882, p. 3, Inspection of rookeries. Bunce, 1885, p. xxiv.

72 *Chronicle*, 23 April 1903, p. 6, Gambling in Chinatown; 12 May 1903 p. 5, Chinese conspiracies to murder. *Herald*, 16 March 1887, p. 11, City buildings unfit for habitation.

73 *Overland Monthly*, quoted in Bronson, 1959, p. 171. Walters, 1901a, pp. 12, 20. *Daily Telegraph*, 9 February 1889, p. 6, Some city rookeries; 19 November 1884, p. 4, Condemned buildings.

9

Faces of Degeneration[1]

Travelling imaginatively through the topsy-turvy territory of the slum, readers are invited to gaze upon the faces of its inhabitants. A remarkable spectacle unfolds: 'All sorts of brows and faces can be seen.' Most are 'hideous and startling': the 'faces ... look ghastly ..., expressionless and semi-savage'. These are plainly not the faces of socially credible individuals, but of theatrically believable human types who seem appropriate to the stylized settings in which they are cast. The slums of newspaper representation are 'filled with the lowest and most degraded *types* of humanity'. Here are to be found 'the worst types of the poor'.[2] They show slum life to be 'low life, the lowest of the low'. The faces of these slumland characters personify 'the under stratum', 'the residuum', and consequently 'Crime and cunning are stamped indelibly on most of the faces.' They are unambiguously 'the outcasts of civilisation'.[3]

The newspapers' representations of slumland physiognomy substantiated popular belief that slum environments made slum-dwellers their slaves. Newspaper story-tellers cautioned that the 'many thrifty and respectable people' who were driven by poverty to live within the territory of the slum faced inevitable 'contamination' from their 'lawless and depraved' neighbours. Walters remarks of the slumland types he encountered that

In some of the obscure neighbourhoods nine women out of ten are the fallen and abandoned creatures who haunt the streets at night, and nine out of ten of the men are bullies and blackguards who prey upon them, or consort with them, or are ready for all species of vice and crime. Among these the hard-working parents of little children are often forced to dwell, and the innocents breathe in the putrid atmosphere, imbibe the filth, and become familiar with the most forbidden sins, before they are in their teens.[4]

Such story-lines dramatically echoed recurring expressions of concern by social workers, police, churchmen, housing reformers, and sanitarians that the 'sordid surroundings' of slums encouraged widespread demoralization and 'the rapid growth of the criminal classes'. In 1901 the editor of the *Birmingham Daily Gazette* pointed a finger at the grim moral of *Scenes in*

Slum-Land: 'Forced into these infernos by poverty, thousands of clean-minded, decent people sink to the level of their surroundings.'[5]

Slums were generally perceived as the territorial heartlands of an ever-swelling 'urban degeneracy'.[6] Worries that urban decadence, nurtured by debased slumland subcultures, would sap the ethics and enterprise of modern cities and nation states had increasingly occupied the attention of bourgeois social commentators since the middle of the nineteenth century. By the turn of the twentieth century worries about urban degeneration considerably influenced the social and physical sciences, and — through the pseudo-science of eugenics — were increasingly influencing social-reform discourse, popular opinion, and public policy-making. A member of the British Royal Commission into the Housing of the Working Classes had suggested in 1884 that slum neighbourhoods each comprised 'a little colony ... quite apart from ... general public opinion'. Such slum living, said the Conservative leader, the Marquis of Salisbury, was 'deleterious and ruinous to the moral progress and development of the race'. In Birmingham, John Nettlefold argued that the city's slum problem was symptomatic of broader challenges to 'industrial progress, and national physique'.[7] Commenting on expressions of concern that each new generation of slum dwellers displayed a 'reversion towards an earlier and lower ethnic form', the *Sydney Morning Herald* suggested in 1887 that the process might not only be shaping physical appearance but 'the intellectual and moral being' as well. A prominent Chicago housing reformer warned in 1917 that slums were 'producing a degenerate race'.[8]

By giving faces to these phantoms of bourgeois slumland imagination, journalists dramatically distilled the indeterminacies of definition about big-city living. Here were personifications of unquestionably intolerable conditions and life choices. The stories canvassed support for bourgeois reform agendas, because the physiognomical stereotypes pithily communicated the reformers' messages to mass audiences. Thus, sensational stories in the San Francisco press about the inhabitants of Chinatown were bracketed with predictions that if 'the people of San Francisco realized what a hotbed of disease and vice it is they would rise up and sweep it into the bay.'[9] More importantly, the slumland types entertained. The caricatures — easily recognizable as the faces of a race apart — had been popularized in theatre, fiction, and illustration since the first half of the nineteenth century. Their effect was to consolidate and extend bourgeois common sense. The roles performed by the characters in slumland dramatize elements from the varied representations of urban society in general discourse, echoing the more persistent expressions of concern, but diffusing them by superimposing the familiar frames of progress or decay, order or chaos, normal folk and savages. Although the characters in slumland are made to challenge the core values of bourgeois culture, even in slumland there are pockets of normalcy to confound the assaults by reasserting the continuing relevance of values drawn from the audience's everyday lives. Homeliness and family-centred morality are reasserted to quash the equation of urbanization with social polarization and moral decay. Duty, obligations, and citizenship are urged as palliatives for the shallow ethics which tinged capitalist progress.

The characters who play out these themes in the topsy-turvy setting of the slum were immediately recognizable to audiences from the resonances which they sounded with other forms of popular entertainment — dating back to the eighteenth-century urban novels of Defoe, Smollett, and Fielding — and with strands of discourse in the everyday world. They were readily assimilable into four image-laden categories which corresponded with clusters of belief recurring in the social dramas of city life: Woman, Foreigner, Landlord, and Child.

Woman

Woman is the principal player encountered by the explorers in slumland. Women were the inner-city residents most often encountered by slummer investigators by day, because male wage earners were away at their places of work. Men of the slum are consequently represented as shadowy types — such as the furtive forms of highbinder assassins in Chinatown — or are given greater definition as 'men of the lounging and unshaven class, strong but idle'.[10] It is not the social category, women, but a gender type, woman, who dominates the newspaper performances. She is spokesperson for the slum: direct speech is limited almost exclusively to her. She, in the guise of good and bad woman, visualizes most systematically the represented strengths of bourgeois lifestyles over those of the slum. She, in the role of housewife and street woman, comes to personify the promise of the modern city and the nightmare images of the city gone wild.

Woman simplifies complex social questions by translating them into familiar patriarchal frameworks of belief. Basic to those frameworks was the conviction that 'Men, everywhere throughout the wide range of civilization, have exhibited ... pride in the construction of the dwelling — the home.' That conviction enshrined *home* as 'one of our sweetest and most expressive words'. It was a truism that woman was the homemaker. Through her were made happy families, and from happy families were built healthy communities. It followed that healthy family life 'lies at the root of the wellbeing of society.' Woman was thus conventionally represented as 'the balance-wheel of the machinery of society ... In men's childhood, how potent [is] the influence of mother.'[11]

Newspaper tales represented as jewels those good homekeepers within slumland who abided by bourgeois canons of domesticity, cleanliness, and cosy household ornamentation. The boundaries between respectability and degeneracy are signified by 'busy housewives ... mopping'. The tourists 'find in some spots evidence of what would have been cleanliness if it could. Tidy little womanly arts had been exercised to make rooms look neat the ceilings of which were falling in small cubes of plaster and the walls of which were propped up with quartering and black with grime.' In such homeplaces 'the attempts at refinement and ornamentation were very marked. Flowers, pictures and nicknacks were placed wherever an opportunity offered, and bore evidence of being carefully tended.'[12] The good woman is cast in order to represent the home lives of the deserving poor, those families of 'honest toilers who had striven their hardest against ill-fortune and sickness.' In such homeplaces the explorers might discover 'an industrious, respectable woman' struggling to make ends meet, and lamenting 'the want of a husband to make things better', because these are situations and roles to which the audience is accustomed from recurring discussions of legitimate poverty and charitable works.[13] These families, clearly, 'are honest, self-respecting, worthily aspiring.' Yet the personal cost of their clinging to decent standards is to be read in the 'wan, drawn faces of the women'. In one such family, glimpsed in *Scenes in Slum-Land*, the consumptive husband — just released from hospital — is out looking for work: 'A white-faced young woman with tear-stains on her cheek, with the remains of prettiness on a face prematurely lined with care, rose to meet us, carrying a baby in her arms, a bright little thing holding a hard crust in its soft tiny hand.'[14]

Womanly 'thrift and cleanliness' in slumland are, however, 'only exceptions to the rule'. The good homemaker is contrasted with her slovenly neighbours. The change is immediately evident in the women's faces: the slumland type are 'frowsy', with 'tousled hair'. Closer scrutiny shows them to be 'coarse-featured, unkempt, and blear-eyed'.[15] They are inadequate housekeepers who perpetuate slum living by their inability to budget sensibly for their families. Journalists in Sydney exclaimed that even in some of the most degraded neighbourhoods 'there were no tokens of want. Even where dirt reigned there was no lack of food, and that of a kind, too, in the way of superiority not seen in more pretentious places.' Copying from British discourse on urban social problems, which maintained that 'quite nine-tenths of ... poverty is caused through drink and gambling', colonial apologists often thus blamed working-class poverty upon reckless household spending on 'luxuries' beyond their station: 'indulgence in feeding, [and] abuse of ... liquors and tobacco'.[16] With sensible household budgeting, so it was said, commodious suburban cottage homes would be within their means. Woman's shortsightedness was symptomatic of slipshod habits in general. Dirty slums and 'untidy women' went hand in hand: with such housekeeping, who could doubt the predictions that slum-dwellers 'will lose all pride in home'? The bad woman's children, neglected, roamed unsupervised through the streets. Meantime she would, if confronted with a basic household chore like clearing a blocked drain, 'waste an hour in talk, but will not take a broom in her hand and clear away the stagnant slops.'[17]

Representations of slumland as dirty, overcrowded, and destructive to home life are often introduced by these sullen unwomanly women, with 'hard faces and knotted hands, defiant of mien, bitter of tongue':

Miss Price ... better [-known] as John Bull, owing doubtless from her bluff and tough aspect ... did not look too kindly on his Worship, and seemed at first as if she intended to personally resent his intrusion, but a stern cry of 'His Worship the Mayor' ... caused the lady to unfold her copiously tattooed bare arms ... and make a curtsey, half in earnest and half in derision.[18]

Readers readily identified the type, because the bad woman was regularly employed to symbolize urban degeneracy. She starred in the fund-raising rhetoric of church and philanthropic moral rescue societies, and appeared daily in newspaper selections of sordid incidents from the city courts, 'continually drunk, and in company with drunken men'. Her performances in the Sydney press serve to confirm and draw together the many hostile characterizations of slums that were current in bourgeois discourse. Thus she denounces her fellow slum types, the foreigner and the landlord, and concedes the ill health of her surroundings. She is shamed by her inadequacies as homemaker: 'I was just agoing to clean this place up when you's gentlemen come. Do call again in half-an-hour'. Her loose morals are 'most distasteful to ... her ... [and] she is now ashamed ... to go into the streets for fear of meeting "old pals".'[19]

The most frequent representation of woman in the newspaper performances is indeed that of 'fallen womanhood'. The immoral woman was a particularly potent — and universal — synthesizing allegory for all of slumland's abominations. Lloyd's *Lights and Shades in San Fancisco* drew particular attention to the 'vice-worn women, abundantly painted and powdered and gaudily attired ..., [who] may be seen upon the thresholds or lounging by the open windows, half-dead from their excesses'. The 'painted harlots of the slums and alleys' were cast as doorkeepers to slumland in the San Francisco Board of Supervisors' 1885 report on Chinatown: 'The lowest grade of prostitution guards the entrance ... , and the hideous visages that peer through the wickets help to add to the general aspect of degradation and misery that reigns below.' The slum's lowest depths are everywhere visualized in the faces of the 'degraded women' who comprised the city's 'lowest prostitutes'. They had sunk 'to the lowest point of human degradation.'.[20] Comparisons between the faces of the good and bad woman thus complete the contrast between modern city and slum that was captured through images of low-lying hovels and soaring skyscrapers. In women's faces is represented the choice between good and evil in the modern city. On the one hand perform 'young women, untidy, unashamed, with loud voices and ready laughter, with wicked looks and leers, with a fearful mockery upon their lips, in various stages of disgrace and ruin.' On the other hand are 'blear-eyed hags and harlots' that 'had once been women', but who had been 'reduced by drink, debauchery, and opium to the verge of idiocy and premature old age.' In *Scenes in Slum-Land* the connection is explicit: readers are introduced to a back court which is full of 'women of all ages, whose vocation was but too plainly stamped upon their faces. And in the midst of them all were two schoolgirls with their skipping-ropes, happy and innocent. Who dare prophesy what the fate of those two will be in a few years?'[21]

Foreigner

The bad woman associates illicitly with the next slum type, the foreigner. She is found with him in Sydney's Chinatown, 'partially nude and lying stupified from either drink, opium or both.' The foreigner is, like her, attracted to the debaucheries of the city by night. Italian coffee- and fruit-stall owners in Sydney nightly allow their back premises to be 'used for the worst of purposes', and an old French couple run a house of ill fame.[22] Foreigners are potent and unmistakable signifiers of difference: they confirm that borders have indeed been crossed, and that slumland is truly a place of strangers. These associations were engrained in popular culture. The flood of 'less civilized' Irish immigrants into British cities had been identified as a contributing cause of slumland since early in the nineteenth century. It was said in 1840 that Birmingham's slums contained a 'considerable number ... [of] the lower class of Irish'.[23] Late in the century the settlement of Eastern European Jews in London's East End also attracted widespread unfavourable comment. Stereotypes of immigrants were especially current in settler societies such as the Australian colonies and the United States.

Often they were a source of comedy. Amusing Irish stereotypes had figured in American theatre and novels since early in the century. Edward Harrigan's comedies during the 1870s and 1880s about New York low life were filled with Irish-American, African-American, German, and Italian immigrant types. Lincoln Steffens discovered in the ghetto a potent source of 'heart-breaking comedies' while working as a police reporter for the New York *Evening Post*.[24] More often, however, characterizations of immigrants were hostile.

It was commonplace for American writers to blame slums on immigrants. Lemuel Shattuck's vastly influential 1850 sanitary report on Boston had accused immigrants of contaminating the city's 'native inhabitants' by importing foreign poverty, disease, and crime. As the century progressed immigrants were blamed for entrenching corrupt practices in big-city politics, for the mayhem of collective violence such as the 1863 draft riots and Orangemen riots during the early 1870s in New York City, for political terrorism such as Chicago's Haymarket bombing in 1886, and for labour unrest, such as the 1909 general strike by New York sweated garment workers. In 1898 Josiah Strong admonished in his tract *The Twentieth Century* that the swelling immigrant hordes who crowded into urban slums were threatening the survival of American democracy. These hostile characterizations flowed through into the scripts of popular entertainment, especially with the quickening pace of migration late in the century and during the first two decades of the twentieth century: the Irish are low-skilled, brawling, and drunken, the German-Jewish sweater or landlord is a stock villain, Italians are associated with crime and terrorism.[25]

In both the United States and Australia, it is the Chinese who were most frequently made to personify the foreign menace of the slum. Chinese immigrants were conventionally represented in American fiction during the last third of the nineteenth century as exotic exemplars of slumland living. Jacob Riis's stories about New York slum life, *How the Other Half Lives*, *The Children of the Poor*, and *Out of Mulberry Street*, slurred the Chinese as the 'one immigrant group who does not keep step' with other recent arrivals in 'pushing upward from the bottom'. The Chinese, he claimed, had 'fallen out of the ranks'.[26] Popular mobilization against large-scale Chinese immigration in the wake of gold discoveries in California, New South Wales, Victoria, and Queensland, and labour anger at wage undercutting by Chinese workers, meant that 'John Chinaman' was immediately adopted by newspaper audiences as a symbol of alien menace. The anger spilled over in both Australia and California to include the Japanese as well. Australian restrictive legislation to check Chinese migration had been passed by the colonial parliaments during the 1850s, and new laws were enacted in the early 1880s. In Sydney, the 'Chinese question' was repeatedly debated in the press, at public meetings, city council elections, and in the New South Wales Parliament, and an Anti-Chinese League urged resistance against the invading 'Chinese hordes'.[27] In the United States, a rolling series of discriminatory federal laws was enacted between 1880 and 1902, designed to deter Chinese immigration and disrupt permanent settlement. The San Francisco Chinese could not, until just before the First World War, become American citizens or marry Europeans, they could not live outside Chinatown unless they were laundry workers or domestic servants, they could not present testimony in court, and their children were barred from public schools.[28]

In Sydney and San Francisco, the Chinese were represented by the daily press as personifying slumland's smells, filth, and disease. In Sydney, the 'dirty, stinking Chinkies' were accused of having 'congregated so thickly and behaved so filthily' as to constitute 'a positive menace to the health of the city'. Health officials in both cities fuelled these characterizations, contending that the Chinese 'do not seem to fear disease, and have little regard for cleanliness.' In 1900 the *San Francisco Examiner* repeated the City Board of Health's opinion that the Chinese were distinguished from all other immigrant groups in the city by their 'extraordinary repugnance to modern cleanliness and sanitation'.[29] The Chinese, moreover, were blamed for epidemics of slum-bred immorality and crime as well as epidemics of disease. San Francisco's Chief Sanitary Inspector in 1900 called 'Chinatown … a menace to public health, to public morals, and to public decency.' Their districts in Sydney were popularly known as 'moral plague-spots'. Because they seemingly disdained home life and its accompanying 'well-defined family relations', the resulting 'relations of the sexes are chiefly so ordered as to provide for the gratification of the animal proclivities alone.' The evils of illicit sex, gambling and drugs are stamped upon the Chinaman's features: 'pale and emaciated, with his eyes protruding, and giving one the impression that he was more like a ghost than a human being.'[30]

The face of 'John Chinaman' thus mirrors the big city's immoralities. Initially, the quirks of character attributed to him are made to confirm the apparent indeterminacies of urban society. Thus, whereas on the surface he plays the role of 'the humble Chinaman', that role is soon shown to be a deceit. Journalists in Sydney and San Francisco highlighted alleged Chinese subterfuge, noting that alarms were spread ahead of any European's call so that the slumland visitors 'find nothing again but misleading innocence in all its Oriental simplicity'. In every den, they were evidently expected, for a look of intense cunning in the faces of the Chinamen found in them showed that much had been hastily hidden from sight. Enough, however, was seen, which, though perfectly unfit for description, fully proved that vice in its most hideous form fattened and festered in nearly every hovel entered. In some of the yards young girls were standing, whose disordered dress and half-stupified appearance, showed they had but a few minutes before been hurried from scenes that would not bear inspection.

Constructed in this role, the Chinese are made to illustrate the covert and diabolical nature attributed to slumland. Appropriately, the Chinese are said to have a passion for coded meanings. The *San Francisco Examiner* pointed to their love of 'secret and mysterious characters, like the swastika embroidered on clothing', the meaning of which no Europeans could ever agree upon.[31]

By stripping away these deceits, the newspaper stories reveal John Chinaman to be unambiguously bad. The fog of indeterminacy thereby clears. John Chinaman is 'crafty and unscrupulous', 'wily', and 'cunning'. He relishes in 'scheming and trickery'.[32] In thus constructing the type, journalists drew upon long and widely current characterizations. San Francisco's Health Officer had railed against 'unscrupulous, lying and treacherous Chinamen' in the 1870s,[33] as did federal health officials during the plague eradication programme in the early 1900s. Sydney's chief Inspector of Nuisances spoke out through the 1870s about rampant opium-induced promiscuity behind the seemingly innocent façades of Chinese stores. Newspaper play upon these supposed Chinese deceits reached its apogee in San Francisco, where Chinatown was a daily source of high-profile and sensational news. This coverage focused upon the figure of the highbinder, a word copied from early nineteenth-century references to Irish bandits. The city press regularly publicized 'tong wars', punctuated by uneasy truces, between rival Chinese highbinder gangs. In so doing the newspapers theatrically contradicted the deceit that the Chinese 'person-ified meekness, humility, industry and peacefulness', and highlighted them instead as a 'treacherous and lawless and a disturbing element in the community'. Readers' imaginations were enticed with arresting photo-graphs of murder scenes, and illustrations of highbinder hatchet-men creeping through trap doors, and of savage dragons with cocked pistols, in order to introduce new instalments in 'a serial story of crime in which every chapter is red with the blood of murdered men.'[34]

Highbinder violence was linked by the newspapers to protection rackets which preyed upon the unsavoury dealers in gambling and prostitution in Chinatown. The brothels and gambling and opium dens were in turn blamed by city and state politicians, health officials, and the press for contaminating the American host society. Sensational disclosures in the mid-1880s about drug abuse, gambling, and prostitution in Chinatown led to predictions of the 'deterioration of our healthy American race' through 'close intercourse' with Chinese. Scandal-mongering also traced Chinese contamination to corrupt practices in otherwise healthy American institutions. In 1900 and 1901 the *Examiner*'s investigations into Chinatown gambling led to disclosures — confirmed by state investigators — that gambling bosses, opium dealers, and brothel keepers were systematically paying off the police force. Mayor Phelan's police chief was widely censured. Mayor Schmitz's city administration was embarrassed in turn during 1903 when the city press again alleged that Chinese gambling houses paid into a common fund to pay off the police. Banner headlines were accompanied by photographs of policemen surrounded by drawings of sly Chinese, money bags, and dollar signs. Schmitz's Chief of Police was removed in disgrace. The city press trumpeted additional 'Sensational Developments' during 1903 when federal law enforcement officers were also tarred with the brush of Chinese corruption.[35]

Yet traces of normalcy could be discovered even among such outcasts. Sydney newspaper investigators remarked upon examples of 'courtesy' and 'politeness', and pointed out 'neatly dressed' children who 'toddled about what was evidently a happy home'. In 1903 the *San Francisco Chronicle* presented a feature article which profiled a 'Mongolian Housewife' as a good woman: Christianized, neat, industrious, and domesticated.[36]

Landlord

If bourgeois domesticity thus endured in the depths of the slum, common sense suggested that family-centred morality could civilize urban barbarism, and educate even slum-dwellers in healthy respectability and responsibility. Thus was vindicated the cautious social strategies by state and private charity and school agencies to address bourgeois anxieties of big-city chaos by lending paternal guidance and a helping hand to decent working-class families. Performances by the landlord suggested, moreover, that a moral community of healthy families need not be incompatible with capitalist progress if the sense of mutual obligation and duty supposedly found within the family was applied also to the ethics of the city marketplace.

Whereas woman and foreigner evoke disgust and occasional pity, the landlord attracts contempt. The newspaper narrators frequently concede, as they denounce the wretchedness of slumland, that 'the fault lay in most cases with the landlord rather than the tenant.' The landlords of newspaper representation do not live in slumland, but recoiling, 'shun their own property'. They none the less draw fat rents from it, crowding in as many tenants as possible and turning a deaf ear to their pleas for repairs. Landlords are characteristically 'very rich', 'rapacious', and motivated by 'rabid greed'.[37]

Slum landlords in Sydney are occasionally said to be titled, and often their names are bracketed with affluent suburban addresses. At other times community leaders are accused: municipal Aldermen, members of Parliament, of the Improvement Board, and even Dr Henry McLaurin, president of the New South Wales Board of Health. The object is to shame: McLaurin's property was described as a 'startling' and 'disgraceful' discovery, which prompted a hasty letter to the press the next day claiming McLaurin to be 'quite innocent' and condemning his property agent as 'the party to blame'. In San Francisco the press in 1901 pounced on another high-flyer: Mayor Phelan's brother-in-law, Frank J. Sullivan, whose Sullivan Estate in Chinatown was labelled a haunt of prostitutes and highbinders. The *Chronicle* moralized 'that the profits of Chinese depravity were shared by some well-to-do Caucasians. These persons consider themselves very respectable, go to church to show their neighbors that they are quite holy, drop a little of their Chinatown rents in the contribution box, dress stylishly and entertain their society friends.'[38]

Scenes in Slum-Land exploits this two-sidedness into yet another play upon slumland deceit, dramatizing the 'various subterfuges' that had been taken to conceal the identity of landlords. Walters nevertheless amasses a '"Black List" of property-owners', filled with 'names hitherto honoured', but who more aptly were subjects of 'shame and reproach'. The centrepiece of Walters' second series was his disclosure that one foul terrace was owned by a City Alderman who actually sat on the Health Committee. Unionist politicians gleefully supplied the name: Dr Alfred Barratt. The Gladstonian Liberal was not only a long-standing member of the Health Committee, but — supreme irony — had been among the initiators of the improvement scheme as well. Barratt did indeed own the offending property — a block of six houses — although they were not located in slumland proper, but in genteel Edgbaston.[39]

Simplistic representations of the low-cost property rental market as the plaything of a few rich and avaricious slumlords were ingrained in city culture. The landlord crystallized the ambiguous ethics of urban progress. It was, after all, a convenient rationalization for urban social problems: guilt was admitted but was embraced by a straw man. The truly immoral disequilibrium between private and social capital was trivialized. The landlord type had long been popular in English discussions of slums, and was given new prominence in the hotly contested debates about housing policy during the 1880s and 1890s, following publication of *The Bitter Cry of Outcast London*. In the United States, Griscom's seminal New York sanitary report of 1842 set a long-lasting trend when it identified landlords as having the prime responsibility to improve housing conditions. San Francisco's Health Officer in 1877 attached the blame for Chinatown's menacingly insanitary conditions upon 'avaricious landlords', and in 1885 the Board of Supervisors' report on Chinatown demanded that the 'property-owner in Chinatown must be made to feel his responsibility in this matter before Chinatown can ever be brought to a level with common public decency.'[40]

The landlord type is used in the newspaper performances initially to turn bourgeois notions of community and mutual obligation on their heads: they 'live at ease and care not for their fellows.' The landlord personified 'the individual greed that preys upon the misfortunes of the poor and helpless — that dooms to squalor and wretchedness whole households because decency would be unremunerative.' Ironically twisting the jargon of investors' discourse, Sydney's *Evening News* warned that such exploitation threatened to '"pay" in a terrible fashion of its own' with pestilence and moral evil breeding in the slum. In 1900 the *San Francisco Examiner*, spinning stories of highbinder atrocities, postulated that Chinatown 'should have been pulled down long ago, and would have been but that the landlords are a hard-fisted set, who would rather give the people of the city a plague scare every year than spend a few dollars in repairs.'[41]

The slumlord is, however, contrasted with landlord philanthropy. The figure who evokes contempt none the less has the potential to become a force for the moral and social improvement of the city. Reformist agendas had long represented the philanthropic slum landlord as a key figure in the social and moral regeneration of the city. London housing reformers' vision of the paternalistic landlord who presided over neighbourhoods of happy and respectable working-class families — and who, at the same time, shrewdly ensured that every such experiment in housing philanthropy was 'a paying one'[42] — exerted a powerful influence upon the urban bourgeoisie throughout the English-speaking world.

Lobbying for the redevelopment of San Francisco's Chinatown, the *Chronicle* urged in 1900 that the city needed 'public-spirited men' among the Chinatown landlords to initiate the reform process. An important part of the dramatic suspense in the newspapers' slumland story-telling lay in landlords' contrite acknowledgment 'of their duty to their fellow-creatures'. Walters contends that in Birmingham's back courts 'where the landlords have done their duty, have kept the houses in repair, have paved and drained the yards ... we have found the inhabitants, though just as poor as the others, cheerful, persevering, and aspiring.' The editor of the *Birmingham Daily Gazette* argued in the preface to *Scenes in Slum-Land* that the articles had been written in the hope that landlords might 'realise the sacred obligations of their stewardship.' Landlords are represented in the Sydney newspaper texts as being likewise swayed by press publicity to 'subordinate their selfishness to the public good ... Formerly the landlords never looked near their property except ... to call for the rent. Now they attend to the comfort of their tenants, and lovingly inspect any defects or damage in their tenements.'[43]

These recantations were pure theatre, of course, but in tapping the familiar demand for civic responsibility, the entertainments served also to instruct. Recriminations against the city's business leadership, and sermons aimed at the mainstream of bourgeois suburbia, for not engaging themselves sufficiently and disinterestedly in the philanthropic and civic affairs of the city were characteristic features of reformist rhetoric in all English-speaking cities in the late nineteenth century. In 1895 the American sociologist, Albion W. Small, lambasted the well-to-do for pursuing 'arrogant individualism' in defiance of 'the law of mutualism ... and ... reciprocal service' that must reign in a just society.[44]

The landlord's belated acknowledgment of duty is compared by the newspapers to the ethics prevailing in other positions of public trust. In San Francisco, slumland sensationalism became a means of demanding honesty and accountability among elected officials. The Republican and Labour leanings of the daily press made Phelan's Democrat administration an obvious target at the turn of the century: they had 'connived' at police inaction regarding public health ordinances and vice controls. The *Birmingham Daily Gazette* explained that *Further Scenes in Slum-Land*, with its damning attacks upon Cook's Health Committee, was intended to arouse the electorate to make 'their representatives understand that slum reform must no longer be shirked or shelved, but undertaken at once and carried through without faltering.'[45] Notwithstanding the often unsubtle political agendas peddled by the newspapers' managers, the slum tales' plea for public responsibility also carried a message for all readers to apply in their everyday lives. Personal commitment, friendship, and guidance by the bourgeoisie were needed, it was urged, in order to civilize the slum and to restore ethical purpose to urban social progress. The ruthlessness and conflicts of the big city would be tamed by new bonds of trust.

Child

Images of slum children complete the imagined split between modern city and modern Babylon. Yet, at the same time, representations of children crystallize the potential, even in slumland, for regeneration and integration rather than continuing degeneration and polarization. Slumland performances commonly unfold against backdrops of swarming children. Infant tears crystallize slumland wretchedness: 'From every other house comes the screaming or whimpering of babies.' Their faces confirm readers' suspicions of adult neglect and ill use. Slum children — 'abnormally pale', with 'thin, haggard faces' — 'bear too plainly the impress of the horrible surroundings they have always known.' Infants are found sprawling neglected upon the floor, unwashed and undressed. Walters points out 'the pathetic eyes of beaten and neglected children'. He exclaims that these 'poor little mites look at you with the dumb pathos of their big glistening eyes, more eloquent than any words they could utter.'[46]

In the mind's eye, these melodramatic vignettes collapse the implied territorial expansiveness of slumland to the potent personal horizons of the readers' own families. Thus, 'in the midst of filth and dilapidation, a scene of debauchery and drunkenness was relieved by the presence of a sweetly pretty child, a very little thing, who chuckled with delight at our intrusion, and was evidently abundantly satisfied with everything and everybody.' Another foray is rounded off with the exclamation that to 'step into the fresh air after exploring this place was like taking a refreshing bath, and the children's voices singing like a child's hymn in a neighbouring school seemed to bring the extremities of the possible in human matters face to face.' The stories thereby contrast scenes of bizarre otherness, the depths of the slum, with reassuringly familiar images of bourgeois domesticity. The menace of the slum is real, but the sway of its influence is everywhere contested. This recognition, however, is tinged with ambiguity: childhood innocence in such settings is a brittle thing. *Scenes in Slum-Land* notes that,

Lynch's Court, off Clarence Street, Sydney, c.1875

among the throngs of night-time revellers, 'Here and there are little girls crying round their mother's skirts till rudely shaken off; here is a little lad of five, with long curls and big brown eyes, holding his drunken father's hand quite trustfully, but looking into his face with a pathetic dumb wonderment.' Childhood vulnerability could be safeguarded in an ethical community of moral families, housed in leafy suburban homes, but, conversely, will inevitably be nipped in the bud if the moral cohesion of bourgeois community is broken down by greed and selfish indifference.[47]

These newspaper performances appeal not only to readers' family emotions, but to familiar themes in urban fiction, theatre, and illustration, and in reformist discourse on social and moral issues in the big city. All gave emphasis to the plight of children in slumland, and painted bleak pictures of the probable future for slum children 'born and brought up in vice'. It was an idle hope, they said, to expect these 'children ... to grow up uncontaminated by their surroundings.' Unless given moral home lives, they would 'only live to swell the dangerous classes of society.' More than with any other slumland type, said Jacob Riis, 'the child is a creature of environment.' The physiognomy of city youth was claimed to encapsulate the degenerative effects of modern urban living: the type is 'weedy ... , undersized and slight ... He has a repulsive face, low forehead, small eyes, a colourless skin and irregular colourless teeth.'[48] Newspaper story-telling operated within these well-established parameters. The contaminating influence of the slum upon childhood behaviour is a universal theme. In San Francisco, the *Chronicle* in 1903 modified its distaste for Chinatown by featuring the story of a Chinese boy's efforts to pay his way through school. Expressing guarded sympathy for the child, the newspaper noted that 'it seems a shame that his growth should be stunted and his mental faculties dwarfed by his cruel environment.'[49]

At the core of the press's pen pictures of slum children is the apparent collapse of healthy home living: 'children ... come stealthily to the place called "home" which they scarcely dare enter until darkness offers them some chance of protection from violence. These slum-children are the most pitiable element of slum-life. They creep about like ill-used animals; and a little lower than the animals they are appraised.'[50] Small wonder that children should become as brutalized as their elders. Children's games in slumland are represented as bizarre and repugnant: 'boys ... up to their knees in a mass of decayed and putrified vegetation', children chanting 'the small-pox! the small-pox!' as they dance around the inspectors, youths playing street football, 'full of desperate energy, good humoured yet perfectly savage, cursing and swearing, rolling over in the dust.'[51] The children graduate, with accumulating years and slumland experience, to street crime, immorality, and uncouth behaviour. The *San Francisco Examiner* tells how a 'young Chinese boy, too old to find amusement in the innocent and harmless game of shuttlecock, took his first lesson in highbindery last night': luring a victim into a dark hallway, where he is shot to death by highbinders. *Scenes in Slum-Land* recoils from the sight of adolescents, 'obviously "courting." Their terms of endearment are loathsome; their language is filthy; their conduct is gross, and it is as well not to watch them closely.' Readers of Sydney's *Evening News* imaginatively penetrate 'dark and dirty dens, with oily Chinese and brazen-faced animal looking girls of our own race.' Sensational representations of children 'forced to the lowest depths' were especially common and long lived in San Francisco, in accounts — circulated since the 1870s by government investigators, reform societies, and the press — of the brothel trade in adolescent Chinese girls. These 'poor creatures, children in years, children in mind, know no other life than a life of shame.'[52]

Bourgeois reformers played upon the spectacle of contamination in order to mobilize community support to rescue the children of the slums. Riis insisted that children born in the slum were not 'predestined' to die there. They must, he said, be raised 'into useful citizens'.[53] Philanthropic societies and asylums for slum children were regularly featured during the nineteenth century by the city press, which applauded the efforts of bourgeois ladies' committees to supervise the instruction of boys in manual trades and girls in needlework, and both in the private and civic responsibilities of homeliness and respectability. The efforts of child rescue societies, baby health centres, kindergartens, and of the burgeoning urban playgrounds and Boy Scouts movements were publicized by the press throughout the first quarter of the twentieth century.

Entertainers popularized the reformers' message. A stream of novels about the rescue of neglected city children consolidated belief that children's nature was essentially plastic. Slummer journalists also played with this theme. Contrasts drawn between the children of decent and debauched homes are common: some, the pride of respectable homes, are 'robust' and 'neatly dressed'; others are neglected, and appear 'unwashed and ill-clad'. Rescue work — designed to 'efface from ... [the] childish mind all reminiscences of the old evil life' — is also emphasized. In 1886 the Sydney *Evening News* noted the poignancy felt by the mayoral inspection party on finding a 'poor little thing' about 18 months old living in the midst of squalor: 'by request of the Mayor, Mr. Seymour [the Inspector of Nuisances] made some inquiries, and left a sum of money to be expended for the benefit of the child. The mother at first declined to accept it, but gave way at length, and appeared to be much affected.' San Francisco newspapers early in the twentieth century frequently dramatized the efforts of evangelical rescue societies to wrench young Chinese women away from the 'shameful lives they are required to live ... in the slave dens of San Francisco.'[54]

Dramatizations of child-saving have a central place in the story-lines of newspaper slumland sensationalism. The dramas clearly signal the inexorable triumph of bourgeois decency over the challenges thrown in its way by slumland degeneracy. That childhood innocence might endure in the slum and transcend this repugnant setting to mature into responsible adulthood left the worst abuses of the other slumland types looking feeble in comparison. The performances rest, in part, upon the familiar proposition that the malleable young could still be helped even if adult generations of slum-dwellers were beyond redemption. In another sense, the image of the child carries with it a promise of even wider slumland regeneration.

Childish traits were commonly applied in popular writings to the other types residing in slumland: the ignorance and uncouthness attributed to the urban poor were construed as symptoms of childlike simplicity.[55] By implication, the analogy of successful child-rearing carried with it the implication that rehabilitation of slumland types as useful members of the wider community was as feasible an undertaking for paternal civic leaders as was responsible child-rearing in the readers' own homes.

Notes

1 See Pick, 1989; also Cowling, 1989.
2 Walters, 1901a, p. 4. Lloyd, 1876, p. 254. *Daily Telegraph*, 28 May 1880, p. 3, The City Improvement Act (my italics). Walters, 1901a, p. 8.
3 Wilson, 1906, p. 179. *Evening News*, 17 May 1881, p. 2, Another sanitary crusade. Walters, 1901a, p. 18. Walters, 1901a, p. 8. *Herald*, 29 April 1884, p. 5, Condemnation of tenements.
4 *Evening News*, 10 September 1884, p. 6, The slums of Sydney. Walters, 1901a, pp. 11, 12.
5 *Australian Churchman*, 29 November 1883, Homes for the poor. Walters, 1901a, preface.
6 Strong, 1907, p. 132.
7 *BPP*, 1884–5, question 12,531, p. 456. *BPD*, 1884, volume 284, p. 1690. *Daily Post*, 21 October 1903, p. 4, Birmingham City Council.
8 *Herald*, 22 October 1887, p. 11. Charles B. Ball, quoted in Philpott, 1978, p. 108.
9 *Chronicle*, 3 July 1900, p. 12, Chinatown problem should be solved, say the merchants.
10 Walters, 1901a, p. 6.
11 California State Board of Health, 1879, p. 72. *Daily Telegraph*, 9 February 1884, p. 4, The enrichment of home life. *Australian Churchman*, 19 May 1881, p. 73, Overgrowth of cities. *Australian Witness*, 26 August 1876 p. 5, The family.
12 Walters, 1901a, p. 11. *Evening News*, 21 February 1881, p. 2, Mayoral inspection of dilapidation. *Daily Telegraph*, 7 January 1881, p. 3, The rookeries of the city.
13 Walters, 1901a, p. 20. *Daily Telegraph*, 7 January 1881, p. 3, The rookeries of the city; 29 April 1881, p. 5, The rookeries on the Rocks.
14 Walters, 1901a, pp. 9, 16, 10.
15 *Daily Telegraph*, 13 June 1882, p. 3, Inspection of rookeries; 10 May 1881, p. 3, The rookeries of Sydney. Walters, 1901a, pp. 4, 6.
16 *Daily Telegraph*, 15 January 1884, p. 6, Inspection and condemnation of rookeries. *BPP*, 1909, p. 395. *Weekly Advocate*, 19 January 1884, p. 340, The dark aspects of city life (quoting from G.R. Sims's 'Horrible London' articles). Dr George Dansey, in SCC, LR, 1883, vol. 3, no. 703 (May 1880).
17 Walters, 1901a, p. 3. *Daily Gazette*, 3 April 1901, p. 4, leader. Walters, 1901b, p. 11.
18 Walters, 1901a, p. 8. *Evening News*, 16 March 1887, p. 3, The condemned 'sell'.
19 ibid., 24 April 1888, p. 6, Filth, depravity, and vice: a horrible den. *Daily Telegraph*, 29 April 1884, p. 5, The rookeries on the Rocks. *Evening News*, 16 September 1884, p. 2, Among the rookeries.
20 *Daily Telegraph*, 28 May 1880, p. 3, The City Improvement Act. Lloyd, 1876, p. 82. San Francisco Board of Supervisors, 1885, pp. 59, 21, 14–15. Walters, 1901b, p. 18.
21 Walters, 1901a, pp. 8–9, 12. *Examiner*, 17 February 1885, p. 3, The Chinese quarter. *Evening News*, 21 February 1881, Mayoral inspection of dilapidation.

Daily Telegraph, 28 May 1880, p. 3, The City Improvement Act; and see The Bancroft Company, 1893, p. 3.

22 *Evening News*, 1 February 1881, p. 2, Human styes in Sydney. *Daily Telegraph*, 9 February, 1889, p. 6, Some city rookeries.

23 Wohl, 1977, p. 9. *BPP*, 1840, question 3021, p. 180.

24 Fine, 1977, p. 29; see Bremner, 1956, pp. 96–8.

25 Shattuck, 1948, p. 205. Buder, 1990, pp. 157–8. See Burchell, 1979.

26 Riis, 1892, pp. 8–9.

27 *Evening News*, 14 November 1887, The Anti-Chinese League. See Price, 1974; Evans, Saunders, Cronin, 1975; Markus, 1979; Cronin, 1982.

28 See Issel, Cherny, 1986; Kazin, 1987; Kraut, 1982, pp. 160–2.

29 *Evening News*, 12 March 1888, p. 4, A fever bed. *Herald*, 10 May 1881, p. 5, News of the day. *Evening News*, 1 May 1888, p. 6, The Chinese curse. San Francisco Department of Public Health, 1890, p. 316. *Examiner*, 4 July 1900, p. 9, Health Board has report on plague. See Trauner, 1974, pp. 1–19.

30 Dr W.S. Chalmers, in San Francisco Department of Public Health, 1901a, p. 74. *Evening News*, 16 April 1888, p. 4, Chinese dens. San Francisco Board of Supervisors, 1885, pp. 8–9. *Evening News*, 25 August 1885, p. 4, More rookeries condemned.

31 *Examiner*, 9 March 1900, p. 6, The Chinatown quarantine. *Daily Telegraph*, 1 February 1881, p. 3, The rookeries of the city. *Sunday Examiner Magazine*, 18 March 1900, Why Chinese murderers escape.

32 *Chronicle*, 28 October 1904, p. 6, Chinese false impersonation; 25 September 1903, p. 16, Arch conspirator said to be in hands of law. *Examiner*, 17 February 1885, p. 3, The Chinese quarter.

33 Dr J.L. Meares, in San Francisco Department of Public Health, 1877, p. 13.

34 Dobie, 1936, pp. 138–9. *Chronicle*, 17 November 1904, p. 4, Examples of Chinese character; 8 December 1903, p. 6, Another tong war. *Examiner*, 18 January 1900, p. 2, Oriental vengeance like a tiger asleep in Chinatown.

35 Workingmen's Party of California, 1880, p. 14. See illustrations in the *Examiner*, 3 April 1903, p. 3, Mayor and commissioner find corruption in Chinatown and Cogan's squad is removed; and 12 April 1903, p. 1, Police board admits gambling has been permitted. *Chronicle*, 25 Septmeber 1903, p. 16, Arch conspirator said to be in hands of law.

36 *Daily Telegraph*, 1 February 1881, p. 3, The rookeries of the city. *Evening News*, 1 February 1881, p. 2, Human styes in Sydney. *Chronicle Sunday Supplement*, 18 January 1903, How a Chinese family lives: a close-range study of a Mongolian housewife.

37 *Herald*, 23 February 1889, p. 11; 25 January 1883, p. 9. *Evening News*, 13 June 1882 p. 2, Old Sydney dens. Walters, 1901a, pp. 3, 9.

38 *Daily Telegraph*, 23 March 1886, p. 5; and 24 March 1886, p. 3, City rookeries. *Chronicle*, 4 May 1901, p. 14, Attack on Chinese vice.

39 Walters, 1901b, pp. 4, 6, 19. Parish of Edgbaston Poor Rate Books, March 1896, folio 103, volume 2. Barratt owned one front house and five back houses at 24 Waterworks Road.

40 Dr J.L. Meares, in San Francisco Department of Public Health, 1877, p. 9. San Francisco Board of Supervisors, 1885, p. 64.

41 *Daily Telegraph*, 25 February 1885, p. 6, Among the rookeries. *Australian Churchman*, 13 January 1881, p. 170, Cleanliness next to godliness. *Evening News*, 21 December 1887, p. 4, Artisans' dwellings. *Sunday Examiner Magazine*, 18 March 1900, Why Chinese murderers escape.

42 *Australian Churchman*, 13 January 1881, p. 170, Cleanliness next to godliness.

43 *Chronicle*, 3 July 1900, p. 6, Rebuilding Chinatown. *Herald*, 7 January 1881, p. 6, Marking tenements for demolition. Walters, 1901a, p. 22. *Evening News*, 18 August 1880, p. 2, Improving the city.

44 Private business is a public trust, *American Journal of Sociology* (November 1895), quoted in White, 1989, p. 170.

45 *Examiner*, 30 April 1901, p. 14, It would be better to help; *Chronicle*, 11 July 1900, p. 6, The root of the Chinatown evil. Walters, 1901b, preface.

46 Walters, 1901a, pp. 4, 16. *Evening News*, 24 March 1886, p. 4, Poverty in Sydney. *Daily Telegraph*, 10 May 1881, p. 3, The rookeries of Sydney. Walters, 1901a, pp. 9, 16–17.

47 *Daily Telegraph*, 29 April 1884, p. 5, The rookeries on the Rocks. *Evening News*, 17 May 1881, p. 2, Another sanitary crusade. Walters, 1901b, p. 24.

48 The Reverend R.G. Paterson in the *Herald*, 4 September 1877, p. 5, Sydney Ragged Schools. *Evening News*, 10 September 1884, p. 6, The slums of Sydney. *V&P(NSW LA)*, 1875–6, question 247, p. 592. Riis, 1892, p. 4. *The Australian at Home* (1892), quoted in Davison, G., The city-bred child and urban reform in Melbourne 1900–1940, in Williams, 1983, p. 143.

49 *Chronicle Sunday Supplement*, 16 August 1903, p. 5, Chinese boy is running an undertaking establishment to keep himself in school.

50 Walters, 1901a, p. 6. See Lloyd, 1876, p. 299.

51 *Daily Telegraph*, 21 February 1881, p. 4, The city rookeries; 17 September 1881, p. 6, Sydney rookeries. Walters, 1901b, 23.

52 *Examiner*, 26 June 1903, p. 4, Highbinder's art charms young Chinese. Walters, 1901a, p. 28. *Evening News*, 17 May 1881, p. 2, Another sanitary crusade. *Examiner*, 27 April 1901, pp. 1, 14, Phelan's shameless defense of chief Sullivan.

53 Riis, 1892, pp. 4, 8.

54 Siegel, 1981, p. 168. James, 1983, p. 60. *Evening News*, 24 March 1886, p. 4, Poverty in Sydney. *Examiner*, 4 April 1901, p. 9, Life story of a rescued slave.

55 See Bremner, 1956, p. 167.

The just war

James Cuming Walters warned his readers in 1901 that slum children, 'unless *rescued*, ... [will] swell the *ranks* of the despairing or boldly enter the *ranks* of vice.' The passage highlights two recurring themes in slumland representation and reformist rhetoric: rescue and impending battle. As late as 1966, the Victorian Housing Commission could still style Melbourne's supposed slums 'The Enemy Within Our Gates', and propose drastic measures for '*attacking* slum clearance'. To fight the slum, and to liberate its hostages, had for a century been characterized by slumland publicists as just and heroic deeds. These dramatic episodes were immensely attractive to readers, as newspaper management well knew. The resulting entertainments also carried a moral message: because the war was just, it would inevitably result in victory and the collapse of slumland barbarism.[1]

Walters presents himself as seeking to rescue slum-dwellers who still cling to honesty and respectability. His enemies are their brutish neighbours and a neglectful city council. Sydney newspapers cast the municipal officials themselves as rescuers. They are made to act as the wise and imposing spokesmen for the citizens of the modern city. The inspectors have an unerring ability to ferret out otherness as if 'by a kind of instinct'.[2] Their common-sense questions and judgements identify the guilty: the debauched woman, the uncaring landlord, the leering Chinaman, the loafish young larrikin. The inspectors provide money, medication, and jobs for the deserving, and insist that landlords adequately repair houses that are still habitable. Their decisions to condemn insanitary buildings are grudgingly endorsed even by the other-siders, and are represented as victories over self-interest and short-sightedness.

This liberation theme was especially played upon by the San Francisco press in lurid coverage of the exploits of Christian 'rescue missionaries in Chinatown'. The daily press revelled in sensational tales about the efforts of imprisoned girls 'to escape from the barred and guarded brothels' of highbinder gangs. Journalists lauded the efforts by Donaldine Cameron at the Presbyterian Mission Home, and Margaret Lake, superintendent of the Methodist Rescue Home, to 'free ... San Francisco's twentieth century serfs' — many of them 'mere children' — from highbinder 'tyranny'. They dramatized scenes in which the rescue workers snatched terrified young women from the 'chattering ... highbinders [who] pressed toward and swarmed around' them. When federal law enforcement officers also intervened against the Chinatown brothels in 1901, the city press styled them 'the rescue brigade', and carried headline news of their search for 'slave girls'. San Franciscans were 'brought up on melodramas based on the rescue of beautiful white women from opium dens.'[3]

To undertake such rescue work was to embark upon incursions into enemy territory. The incursions herald all-out assaults across the borders of the slum. The analogies thus serve not only to reinforce the slumland threshold in popular imagination,[4] but to foreshadow the slum's collapse. Metaphors of military conquest pepper newspaper features about slums and the discourse of slum reform. Headlines in the Sydney press characterize municipal sanitary inspections as an 'Attack' upon slumland, and the stories liken the municipal inspections to 'invasions of the unsavory regions'.[5] The *Birmingham Daily Mail* cheered on the 'little army of sanitary inspectors, here there and everywhere, [who] are zealously engaged in battling with disease, and driving it back into a few wretched corners where it can still lurk defiantly, but where it will be powerless to lurk much longer.' The concluding article in *Scenes in Slum-Land* is entitled 'A Call to Battle and Reform'. Walters is depicted as the commandant of an 'anti-slum campaign'. In San Francisco, likewise, the daily press described how police squads 'invaded' Chinatown as they scoured the lanes for gambling dens. The *Examiner* referred to its stories of Chinatown vice in terms of the '"Examiner's" Warfare on Chinese'. In New York, meanwhile, Jacob Riis published ringing calls to arms in 1900 and 1902, entitled *Ten Years' War* and *The Battle with the Slum*.[6]

Story-lines deliberately echoed the heroic encounters between gallant knights and rogues which were the staple of popular historical novels. The assault on the slum is pictured as carrying the fight right up to the gates of the enemies' citadel. It was not unusual in San Francisco to liken the dwellings of Chinatown as each an 'impregnable fortress', and recurring threshold tales cast the police as besieging warriors, battering down the defences of slumland garrisons. During anti-plague operations in 1900, the *Examiner* suggested repeatedly that 'Chinatown resembles a besieged city.'[7]

Telling the story of the battle with the slum also imitated newsmaking about European imperialism. Walter's Birmingham greets its returning heroes from the Boer War with 'tremendous huzzas'. Australians shared the glow of British imperial glories, and clamoured for annexations of their own in the South Pacific. Californians looked with pride at the new American territories of Hawaii and the Philippines, which had been seized during the Spanish–American War. The San Francisco *Examiner* translated to its coverage of Chinatown plague-eradication measures in 1900 the same language it used in other news columns to cover military operations in China between the Boxer rebels and the allied expeditionary forces. The newspaper described its Chinatown reporter as a war correspondent, and announced sensationally that he had penetrated its 'borders ... [and] immured himself in Chinatown that he may get at the actual facts.'[8] Headlines in the Sydney press frequently referred to the municipal house-to-house inspections as *raids*, as did San Francisco newspaper coverage of police activities against gambling in Chinatown.

Public memory of imperialist triumphs served to picture these confrontations between the invaders and defenders of slums as unequal encounters between manliness and savagery. Sydney's *Evening News* described the municipal inspectors as 'hunting up' slumland horrors, a phrase which readers recognized from the language applied to frontier skirmishes between the mounted police and bands of outlaws or aboriginals. Walters characterizes slum-dwellers as a 'horde', and announces that to penetrate far into their territory is to be 'assailed with the hideous cries of the half-wild creatures'.[9]

To wage war on this kingdom of darkness is a moral necessity. The fight is just because the opposing forces are recruited from beyond the boundaries of civilization and decency. As Walters explains, 'these people in the slums have lost their anchorage.' The Sydney *Evening News* styled them 'wretched pagans'.[10] In San Francisco, Birmingham, and Sydney, newspaper tales of expeditions into slumland by police and sanitary officials are therefore constantly represented as *crusades* against heathen territories. The metaphor of the crusade is ingrained in slumland representation. It made for good entertainment. Read against a backdrop of community pride in European expansion, it also carried an unmistakable message. The battle with the slum was a just war because it carried civilization to the savages, and transformed the newly occupied territories from blighted wilderness into sites for useful industry. *Further Scenes in Slum-Land* typifies the style: 'revisiting some of the dark places we had described in previous articles ... It seemed as if some fairy had been at work, and with a wave of the wand had changed the aspect of the whole region. Some of the gloomiest spots had become bright and cheerful, the foul spots clean, the plague spots wholesome.'[11] Bourgeois common sense is ascendent. The modern city has triumphed over the slum.

Notes

1   Walters, 1901a, p.6. Housing Commission of Victoria, 1966, n.p. (my italics).
2   *Evening News*, 21 February 1881, p.2, Mayoral inspection of dilapidation.
3   *Examiner*, 26 April 1901, p.2, Christian workers applaud crusade of 'The Examiner'; 5 April 1901, p.7, Risks her life to rescue other slaves in Chinatown; 23 March 1901, p.3, Hideous tyranny of slave dealers darkens fair fame of California; 11 November 1903, p.7, Slave girl eludes her highbinder pursuers. *Chronicle*, 21 April 1901, p.12, Government lays strong hand on Chinese slave trade. Dobie, 1936, pp. 246-7.
4   See chapter 7.
5   *Evening News*, 28 May 1880, p.3, The homes of the larrikins; 17 May 1881, p.2, Another sanitary crusade.

6 *Daily Mail*, 3 July 1877, p.2, leader. Walters, 1901a, p.30. *Manchester City News*, Mr. J. Cuming Walters: a journalist's long and varied career, no date (1931), in BCL. *Chronicle*, 5 April 1903, p.16, Chinese fear the new police squad. *Examiner*, 26 April 1901, p.2, Christian workers applaud crusade of 'The Examiner'. See Riis, 1900; 1902.

7 *Chronicle Sunday Supplement*, 18 January 1903, How a Chinese family lives. *Examiner*, 31 May 1900, p.3, Strict quarantine Chinatown district; also 11 March 1900, p.14, Quarantine of Chinatown raised; 16 June 1900, p.5, Court decrees the raising of quarantine.

8 Walters, 1901b, p.22. *Examiner*, 6 June 1900, p.2, Volunteered to face death to get the news. During 1904, newspaper accounts of anti-slum campaigns in the city were likewise coloured by their simultaneous coverage of the Russo-Japanese War.

9 *Evening News*, 8 July 1880, p.2, Another raid on the hovels and rookeries of the city. Walters, 1901a, p.10. Walters, 1901b, p.23.

10 Walters, 1901a, p.18. *Evening News*, 27 May 1880, p.2, Through the city styes and stews.

11 Walters, 1901b, p.25.

Bibliography

Abrams, C., 1965, *The city is the frontier*, Harper and Row, New York.

Annan, T., 1900, *Photographs of old closes, streets, etc., taken 1868-1877*, third edition, City of Glasgow Improvement Trust, Glasgow.

Anon, n.d. (1902), *Complimentary banquet given to Hon. James D. Phelan, by the officials of the city of San Francisco, Saturday evening, December 28, 1901*, Cubery and Company, San Francisco.

(1908), *Modern San Francisco*, Western Press Association, San Francisco.

Balfour, M., 1985, *Britain and Joseph Chamberlain*, Allen and Unwin, London.

The Bancroft Company, 1893, *Chinatown*, Bancroft Company, San Francisco.

Bancroft, H.H., 1907, *Some cities and San Francisco and resurgam*, Bancroft Company, New York.

Banks, C.E., Read, O., 1906, *The history of the San Francisco disaster and Mount Vesuvius horror*, C.E. Thomas, San Francisco.

Barth, G., 1980, *City people: the rise of modern city culture in nineteenth-century America*, Oxford University Press, New York.

1988, *Instant cities: urbanization and the rise of San Francisco and Denver*, University of New Mexico Press, Albuquerque.

Bass, T.J., 1898 (?), *Every day in blackest Birmingham*, BCL.

1903, *Hope in shadow land*, BCL.

BCL, Photographs of buildings removed under the Birmingham improvement scheme of 1875, c. 1882–84 (reference 311911).

Bean, W.,1972, *Boss Ruef's San Francisco: the story of the Union Labor Party, big business, and the graft prosecution*, University of California Press, Berkeley and Los Angeles.

Beebe, L., Clegg, C., 1960, *San Francisco's golden era: a picture story of San Francisco before the fire*, Howell-North Books, Berkeley.

Birmingham Liberal Association, Rotton Park Ward, 1879, *The improvement scheme and the coming elections: a speech by Councillor R. Tangye, delivered in Clark Street Board Schools on Monday August 25th 1879*, BCL.

Board of Trade of San Francisco, 1893, *Sixteenth Annual Report*, San Francisco.

1899, *Twenty-second Annual Report*, San Francisco.

1901, *Twenty-fourth Annual Report*, San Francisco.

Borough of Birmingham, 1875a, *A short history of the passing of the Birmingham (Corporation) Gas Act, and the Birmingham (Corporation) Water Act, with the speeches of the Mayor Joseph Chamberlain Esquire (in support of these measures) and also in favour of the adoption of the Artisans' and Labourers' Dwellings Improvement Act*, BCL.

1875b, *The Artisans' and Labourers' Dwellings Act 1875: proceedings on the adoption by the Council of a scheme for the improvement of the Borough, with the speeches of the Mayor, Joseph Chamberlain Esquire, and the chairman of the Improvement Committee, Mr Councillor White, in support thereof*, BCL.

1878, *The progress of the Birmingham improvement scheme: a speech delivered by Alderman Chamberlain M.P. at a special meeting of the Council held on the 11th of June 1878*, BCL.

Boyd, C.W. (ed.), 1914, *Mr. Chamberlain's speeches*, Constable, London.

BPP, 1840, volume 11, Report from the Select Committee on the Health of Towns.

1844, volume 17, First Report of the Commissioners for Inquiring into the State of Large Towns and Populous Districts.

1845, volume 18, Second Report of the Commissioners for Inquiring into the State of Large Towns and Populous Districts.

1866, volume 33, Eighth Report of the Medical Officer of the Privy Council.

1870, volume 38, Twelfth Report of the Medical Officer of the Privy Council.

1871, volume 35, Second Report of the Royal Sanitary Commission.

1874, volume 52, Royal College of Physicians, Memorial on the Condition of the Dwellings of the Poor in London; and Council of the Charity Organization Society, Memorial on the Improvement of the Dwellings of the Poor in London.

1880, volume 26, Ninth Report of the Local Government Board.

1882, volume 7, Report from the Select Committee on Artisans' and Labourers' Dwellings.

1884–5, volume 30, First Report of the Royal Commission into the Housing of the Working Classes.

1908, volume 107, Report of the Inquiry by the Board of Trade into Working Class Rents, Housing and Retail Prices, together with the Standard Rates of Wages Prevailing in Certain Occupations in the Principal Industrial Towns of the United Kingdom.

1909, volume 41, Royal Commission on the Poor Laws and Relief of Distress.

Bremner, R.H., 1956, *From the depths: the discovery of poverty in the United States*, New York University Press, New York.

Briggs, A., 1952, *History of Birmingham*, volume 2, Oxford University Press, London.

British Association for the Advancement of Science, 1950, *Birmingham and its regional setting: a scientific survey*, Local Executive Committee of the British Association for the Advancement of Science, Birmingham.

Bronson, W., 1959, *The earth shook, the sky burned*, Doubleday and Company, New York.

Buder, S., 1990, *Visionaries and planners: the garden city movement and the modern community*, Oxford University Press, New York.

Bunce, J.T., 1878, *History of the Corporation of Birmingham*, volume 1, Cornish Brothers, Birmingham.

1885, *History of the Corporation of Birmingham*, volume 2, Cornish Brothers, Birmingham.

Burchell, R.A., 1979, *The San Francisco Irish, 1848–1880*, Manchester University Press, Manchester.

Burnett, J., 1978, *A social history of housing, 1815-1970*, David and Charles, Newton Abbot.

Byington, L.F., Lewis, O. (eds), 1931, *The history of San Francisco*, volume 1, S.J. Clarke Publishing Company, Chicago and San Francisco.

Cadbury, E., Matheson, M.C., Shann, G., 1909, *Women's work and wages: a phase of life in an industrial city*, 2nd edition, T. Fisher Unwin, London.

California Promotion Committee, 1903, *San Francisco and its environs*, San Francisco.

California State Board of Health, 1879, *Fifth Biennial Report of the State Board of Health of California*, 1878-9, Sacramento.

1903, *Monthy Circular of the California State Board of Health* (March).

1906a, *Monthly Bulletin*, 1 (11).

1906b, *Monthly Bulletin*, 2 (4).

1907a, *Monthly Bulletin*, 3 (3).

1907b, *Monthly Bulletin*, 3 (6).

1908, *Monthly Bulletin*, 3 (8).

1909, *Monthly Bulletin*, 5 (5).

1913, *Twenty-second Biennial Report of the State Board of Health of California, 1910-1912*, Sacramento.

Chamberlain, J., 1874, The new page of the liberal programme, *Fortnightly Review*, new series, 16 (94): 405-29.

1877, A new political organization, *Fortnightly Review*, 22 (127): 126-34.

1878, The caucus, *Fortnightly Review*, 24 (143): 721-41.

1883, Labourers' and artisans' dwellings, *Fortnightly Review*, 34 (204): 761-76.

1894, Municipal government: past, present, and future, *The New Review*, 10, (61): 649-61.

City of Birmingham, 1900, *Proceedings of the Council, 1899-1900*, BCL.

1901, *Proceedings of the Council, 1900-1901*, BCL.

1902, *Proceedings of the Council, 1901-1902*, BCL.

1903a, *Proceedings of the Council, 1902-1903*, BCL.

1903b, *Housing of the Working Classes: Report of the Housing Committee to the City Council, 20th October 1903*, BCL.

1904, *Proceedings of the Council, 1903-1904*, BCL.

1907, *Proceedings of the Council, 1906-1907*, BCL.

1913, *Proceedings of the Council, 1912-1913*, BCL.

1914, *Report of the Special Housing Inquiry Committee*, BCL.

City of Sydney, 1889, *Proceedings of the Municipal Council of the City of Sydney During the Year 1888*, SCCA.

1890, *Proceedings of the Municipal Council of the City of Sydney During the Year 1889*, SCCA.

1901, *Proceedings of the Municipal Council of the City of Sydney During the Year 1900*, SCCA.

1902, *Proceedings of the Municipal Council of the City of Sydney During the Year 1901*, SCCA.

Coghlan, T.A., 1897, *The wealth and progress of New South Wales, 1896-7*, Government Printer, Sydney.

Cole, T., 1981, *A short history of San Francisco*, Lexikos, San Francisco.

Coleman, B.I. (ed.), 1973, *The idea of the city in nineteenth-century Britain*, Routledge and Kegan Paul, London.

Cowling, M., 1989, *The artist as anthropologist: the representation of type and character in Victorian art*, Cambridge University Press, Cambridge.

Crespi, A.J.H., 1889, The progress of modern Birmingham, *National Review*, 13: 386-411.

Cronin, K., 1982, *Colonial casualties: Chinese in early Victoria*, Melbourne University Press, Melbourne.

Cross, R.A., 1885, Housing the poor, *Nineteenth Century*, 17 (100): 926-47.

Cruden, A., n.d., *A complete concordance to the Old and New Testament*, Frederick Warne and Company, London.

Curson, P.H., 1985, *Times of crisis: epidemics in Sydney, 1788-1900*, Sydney University Press, Sydney.

Davison, G., 1983, The city-bred child and urban reform in Melbourne 1900-1940, in Williams, P. (ed.), *Social process and the city*, George Allen and Unwin, Sydney, pp.143-74.

Davison, G., Dunstan, D., McConville, C. (eds),1985, *The outcasts of Melbourne: essays in social history*, Allen and Unwin, Sydney.

Dent, R.K., 1894, *The making of Birmingham: being a history of the rise and growth of the midland metropolis*, J.L. Allday, Birmingham.

Disturnell, W.C., 1883, *Disturnell's strangers' guide to San Francisco and vicinity*, W.C. Disturnell, San Francisco.

Dobie, C.C., 1936, *San Francisco's Chinatown*, D. Appleton-Century Company, New York.

Dolman, F. (ed. Lees, L., Lees, A.), 1985, *Municipalities at work: the municipal policy of six great towns and its influence on their social welfare* (first published 1895), Garland Publishing, New York.

Duffy, J., 1974, *A history of public health in New York city, 1866-1966*, Russell Sage Foundation, New York.

Dunlap, G.A., 1965, *The city in the American novel, 1789-1900*, Russell and Russell, New York.

Dunleavy, P., 1981, *The politics of mass housing in Britain, 1945-1975*, Clarendon Press, Oxford.

Dyos, H.J., 1957, Urban transformation: a note on the objects of street improvement in Regency and early Victorian London, *International review of social history*, 2 (2): 259-65.

1967, The slums of Victorian London, *Victorian Studies*, 11 (1): 5-40.

Dyos, H.J., Wolff, M. (eds), 1973, *The Victorian city: images and realities*, Routledge and Kegan Paul, London.

Edgar, A. (ed.), 1869, *Transactions of the National Association for the Promotion of Social Science*, Longmans, Green, Reader, and Dyer, London.

Edgbastonia, 1904, The Reverend Thomas J. Bass, 4 (272): 3-7.

1907, Councillor J.S. Nettlefold, J.P., 27 (310): 325-9.

Englander, D., 1983, *Landlord and tenant in urban Britain, 1838-1918*, Clarendon Press, Oxford.

Evans, R., Saunders, K., Cronin, K., 1975, *Exclusion, exploitation and extermination: race relations in colonial Queensland*, Australia and New Zealand Book Company, Sydney.

Fallows, J.A., Hughes, F., 1905, *The housing question in Birmingham*, BCL.

Fine, D.M., 1977, *The city, the immigrant and American fiction, 1880-1920*, Scarecrow Press, Metuchen, New Jersey.

Fitzgerald, S., 1987, *Rising damp: Sydney, 1870-90*, Oxford University Press, Melbourne.

Fowler, F.E.T., 1975, *Southern lights and shadows*, Sydney University Press, Sydney (first published in London, 1859).

Fraser, D., 1976, *Urban politics in Victorian England: the structure of politics in Victorian cities*, Leicester University Press, Leicester.

Fraser, D., Sutcliffe, A. (eds), 1983, *The pursuit of urban history*, Edward Arnold, London.

Frazer, W.M., 1950, *A history of English public health*, Bailliere, Tindall and Cox, London.

Freeman, J., 1888, *Lights and shadows of Melbourne life*, Sampson Low, Marston, Searle, and Rivington, London.

Fried, L.F., 1990, *Makers of the city*, University of Massachusetts Press, Amherst.

Garvin, J.L., 1935, *The life of Joseph Chamberlain*, volume 1, Macmillan, London.

Gaskell, S. M. (ed.), 1990, *Slums*, Leicester University Press, Leicester.

Gates, R.A., 1987, *The New York vision: interpretations of New York city in the American novel*, University Press of America, Lantham.

Gennep, A. van, 1960 (trans. Vizedom, M.B., Caffee, G.L.), *Rites of passage*, Routledge and Kegan Paul, London.

Genthe, A., Irwin, W., 1909, *Pictures of old Chinatown*, Moffat, Yard and Company, New York.

Gibbs, Shallard and Company, 1884, *Illustrated guide to Sydney and its suburbs, and to favourite places of resort in New South Wales*, fourth edition, Gibbs, Shallard and Company, Sydney.

Gilbert, B.B., 1966, *The evolution of national insurance in Great Britain: the origins of the welfare state*, Michael Joseph, London.

Gilman, S.L., 1985, *Difference and pathology: stereotypes of sexuality, race, and madness*, Cornell University Press, Ithaca.

Gordon and Gotch, 1888, *The Australian handbook*, Gordon and Gotch, London and Sydney.

Gould, S.J., 1989, *Wonderful life: the burgess shale and the nature of history*, W.W. Norton and Company, New York.

Greer, S., 1965, *Urban renewal and American cities: the dilemma of democratic intervention*, Bobbs-Merrill, Indianapolis.

Harris, F., Chamberlain, J., 1883, The radical programme, III: the housing of the poor in towns, *Fortnightly Review*, 34 (202): 587-600.

Hawkes, H., 1878, *The Birmingham Landlords' and Ratepayers' Mutual Protection Association: speech of Henry Hawkes Esquire J.P., Coroner for Birmingham at the annual dinner May 29th 1878*, Birmingham Gazette, Birmingham.

Heath, F.R., 1876, *Artisans' dwellings and the Birmingham improvement scheme*, F. Grew, Birmingham.

Hennock, E.P., 1956, The role of religious dissent in the reform of municipal government in Birmingham, 1865-1876, Ph.D. thesis, University of Cambridge.

Hergenhan, L.T. (ed.), 1972, *A colonial city: high and low life — selected journalism of Marcus Clarke*, University of Queensland Press, Brisbane.

Hill, O., 1869, Organized work among the poor: suggestions founded on four years' management of a London court, *Macmillan's Magazine*, 20: 219-26.

———— 1883, *Homes of the London poor*, 2nd edition, Macmillan, London; reprinted in Chaloner, W.H. (ed.), 1970, *Octavia Hill and Andrew Mearns, homes of the London poor and the bitter cry of outcast London*, Frank Cass and Company, London.

———— 1891, Our dealings with the poor, *Nineteenth Century*, 30 (174): 161-70.

Himmelfarb, G., 1984, *The idea of poverty: England in the industrial age*, Knopf, New York

Hittell, J.S., 1888, *A guide-book to San Francisco*, Bancroft Company, San Francisco.

Housing Commission of Victoria, 1966, *The enemy within our gates*, Housing Commission of Victoria, Melbourne.

Howe, R. (ed.), 1988, *New houses for old: fifty years of public housing in Victoria, 1938-1988*, Ministry of Housing and Construction, Melbourne.

Hunter, R., 1904, *Poverty*, Macmillan, New York.

Irwin, W., 1906, *The city that was: a requiem of old San Francisco*, B. W. Huebsch, New York.

Issel, W., Cherny, R.W., 1986, *San Francisco, 1865-1932: politics, power, and urban development*, University of California Press, Berkeley and Los Angeles.

James, J.S. (ed. Cannon, M.), 1983, *The vagabond papers*, Hyland House, Melbourne (first published 1877-8).

Jones, G.S., 1984, *Outcast London: a study in the relationship between classes in Victorian London*, Penguin Books, Harmondsworth (first published in 1971 by Oxford University Press).

Jones, M.A., 1972, *Housing and poverty in Australia*, Melbourne University Press, Melbourne.

Kasson, J.F., 1976, *Civilizing the machine: technology and republican values in America 1776–1900*, Grossman, New York.

Kazin, M., 1987, *Barons of labor: the San Francisco building trades and union power in the progressive era*, University of Illinois Press, Urbana.

Keating, P. (ed.), 1976, *Into unknown England, 1866-1913*, William Collins Sons and Company, Glasgow.

Keeler, C., 1906, *San Francisco through earthquake and fire*, Paul Elder and Company, San Francisco.

Kellogg, P.U. (ed.), 1974, *The Pittsburgh district civic frontage*, Arno Press, New York (first published in 1914 by the Russell Sage Foundation).

Kelly, M., 1978, Picturesque and pestilential: the Sydney slum observed, 1860-1900, in Kelly (ed.), *Nineteenth-century Sydney: essays in urban history*, Sydney University Press, Sydney, pp.66-80.

Kendig, H., 1979, *New life for old suburbs: post-war land use and housing in the Australian inner city*, George Allen and Unwin, Sydney.

Klein, M., Kantor, H.A., 1976, *Prisoners of progress: American industrial cities, 1850-1920*, Macmillan, New York.

Knapp, J.M. (ed.), 1895, *The universities and the social problem: an account of the university settlements in East London*, Rivington Percival and Company, London.

Kraut, A.M., 1982, *The huddled masses: the immigrant in American society, 1880-1921*, Harlan Davidson, Arlington Heights.

Lambert, J.R., 1970, *Crime, police, and race relations: a study in Birmingham*, Oxford University Press, London.

Lane, J. B., 1974, *Jacob A. Riis and the American city*, Kennikat Press, Port Washington.

Lane, W., 1980, *The workingman's paradise: an Australian labour novel*, Sydney University Press, Sydney (first published in Brisbane, 1892).

Lane-Claybon, J.E., 1920, *The child welfare movement*, G. Bell and Sons, London, appendix 7: Housing and sanitary conditions in relation to mortality rates in Birmingham.

Larcombe F.A., 1976, *The stabilization of local government in New South Wales, 1858-1906*, Sydney University Press, Sydney.

Lees, A., 1985, *Cities perceived: urban society in European and American thought, 1820-1940*, Manchester University Press, Manchester.

Lewis, O., 1966, *San Francisco: mission to metropolis*, Howell-North Books, Berkeley.

Linthicum, R., 1906, *San Francisco earthquake horror*, Hubert D. Russell, Chicago.

Lloyd, B.E., 1876, *Lights and shades in San Francisco*, A. L. Bancroft and Company, San Francisco.

Lubove, R., 1962, *The progressives and the slums: tenement housing reform in New York city, 1890-1917*, University of Pittsburgh Press, Pittsburgh.

Macdonald, J., 1886, Birmingham: a study from the life, *Nineteenth Century*, 22, (114): 234-54.

McDonald, T.J., 1986, *The parameters of urban fiscal policy; socioeconomic change and political culture in San Francisco, 1860-1906*, University of California Press, Berkeley and Los Angeles.

MaCulla, D., 1973, *Victorian and Edwardian Birmingham from old photographs*, B.T. Batsford, London.

Markus, A., 1979, *Fear and hatred: purifying Australia and California, 1850-1901*, Hale and Iremonger, Sydney.

Marqusee, M., 1988, *New York: an illustrated anthology*, Conran Octopus, London.

Massachusetts State Board of Health, 1873, The homes of the poor in our cities, *Public Documents of Massachusetts*, 4 (31): 396-441.

Mayne, A.J.C., 1981, 'A most pernicious principle': the local government franchise in nineteenth-century Sydney, *Australian Journal of Politics and History*, 27 (2): 160-71.

1982, *Fever, squalor and vice: sanitation and social policy in Victorian Sydney*, University of Queensland Press, Brisbane.

1988, 'The dreadful scourge': responses to smallpox in Sydney and Melbourne, 1881-2, in MacLeod, R., Lewis, M. (eds), *Disease, medicine and empire: perspectives on western medicine and the experience of European expansion*, Routledge, London.

1990, Representing the slum, *Urban History Yearbook*, 17: pp.66-84.

1991a, *Representing the slum: popular journalism in a late nineteenth-century city*, Melbourne University History Monograph Series, Melbourne.

1991b, An Italian traveller in the antipodes: an historical rite of passage, *Australian Cultural History*, 10: 58-68.

Mearns, A. (ed. Wohl, A.S.), 1970, *The bitter cry of outcast London*, Leicester University Press, Leicester (first published 1883).

Meisel, M., 1983, *Realizations: narrative, pictorial, and theatrical arts in nineteenth-century England*, Princeton University Press, Princeton.

Merchants Exchange, 1907, *Annual Report of the Merchants Exchange for the Year Ending June 30, 1907*, Commercial Publishing Company, San Francisco.

1908, *Annual Report of the Merchants Exchange for the Year Ending June 30, 1908*, Commercial Publishing Company, San Francisco.

1909, *Annual Report of the Merchants Exchange for the Year Ending June 30, 1909*, Commercial Publishing Company, San Francisco.

Mitchell, B.R., 1981, *European historical statistics, 1750-1975*, second edition, Macmillan, London.

1983, *International historical statistics: the Americas and Australia*, Macmillan, London.

Mollenkopf, J.H. (ed.), 1988, *Power, culture, and place: essays on New York City*, Russell Sage Foundation, New York.

Moore, S.F., Myerhoff, B.G. (eds), 1975, *Symbol and politics in communal ideology: cases and questions*, Cornell University Press, Ithaca.

Muscatine, D., 1975, *Old San Francisco: the biography of a city from early days to the earthquake*, G.P. Putnam's Sons, New York.

Nadel, I.B., Schwarzbach, F.S. (eds), 1980, *Victorian artists and the city: a collection of critical essays*, Pergamon Press, New York.

Nettlefold, J.S., 1905, *A housing policy*, Cornish Brothers, Birmingham.

n.d. (1906), *A housing policy; to which is added a lecture on housing reform delivered in the Town Hall Birmingham, Wednesday March 28 1906*, Cornish Brothers, Birmingham.

1908a, *Birmingham municipal affairs: a message to the citizens: a series of special articles by Councillor Nettlefold and a leading article by the editor of the 'Gazette'*, Birmingham Printers, Birmingham.

1908b, *Practical housing*, Garden City Press, Letchworth.

1910, *Practical housing*, second edition, T. Fisher Unwin, London, and Garden

City Press, Letchworth.

1911, *A campaign for lower rates and a better Birmingham*, Birmingham News and Printing Company, Birmingham.

1914, *Practical town planning*, St Catherine Press, London.

Newton, K., 1976, *Second city politics: democratic process and decision-making in Birmingham*, Clarendon Press, Oxford.

Older, F., 1919, *My own story*, Call Publishing Company, San Francisco.

Olsen, D.J., 1979, *The growth of Victorian London*, Penguin Books, Harmondsworth (first published 1976).

Osborne, G.H., 1907, Birmingham newspaper scrapbook, 1867-1907, BCL.

Park, A.G., 1906, *The city beautiful: San Francisco past, present and future*, Houston and Harding, Los Angeles.

Partridge, E., 1966, *Origins: a short etymological dictionary of modern English*, Routledge and Kegan Paul, London.

Paterson, J.T., 1981, *America's struggle against poverty, 1900-1980*, Harvard University Press, Cambridge.

Philpott, T.L., 1978, *The slum and the ghetto: neighborhood deterioration and middle-class reform, Chicago, 1880-1930*, Oxford University Press, New York.

Pick, D., 1989, *Faces of degeneration: a European disorder*, Cambridge University Press, Cambridge.

Pike, B., 1981, *The image of the city in modern literature*, Princeton University Press, Princeton.

Pimlott, J.A.R., 1935, *Toynbee hall: fifty years of social progress, 1884-1934*, J. Dent and Company, London.

Plunz, R., 1990, *A history of housing in New York city: dwelling type and social change in the American metropolis*, Columbia University Press, New York.

Poole, A., 1975, *Gissing in context*, Macmillan, London.

Price, C., 1974, *The great white walls are built: restrictive immigration to North America and Australasia, 1836-1888*, Australian National University Press, Canberra.

Pugh, R.B. (ed.), 1964, *The Victoria history of the counties of England*, Oxford University Press, London.

Ralph, J., 1890, The best-governed city in the world, *Harper's New Monthly Magazine*, 81 (481): 99-111.

Raymond, W.J., 1886, *Horrors of the Mongolian settlement, San Francisco, Cal.: enslaved and degraded race of paupers, opium-eaters and lepers*, Cashman, Keating and Company, Boston.

Rex, J., Moore, R., 1967, *Race, community, and conflict: study of Sparkbrook*, Oxford University Press, London.

Rieder, M., 1904, *San Francisco and vicinity*, M. Rieder, Los Angeles.

Riis, J.A., 1971, *How the other half lives: studies among the tenements of New York*, Dover Publications, New York (first published 1890).

1892, *The children of the poor*, Charles Scribners, New York.

1900, *Ten years' war: an account of the battle with the slums*, Houghton, Mifflin and Company, New York.

1902, *The battle with the slum*, Macmillan, New York.

1904, *Theodore Roosevelt: the citizen*, Johnson, Wynne Company, Washington, DC.

Roberts, A.M.S., 1979, City improvement in Sydney: public policy 1880-1900, Ph.D. thesis, University of Sydney.

Robertson, J.D., n.d. (*c.*1895), *San Francisco and suburbs*, Robertson Publishing Company, San Francisco.

Roe, J. (ed.), 1980, *Twentieth century Sydney: studies in urban and social history*, Hale and Iremonger, Sydney.

San Francisco Board of Supervisors, 1875, *Report of the Health Officer of the City and County of San Francisco for the Fiscal Year Ending June 30th, 1875*, Spaulding and Barto, San Francisco.

1877, *Report of the Health Officer of the City and County of San Francisco for the Fiscal Year ending June 30th, 1877*, Spaulding and Barto, San Francisco.

1885, *Report of the Special Committee of the Board of Supervisors of San Francisco on the Condition of the Chinese Quarter and the Chinese in San Francisco*, P.J. Thomas, San Francisco.

1908-9, *Souvenir — Portola: Public Work of San Francisco Board of Supervisors Since 1906*, Supplement to Municipal Reports, San Francisco.

San Francisco Chamber of Commerce, 1875, *Twenty-fifth Annual Report of the Chamber of Commerce of San Francisco*, C.A. Murdock and Company, San Francisco.

1893, *Forty-third Annual Report of the Chamber of Commerce of San Francisco*, Commercial Publishing Company, San Francisco.

1901, *Fifty-first Annual Report of the Chamber of Commerce of San Francisco*, Commercial Publishing Company, San Francisco.

1902, *Fifty-second Annual Report of the Chamber of Commerce of San Francisco*, Commercial Publishing Company, San Francisco.

1907, *Fifty-sixth and Fifty-Seventh Annual Reports of the Chamber of Commerce of San Francisco*, Neal Publishing Company, San Francisco.

1908, *Fifty-eighth Annual Report of the Chamber of Commerce of San Francisco*, Neal Publishing Company, San Francisco.

1909, *Fifty-ninth Annual Report of the Chamber of Commerce of San Francisco*, Neal Publishing Company, San Francisco.

San Francisco Department of Public Health, 1877, *Report of the Health Department of the City and County of San Francisco for the Fiscal Year Ending June 30th, 1877*, George Spaulding and Company, San Francisco.

1879, *Report of the Health Department of the City and County of San Francisco for the Fiscal Year Ending June 30, 1879*, W.M. Hinton and Company, San Francisco.

1881, *Report of the Health Department of the City and County of San Francisco for the Fiscal Year Ending June 30, 1881*, George Spaulding and Company, San Francisco.

1882, *Report of the Health Department of the City and County of San Francisco for the Fiscal Year Ending 30 June 1882*, George Spaulding and Company, San Francisco.

1885, *Report of the Health Department of the City and County of San Francisco for the Fiscal Year Ending June 30, 1885*, W.M. Hinton and Company, San Francisco.

1890, *Report of the Health Department of the City and County of San Francisco for the Fiscal Year Ending June 30, 1890*, W.M. Hinton and Company, San Francisco.

1896, *Report of the Health Department of the City and County of San Francisco for the Fiscal Year Ending 30 June 1896*, Hinton Printing Company, San Francisco.

1901a, *Biennial report of the Board of Health of the City and County of San Francisco for the Fiscal Years 1898-1899 and 1899-1900*, Hinton Printing Company, San Francisco.

1901b, *Annual Report of the Department of Public Health of San Francisco, Cal.*

for the Fiscal Year Ending June 30, 1901, Hinton Printing Company, San Francisco.

1908, *Annual Report of the Department of Public Health of San Francisco, Cal. for the Fiscal Year, July 1, 1907 to June 30, 1908*, Neal Publishing Company, San Francisco.

San Francisco Passenger Department, 1901, *The Santa Fe*, Santa Fe Railroad Company, Chicago.

San Francisco Plague Commission, 1901, Report of the San Francisco Plague Commission, 26 February 1901, in *Public Health Reports*, 19 April 1901, pp.801-16.

Saxton, A., 1971, *The indispensable enemy: labor and the anti-Chinese movement in California*, University of California Press, Berkeley and Los Angeles.

Schiesl, M.J., 1977, *The politics of efficiency: municipal administration and reform in America, 1800-1920*, University of California Press, Berkeley and Los Angeles.

Schultz, S.K., 1989, *Constructing urban culture: American cities and city planning, 1800-1920*, Temple University Press, Philadelphia.

Scobey, D.M., 1989, Empire city: politics, culture, and urbanism in gilded-age New York, Ph.D. thesis, Yale University.

Scott, M., 1969, *American city planning since 1890: a history commemorating the fiftieth anniversary of the American Institute of Planners*, University of California Press, Berkeley and Los Angeles.

Searlight, F.T., 1906, *The doomed city: a thrilling tale*, Laird and Lee, Chicago.

Shapiro, M.J., 1983, *A picture history of the Brooklyn Bridge*, Dover, New York.

Shattuck, L., 1948, *Report of the sanitary commission of Massachusetts*, Harvard University Press, Cambridge (first published 1850).

Siegel, A., 1981, *The image of the American city in popular literature, 1820-1870*, Kennikat Press, Port Washington.

Simey, T.S., Simey, M.B., 1960, *Charles Booth: social scientist*, Oxford University Press, Oxford.

Simon, J., 1897, *English Sanitary Institutions*, second edition, Smith, Elder and Company, London.

Smith, F.B., 1979, *The people's health, 1830-1910*, Australian National University Press, Canberra.

Snyder, R.W., 1989, *The voice of the city: vaudeville and popular culture in New York*, Oxford University Press, New York.

Spearritt, P., 1974, Sydney's 'slums': middle class reformers and the labor response, *Labour History*, 26: 65-81.

1978, *Sydney since the twenties*, Hale and Iremonger, Sydney.

Stead, W.T. (introduction by Wish, H.), 1964, *If Christ came to Chicago*, Living Books, New York (first published 1894).

Steele, R., 1909, *The city that is: the story of the rebuilding of San Francisco in three years*, A.M. Robertson, San Francisco.

Still, B., 1956, *Mirror for Gotham: New York as seen by contemporaries from Dutch days to the present*, New York University Press, New York.

Stout, J.P., 1976, *Sodoms in Eden: the city in American fiction before 1860*, Greenwood Press, Westport.

Strong, J., 1907, *The challenge of the city*, Young People's Missionary Movement, New York.

Sutcliffe, A.R. (ed.), 1974, *Multi-storey living: the British working-class experience*, Croom Helm, London.

Tagg, J., 1988, *The burden of representation: essays on photographies and histories*, University of Massachusetts Press, Amherst.

Todd, F.M., 1909, *Eradicating plague from San Francisco: report of the Citizens' Health Committee and an account of its work*, C. A. Murdock and Company, San Francisco.

Todd, R.E., Sanborn, F.B., 1912, *The report of the Lawrence Survey*, Andover Press, Andover, Massachusetts.

Trachtenberg, A., 1989, *Reading American photographs: images as history — Mathew Brady to Walker Evans*, Hill and Wang, New York.

Trauner, J.B., 1974, The Chinese as medical scapegoats in San Francisco, *Bulletin of the Chinese Historical Society of America*, 9: 1-19.

Turner, V., 1982, *From ritual to theatre: the human seriousness of play*, Performing Arts Journal Publications, New York.

1985, *On the edge of the bush: anthropology as experience*, University of Arizona Press, Tucson.

Turner, V., Bruner, E.M. (eds), 1986, *The anthropology of experience*, University of Illinois Press, Urbana.

Twopeny, R., 1883, *Town life in Australia* (first published London, 1883), republished in 1973 by Penguin Colonial Facsimiles, Melbourne.

Tyler, S., 1906, *San Francisco's great disaster*, P.W. Ziegler, Philadelphia.

United States Public Health Service, 1901, *Public Health Reports*, 15 (1-26), Government Printing Office, Washington, DC.

1902, *Annual Report of the Supervising Surgeon-General of the Marine Hospital Service of the United States for the Fiscal Year 1901*, Government Printing Office, Washington, DC.

1903a, *Public Health Reports*, 18 (1-26), Government Printing Office, Washington, DC.

1903b, *Transactions of the First Annual Conference of State and Territorial Health Officers with the United States Public Health and Marine Hospital Service*, Government Printing Office, Washington, DC.

1904, *Transactions of the Second Annual Conference of State and Territorial Health Officers with the United States Public Health and Marine Hospital Service*, Government Printing Office, Washington, DC.

1905, *Public Health Reports*, 20 (1-26), Government Printing Office, Washington, DC.

1906, *Annual Report of the Surgeon-General of the Public Health and Marine Hospital Service of the United States for the Fiscal Year 1905*, Government Printing Office, Washington, DC.

1909a, *Public Health Reports*, 23 (27-52), Government Printing Office, Washington, DC.

1909b, *Annual Report of the Surgeon-General of the Public Health and Marine Hospital Service of the United States for the Fiscal Year 1908*, Government Printing Office, Washington, DC.

Vamplew, W. (ed.), 1987, *Australians: historical statistics*, Fairfax, Syme and Weldon Associates, Sydney.

V&P(NSW LA), 1859-60, volume 4, Report of the Select Committee on the Condition of the Working Classes of the Metropolis.

1875-6, volume 5, Eleventh Progress Report of the Sydney City and Suburban Sewage and Health Board.

1888-9, volume 2, Statement of the Commissioner for Railways upon Relinquishing Office, October, 1888.

1890, volume 6, Second Report by the Parliamentary Standing Committee on Public Works Relating to the Proposed Railway to Connect the North Shore Railway with Port Jackson at Milson's Point.

Vince, C.A., 1902, *History of the Corporation of Birmingham*, volume 3, Cornish Brothers, Birmingham.

Walker, R.H., 1962, The poet and the rise of the city, *Mississippi Valley Historical Review*, 49: 85-99.

Wallace, A.D., Ross, W.O. (eds), 1958, *Studies in honor of John Wilcox*, Wayne State University Press, Detroit.

Walters, J.C., 1901a, *Scenes in slum-land: pen pictures of the black spots of Birmingham*, Daily Gazette Company, Birmingham.

1901b, *Further scenes in slum-land*, Daily Gazette Company, Birmingham.

Ward, D., 1976, The Victorian slum: an enduring myth? *Annals of the Association of American Geographers*, 66 (2): 323-36.

1989, *Poverty, ethnicity, and the American city, 1840-1925: changing conceptions of the slum and the ghetto*, Cambridge University Press, Cambridge.

Watts, S., 1992, Academe's leftists are something of a fraud, *Chronicle of Higher Education*, 38 (34): A40.

Webb, B., 1938, *My apprenticeship*, Penguin Books, Harmondsworth.

White, D.F., 1989, *The urbanists, 1865-1915*, Greenwood Press, New York.

White, M., White, L., 1962, *The intellectual versus the city: from Thomas Jefferson to Frank Lloyd Wright*, Harvard University Press and MIT Press, Cambridge.

Williams, P. (ed.), 1983, *Social process and the city*, Allen and Unwin, Sydney.

Williams, R.C., 1951, *The United States Public Health Service, 1798-1950*, Commissioned Officers Association of the United States Public Health Service, Washington, DC.

Wilson, J.R., 1906, *San Francisco's horror of earthquake and fire*, National Publishing Company, Philadelphia.

Wohl, A.S., 1977, *The eternal slum: housing and social policy in Victorian London*, Edward Arnold, London.

1991, Social explorations among the London poor: theatre or laboratory? *Revue Française de Civilisation Britannique*, 6 (2): 76-97.

Workingmen's Party of California, 1880, *Chinatown declared a nuisance!* Workingmen's Party of California, San Francisco.

Workmen's Cottages, Lawrence Street, 1893, *Birmingham faces and places*, 5: 191-3.

Wright, G., 1981, *Building the dream: a social history of housing in America*, Pantheon Books, New York.

Yelling, J.A., 1986, *Slums and slum clearance in Victorian London*, Allen and Unwin, London.

Young, J.P., 1912, *San Francisco: a history of the Pacific coast metropolis*, volume 2, S.J. Clarke Publishing Company, San Francisco.

1915, *Journalism in California*, Chronicle Publishing Company, San Francisco.

Index